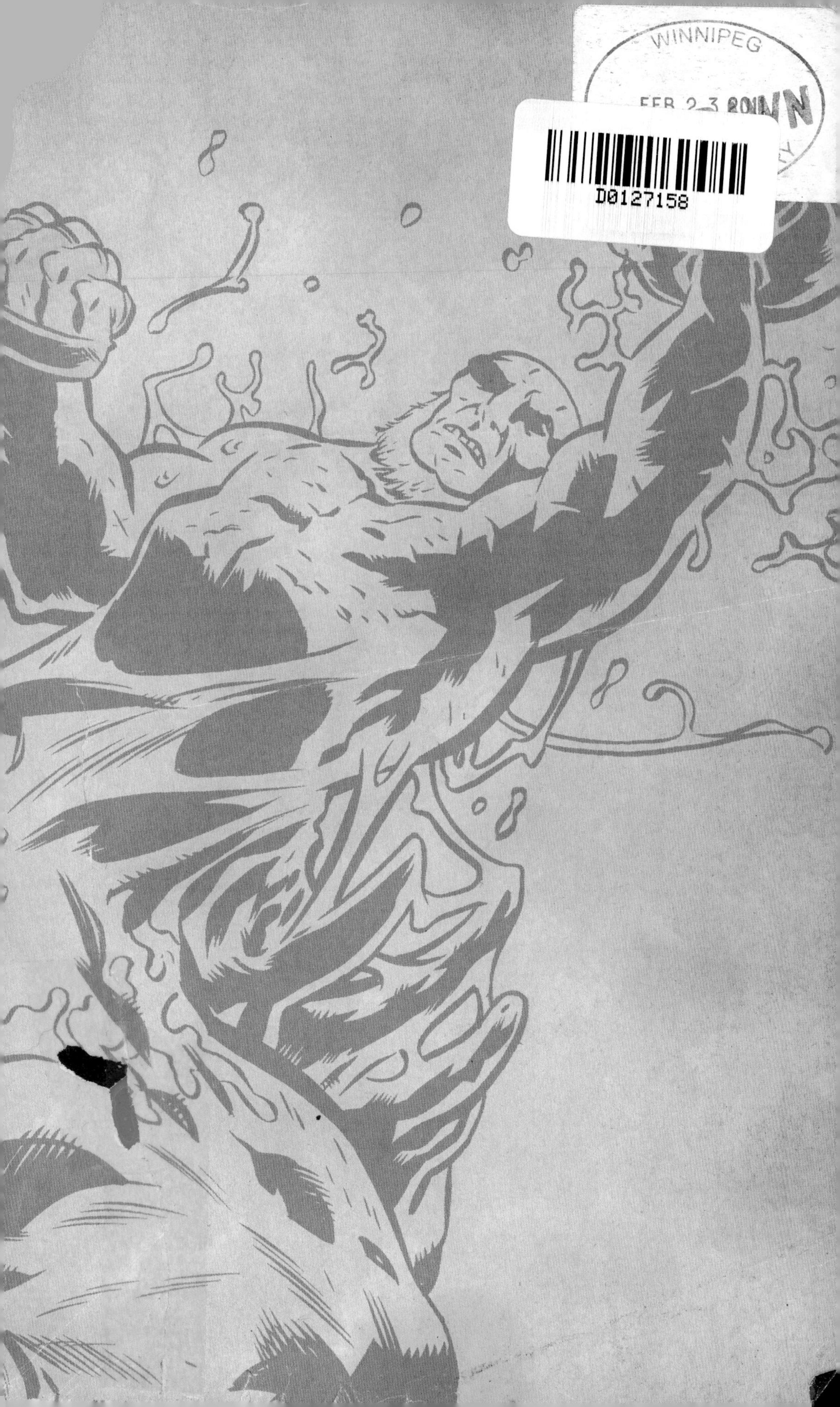

THE ANCHOR

VOLUME ONE: FIVE FURIES

BOOM! STUDIOS

ROSS RICHIE
chief executive officer

MARK WAID
editor-in-chief

ADAM FORTIER
vice president, publishing

CHIP MOSHER
marketing director

MATT GAGNON
managing editor

JENNY CHRISTOPHER
sales director

FIRST EDITION: FEBRUARY 2010
10 9 8 7 6 5 4 3 2 1

PRINTED BY WORLD COLOR PRESS, INC.,
ST-ROMUALD, QC. CANADA. 12/09/09

Office of publication: 6310 San Vicente Blvd, Ste 404, Los Angeles, CA 90048-5457.

A catalog record for this book is available from OCLC and on our website www.boom-studios.com on the Librarians

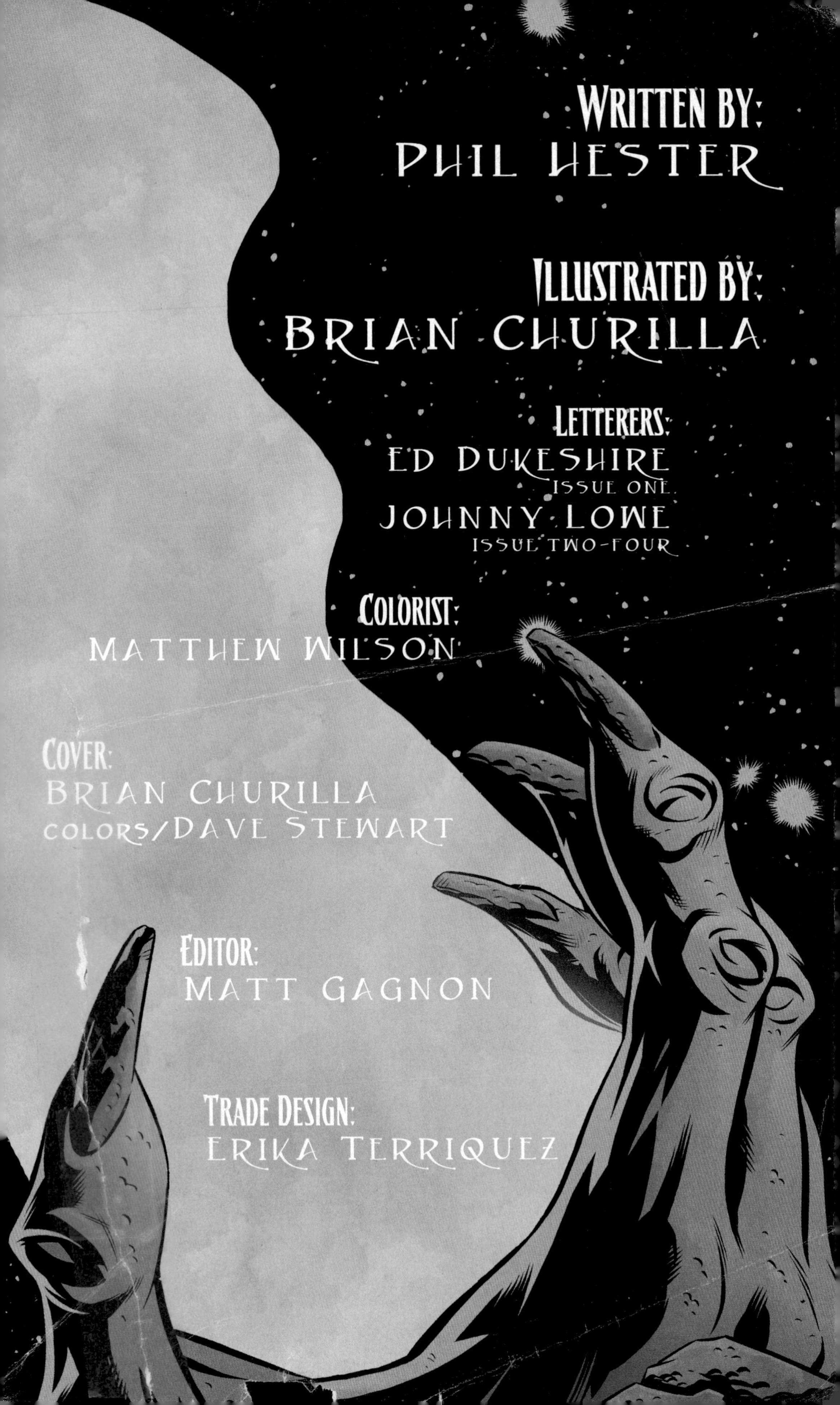

WRITTEN BY:
PHIL HESTER

ILLUSTRATED BY:
BRIAN CHURILLA

LETTERERS:
ED DUKESHIRE
ISSUE ONE
JOHNNY LOWE
ISSUE TWO-FOUR

COLORIST:
MATTHEW WILSON

COVER:
BRIAN CHURILLA
COLORS/DAVE STEWART

EDITOR:
MATT GAGNON

TRADE DESIGN:
ERIKA TERRIQUEZ

CHAPTER ONE

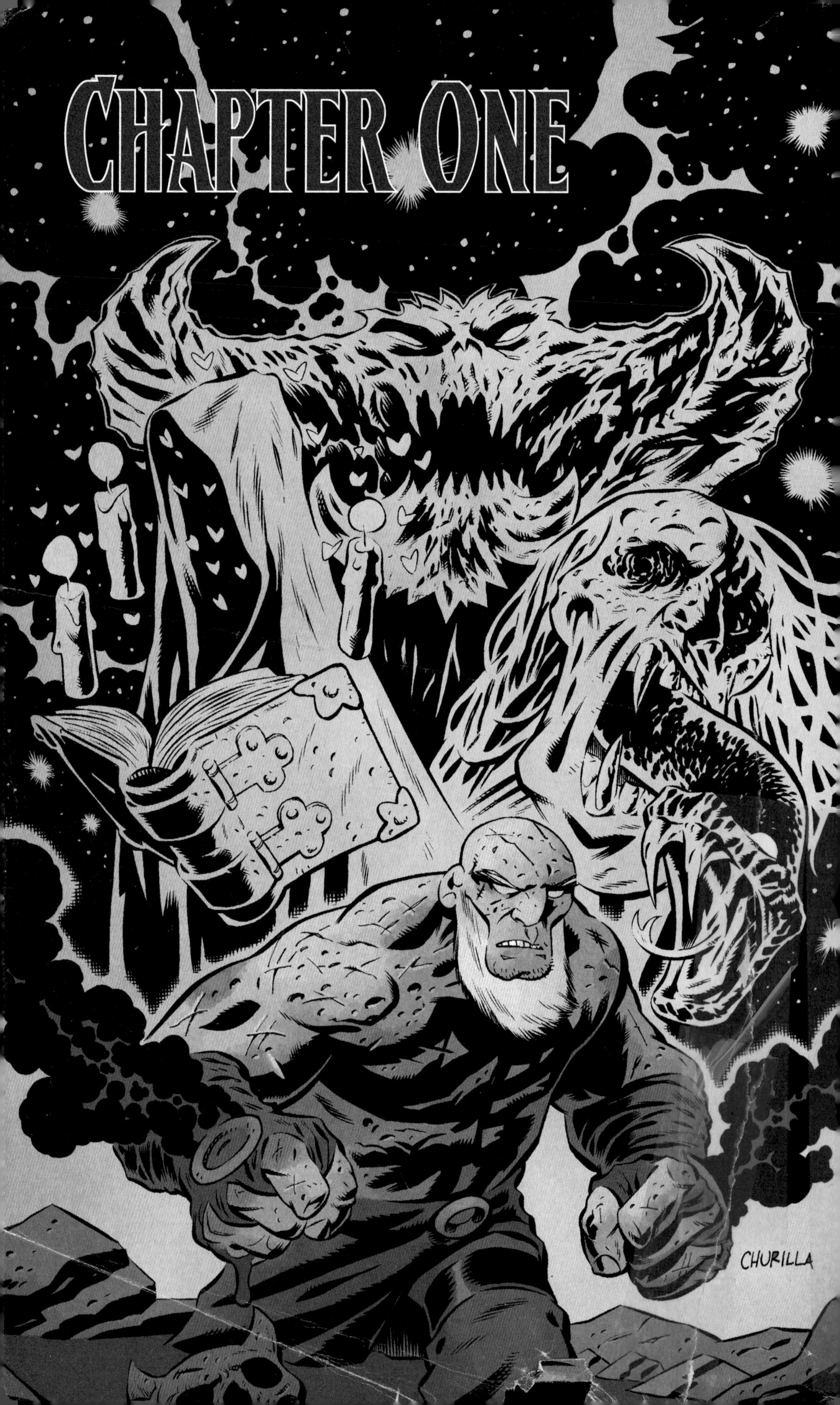
CHURILLA

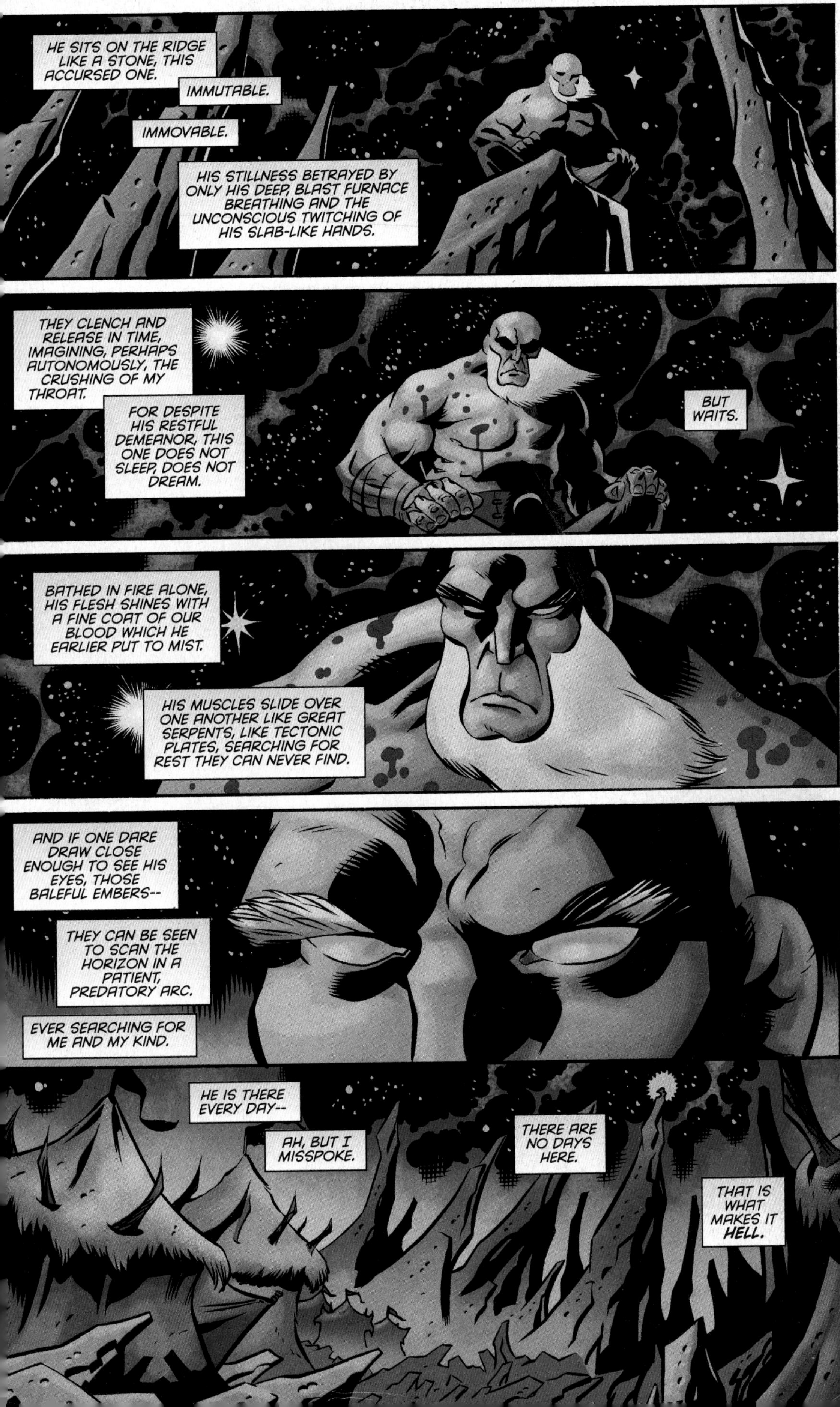
HE SITS ON THE RIDGE LIKE A STONE, THIS ACCURSED ONE.
IMMUTABLE.
IMMOVABLE.
HIS STILLNESS BETRAYED BY ONLY HIS DEEP, BLAST FURNACE BREATHING AND THE UNCONSCIOUS TWITCHING OF HIS SLAB-LIKE HANDS.
THEY CLENCH AND RELEASE IN TIME, IMAGINING, PERHAPS AUTONOMOUSLY, THE CRUSHING OF MY THROAT.
FOR DESPITE HIS RESTFUL DEMEANOR, THIS ONE DOES NOT SLEEP, DOES NOT DREAM.
BUT WAITS.
BATHED IN FIRE ALONE, HIS FLESH SHINES WITH A FINE COAT OF OUR BLOOD WHICH HE EARLIER PUT TO MIST.
HIS MUSCLES SLIDE OVER ONE ANOTHER LIKE GREAT SERPENTS, LIKE TECTONIC PLATES, SEARCHING FOR REST THEY CAN NEVER FIND.
AND IF ONE DARE DRAW CLOSE ENOUGH TO SEE HIS EYES, THOSE BALEFUL EMBERS--
THEY CAN BE SEEN TO SCAN THE HORIZON IN A PATIENT, PREDATORY ARC.
EVER SEARCHING FOR ME AND MY KIND.
HE IS THERE EVERY DAY--
AH, BUT I MISSPOKE.
THERE ARE NO DAYS HERE.
THAT IS WHAT MAKES IT **HELL.**

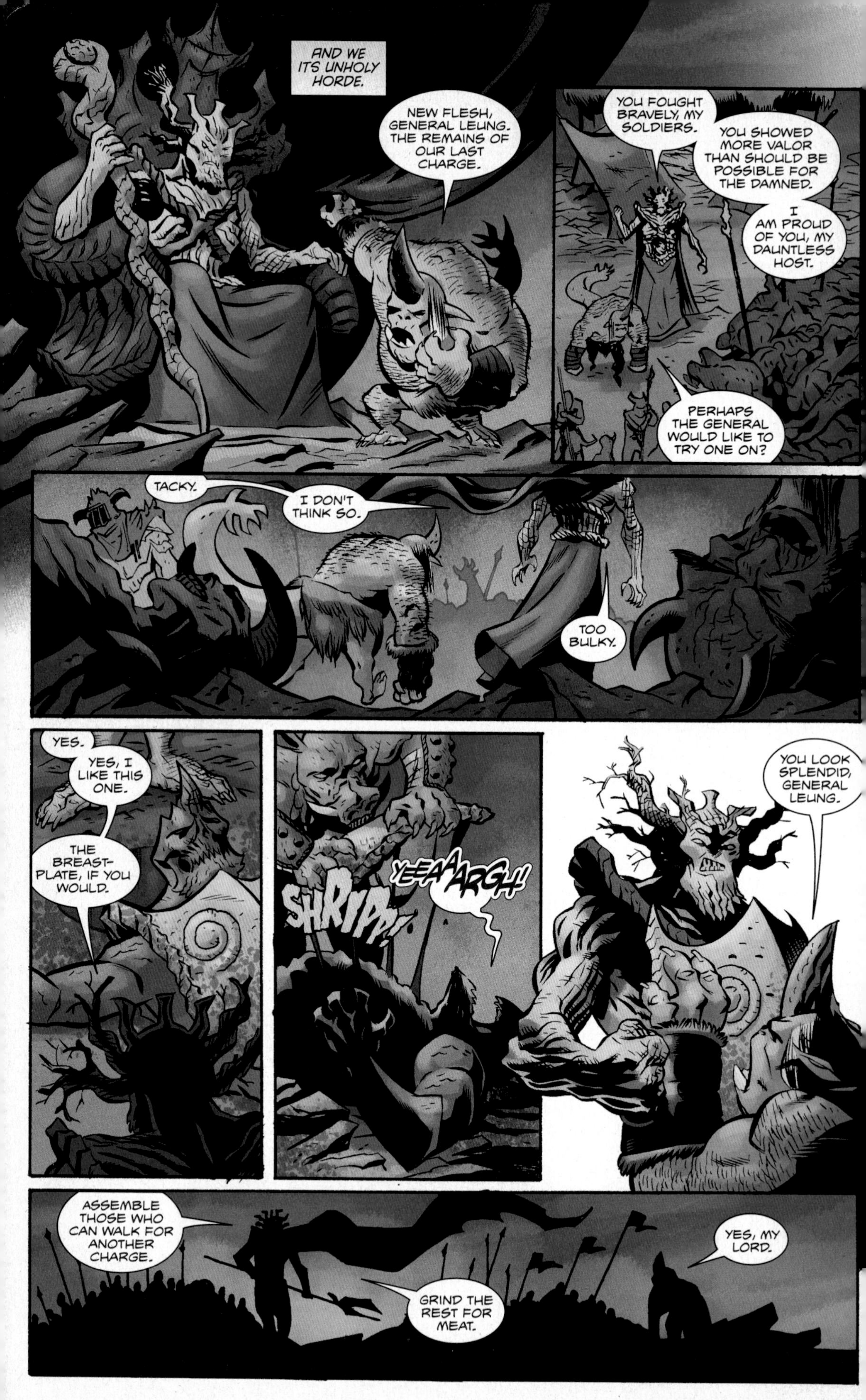
AND WE ITS UNHOLY HORDE.
NEW FLESH, GENERAL LEUNG. THE REMAINS OF OUR LAST CHARGE.
YOU FOUGHT BRAVELY, MY SOLDIERS.
YOU SHOWED MORE VALOR THAN SHOULD BE POSSIBLE FOR THE DAMNED.
I AM PROUD OF YOU, MY DAUNTLESS HOST.
PERHAPS THE GENERAL WOULD LIKE TO TRY ONE ON?
TACKY.
I DON'T THINK SO.
TOO BULKY.
YES.
YES, I LIKE THIS ONE.
THE BREAST-PLATE, IF YOU WOULD.
SHRIPP!
YEEAAARGH!
YOU LOOK SPLENDID, GENERAL LEUNG.
ASSEMBLE THOSE WHO CAN WALK FOR ANOTHER CHARGE.
GRIND THE REST FOR MEAT.
YES, MY LORD.

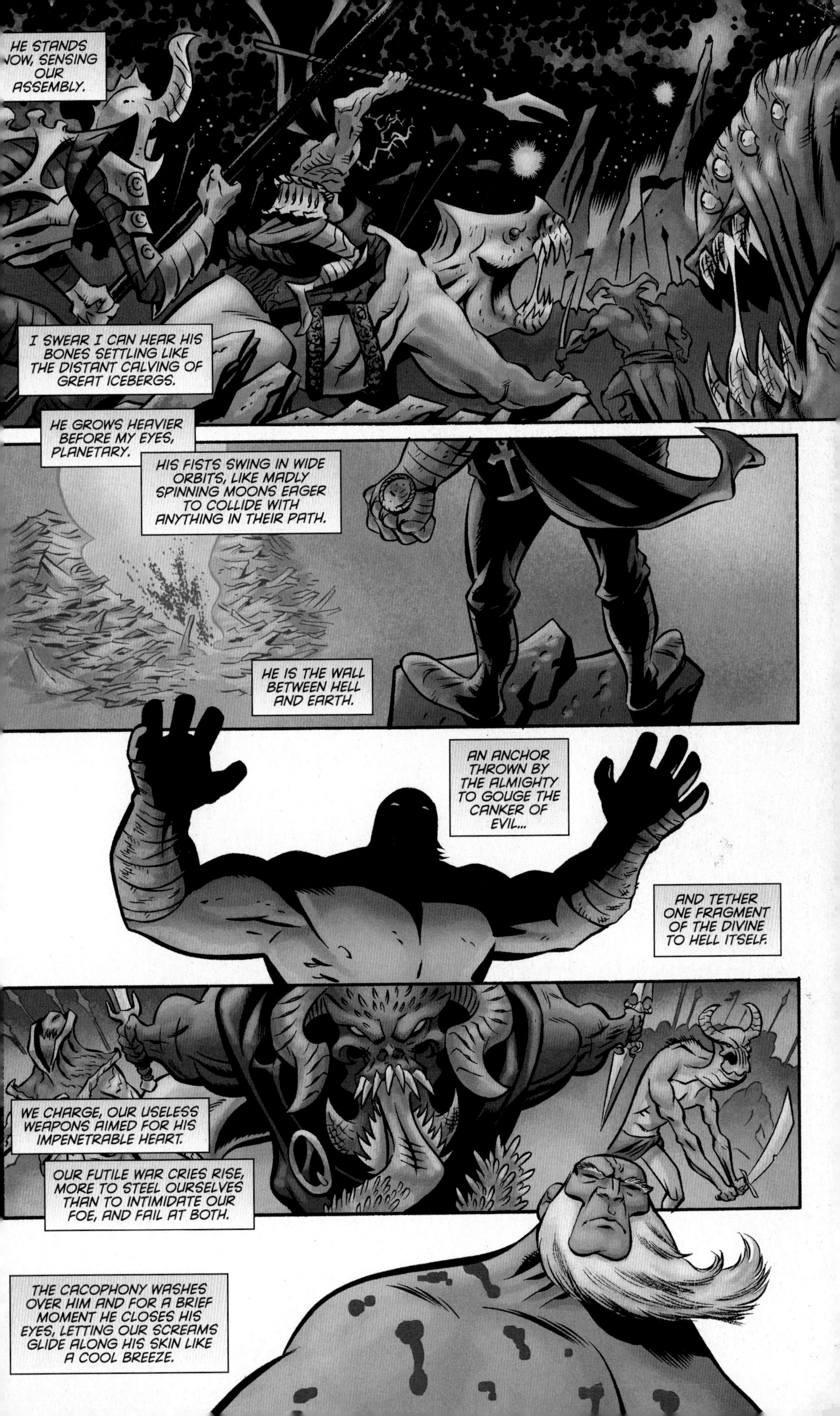
HE STANDS NOW, SENSING OUR ASSEMBLY.
I SWEAR I CAN HEAR HIS BONES SETTLING LIKE THE DISTANT CALVING OF GREAT ICEBERGS.
HE GROWS HEAVIER BEFORE MY EYES, PLANETARY.
HIS FISTS SWING IN WIDE ORBITS, LIKE MADLY SPINNING MOONS EAGER TO COLLIDE WITH ANYTHING IN THEIR PATH.
HE IS THE WALL BETWEEN HELL AND EARTH.
AN ANCHOR THROWN BY THE ALMIGHTY TO GOUGE THE CANKER OF EVIL...
AND TETHER ONE FRAGMENT OF THE DIVINE TO HELL ITSELF.
WE CHARGE, OUR USELESS WEAPONS AIMED FOR HIS IMPENETRABLE HEART.
OUR FUTILE WAR CRIES RISE, MORE TO STEEL OURSELVES THAN TO INTIMIDATE OUR FOE, AND FAIL AT BOTH.
THE CACOPHONY WASHES OVER HIM AND FOR A BRIEF MOMENT HE CLOSES HIS EYES, LETTING OUR SCREAMS GLIDE ALONG HIS SKIN LIKE A COOL BREEZE.

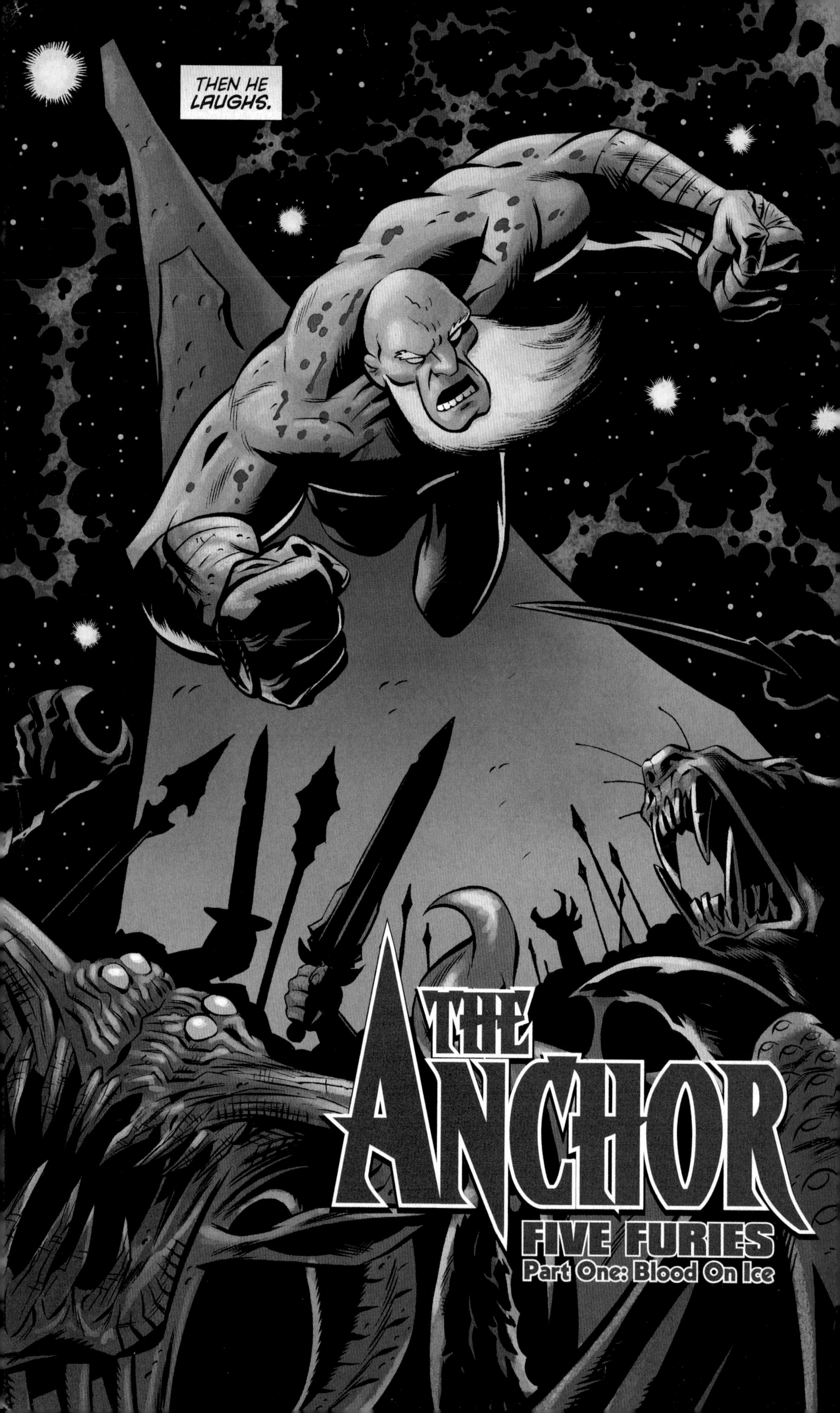
THEN HE LAUGHS.
THE ANCHOR
FIVE FURIES
Part One: Blood On Ice

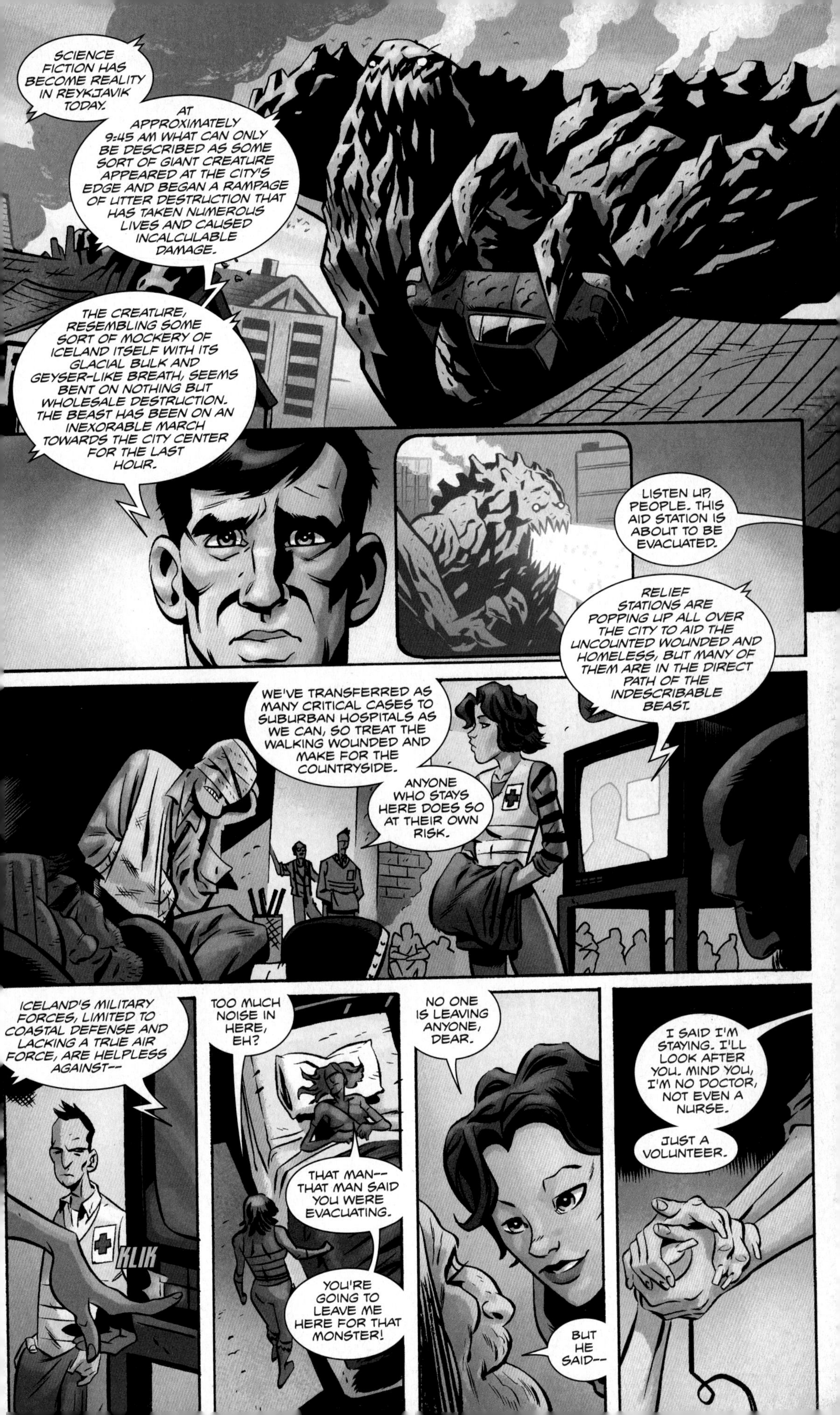
SCIENCE FICTION HAS BECOME REALITY IN REYKJAVIK TODAY.
AT APPROXIMATELY 9:45 AM WHAT CAN ONLY BE DESCRIBED AS SOME SORT OF GIANT CREATURE APPEARED AT THE CITY'S EDGE AND BEGAN A RAMPAGE OF UTTER DESTRUCTION THAT HAS TAKEN NUMEROUS LIVES AND CAUSED INCALCULABLE DAMAGE.
THE CREATURE, RESEMBLING SOME SORT OF MOCKERY OF ICELAND ITSELF WITH ITS GLACIAL BULK AND GEYSER-LIKE BREATH, SEEMS BENT ON NOTHING BUT WHOLESALE DESTRUCTION. THE BEAST HAS BEEN ON AN INEXORABLE MARCH TOWARDS THE CITY CENTER FOR THE LAST HOUR.
LISTEN UP, PEOPLE. THIS AID STATION IS ABOUT TO BE EVACUATED.
RELIEF STATIONS ARE POPPING UP ALL OVER THE CITY TO AID THE UNCOUNTED WOUNDED AND HOMELESS, BUT MANY OF THEM ARE IN THE DIRECT PATH OF THE INDESCRIBABLE BEAST.
WE'VE TRANSFERRED AS MANY CRITICAL CASES TO SUBURBAN HOSPITALS AS WE CAN, SO TREAT THE WALKING WOUNDED AND MAKE FOR THE COUNTRYSIDE.
ANYONE WHO STAYS HERE DOES SO AT THEIR OWN RISK.
ICELAND'S MILITARY FORCES, LIMITED TO COASTAL DEFENSE AND LACKING A TRUE AIR FORCE, ARE HELPLESS AGAINST--
KLIK
TOO MUCH NOISE IN HERE, EH?
THAT MAN--THAT MAN SAID YOU WERE EVACUATING.
YOU'RE GOING TO LEAVE ME HERE FOR THAT MONSTER!
NO ONE IS LEAVING ANYONE, DEAR.
BUT HE SAID--
I SAID I'M STAYING. I'LL LOOK AFTER YOU. MIND YOU, I'M NO DOCTOR, NOT EVEN A NURSE.
JUST A VOLUNTEER.

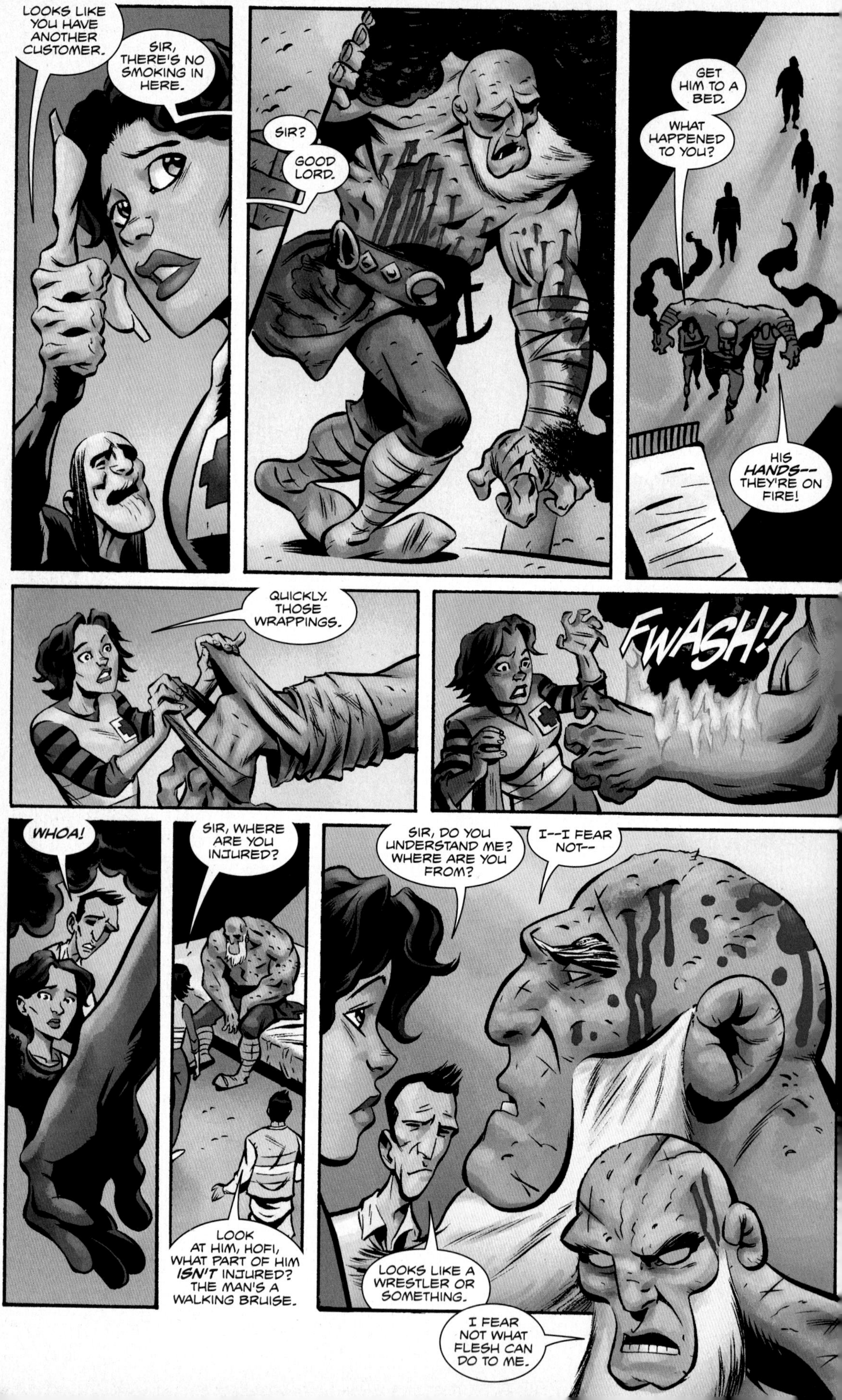
LOOKS LIKE YOU HAVE ANOTHER CUSTOMER.
SIR, THERE'S NO SMOKING IN HERE.
SIR?
GOOD LORD.
GET HIM TO A BED.
WHAT HAPPENED TO YOU?
HIS *HANDS*-- THEY'RE ON FIRE!
QUICKLY. THOSE WRAPPINGS.
FWASH!!
WHOA!
SIR, WHERE ARE YOU INJURED?
LOOK AT HIM, HOFI, WHAT PART OF HIM *ISN'T* INJURED? THE MAN'S A WALKING BRUISE.
SIR, DO YOU UNDERSTAND ME? WHERE ARE YOU FROM?
I--I FEAR NOT--
LOOKS LIKE A WRESTLER OR SOMETHING.
I FEAR NOT WHAT FLESH CAN DO TO ME.

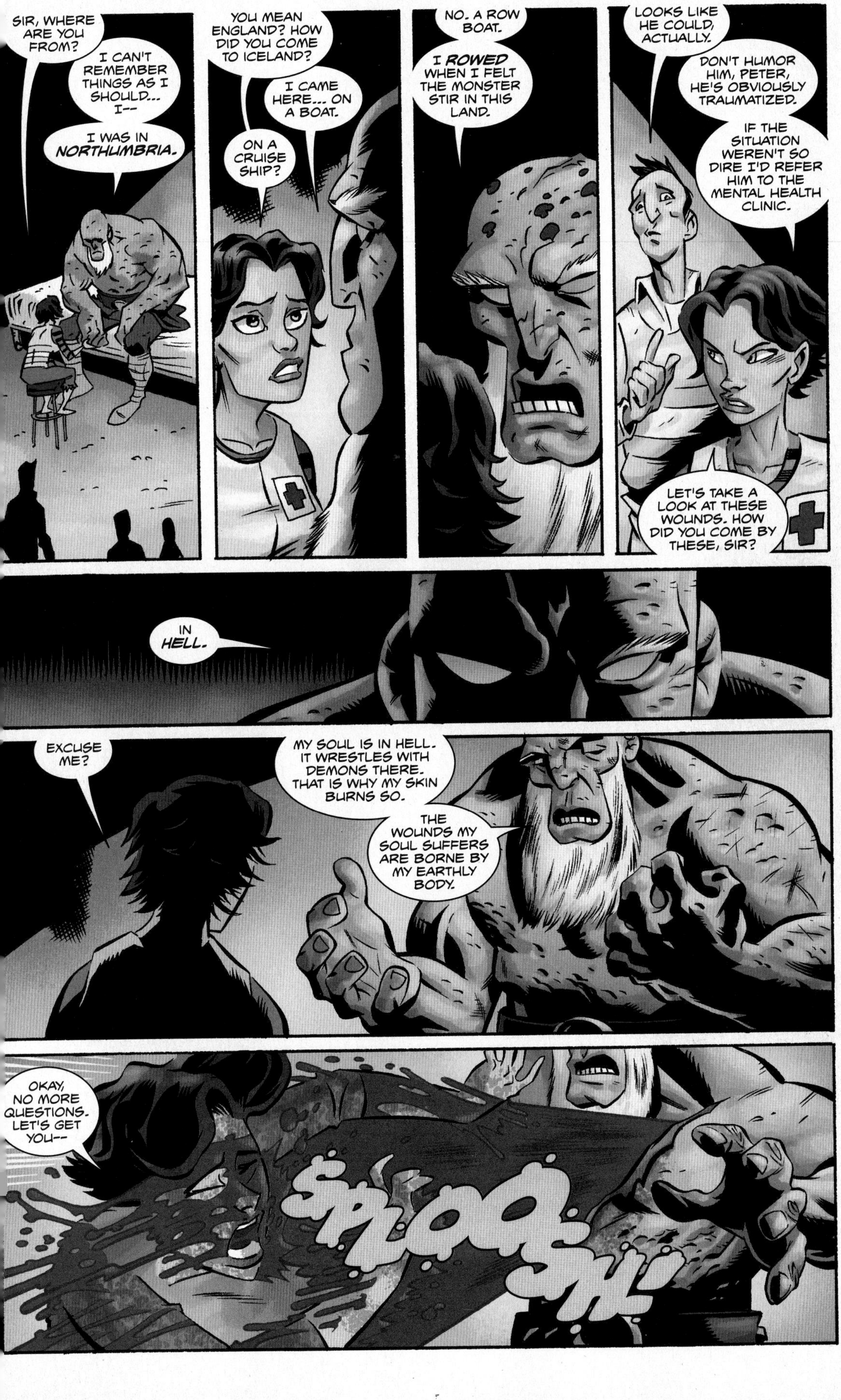
SIR, WHERE ARE YOU FROM?
I CAN'T REMEMBER THINGS AS I SHOULD... I--
I WAS IN NORTHUMBRIA.
YOU MEAN ENGLAND? HOW DID YOU COME TO ICELAND?
I CAME HERE... ON A BOAT.
ON A CRUISE SHIP?
NO. A ROW BOAT.
I ROWED WHEN I FELT THE MONSTER STIR IN THIS LAND.
LOOKS LIKE HE COULD, ACTUALLY.
DON'T HUMOR HIM, PETER, HE'S OBVIOUSLY TRAUMATIZED.
IF THE SITUATION WEREN'T SO DIRE I'D REFER HIM TO THE MENTAL HEALTH CLINIC.
LET'S TAKE A LOOK AT THESE WOUNDS. HOW DID YOU COME BY THESE, SIR?
IN HELL.
EXCUSE ME?
MY SOUL IS IN HELL. IT WRESTLES WITH DEMONS THERE. THAT IS WHY MY SKIN BURNS SO.
THE WOUNDS MY SOUL SUFFERS ARE BORNE BY MY EARTHLY BODY.
OKAY, NO MORE QUESTIONS. LET'S GET YOU--
SPLOOSH!

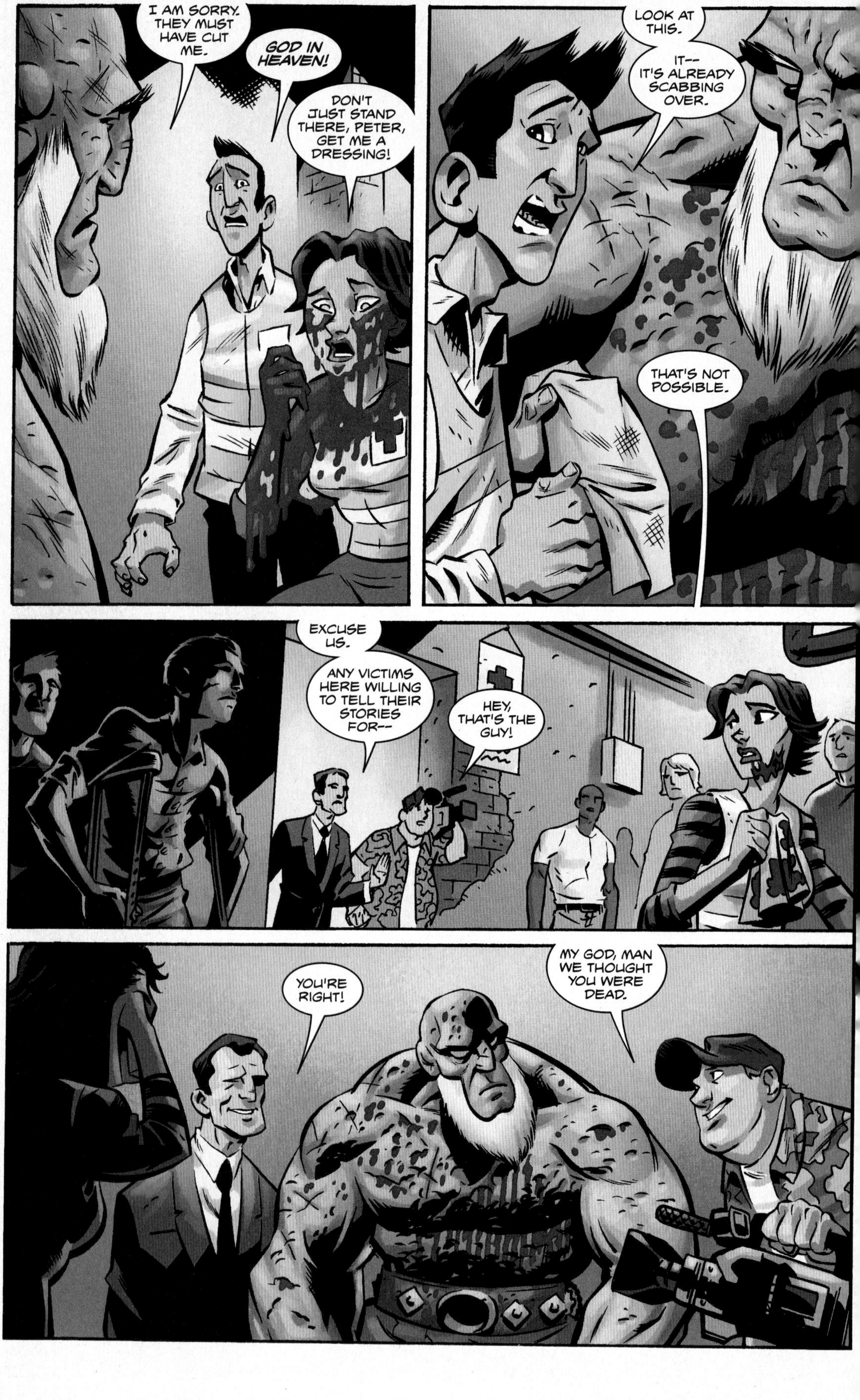
I AM SORRY. THEY MUST HAVE CUT ME.
GOD IN HEAVEN!
DON'T JUST STAND THERE, PETER, GET ME A DRESSING!
LOOK AT THIS.
IT-- IT'S ALREADY SCABBING OVER.
THAT'S NOT POSSIBLE.
EXCUSE US.
ANY VICTIMS HERE WILLING TO TELL THEIR STORIES FOR--
HEY, THAT'S THE GUY!
YOU'RE RIGHT!
MY GOD, MAN WE THOUGHT YOU WERE DEAD.

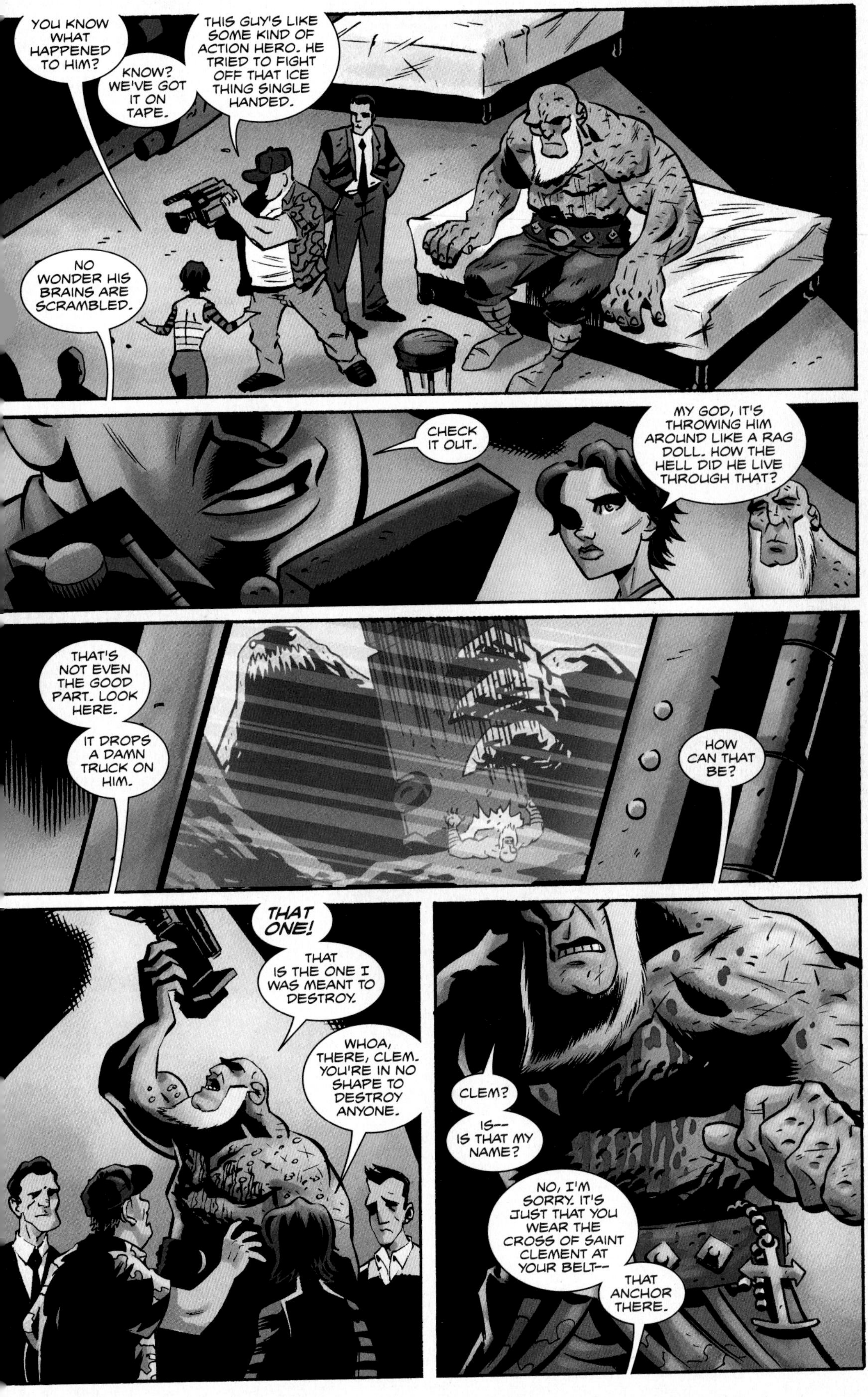
YOU KNOW WHAT HAPPENED TO HIM?
KNOW? WE'VE GOT IT ON TAPE.
THIS GUY'S LIKE SOME KIND OF ACTION HERO. HE TRIED TO FIGHT OFF THAT ICE THING SINGLE HANDED.
NO WONDER HIS BRAINS ARE SCRAMBLED.
CHECK IT OUT.
MY GOD, IT'S THROWING HIM AROUND LIKE A RAG DOLL. HOW THE HELL DID HE LIVE THROUGH THAT?
THAT'S NOT EVEN THE GOOD PART. LOOK HERE.
IT DROPS A DAMN TRUCK ON HIM.
HOW CAN THAT BE?
THAT ONE!
THAT IS THE ONE I WAS MEANT TO DESTROY.
WHOA, THERE, CLEM. YOU'RE IN NO SHAPE TO DESTROY ANYONE.
CLEM?
IS-- IS THAT MY NAME?
NO, I'M SORRY. IT'S JUST THAT YOU WEAR THE CROSS OF SAINT CLEMENT AT YOUR BELT--
THAT ANCHOR THERE.

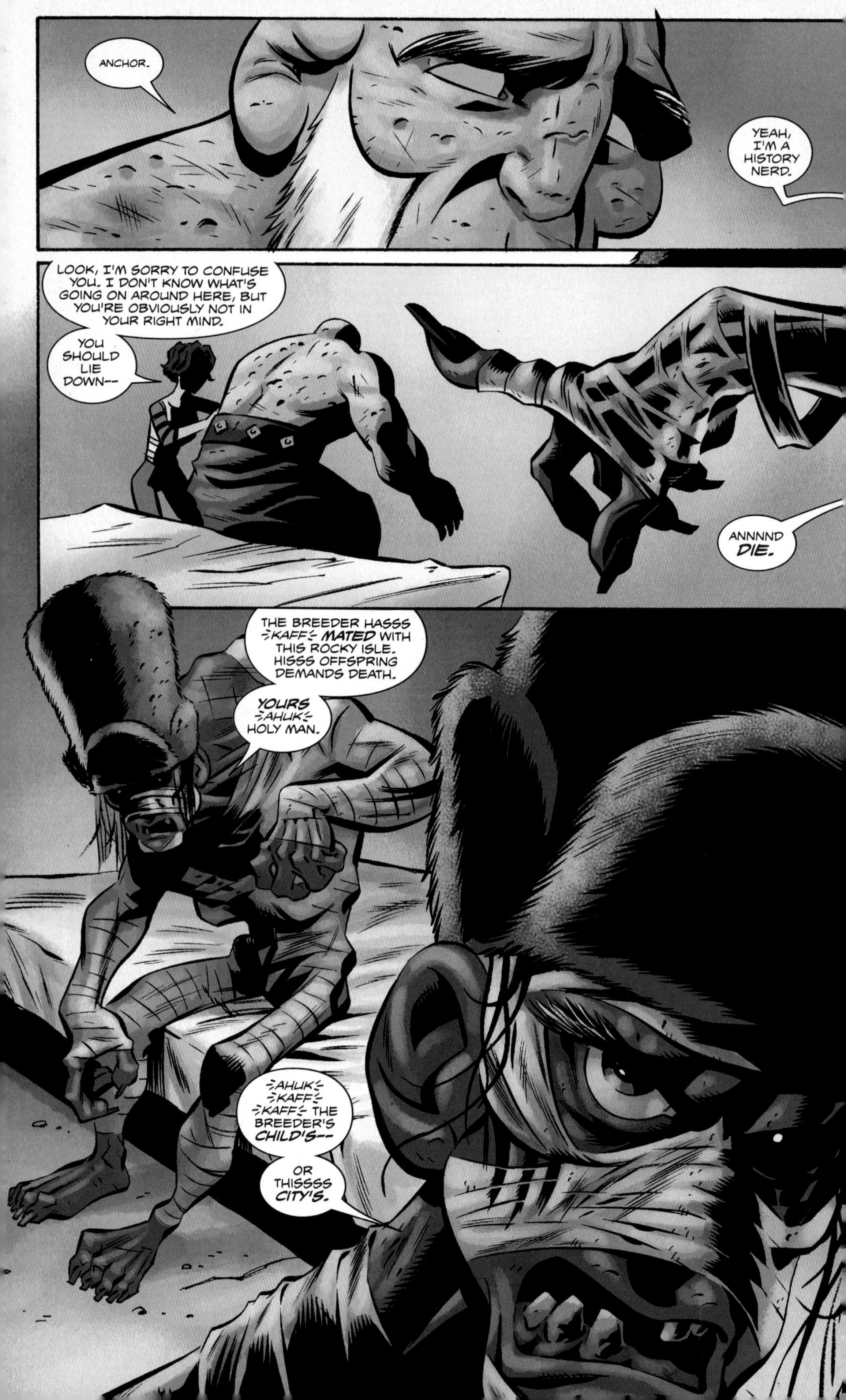
ANCHOR.
YEAH, I'M A HISTORY NERD.
LOOK, I'M SORRY TO CONFUSE YOU. I DON'T KNOW WHAT'S GOING ON AROUND HERE, BUT YOU'RE OBVIOUSLY NOT IN YOUR RIGHT MIND.
YOU SHOULD LIE DOWN--
ANNNND DIE.
THE BREEDER HASSS -KAFF- MATED WITH THIS ROCKY ISLE. HISSS OFFSPRING DEMANDS DEATH.
YOURS -AHUK- HOLY MAN.
-AHUK- -KAFF- -KAFF- THE BREEDER'S CHILD'S--
OR THISSSS CITY'S.

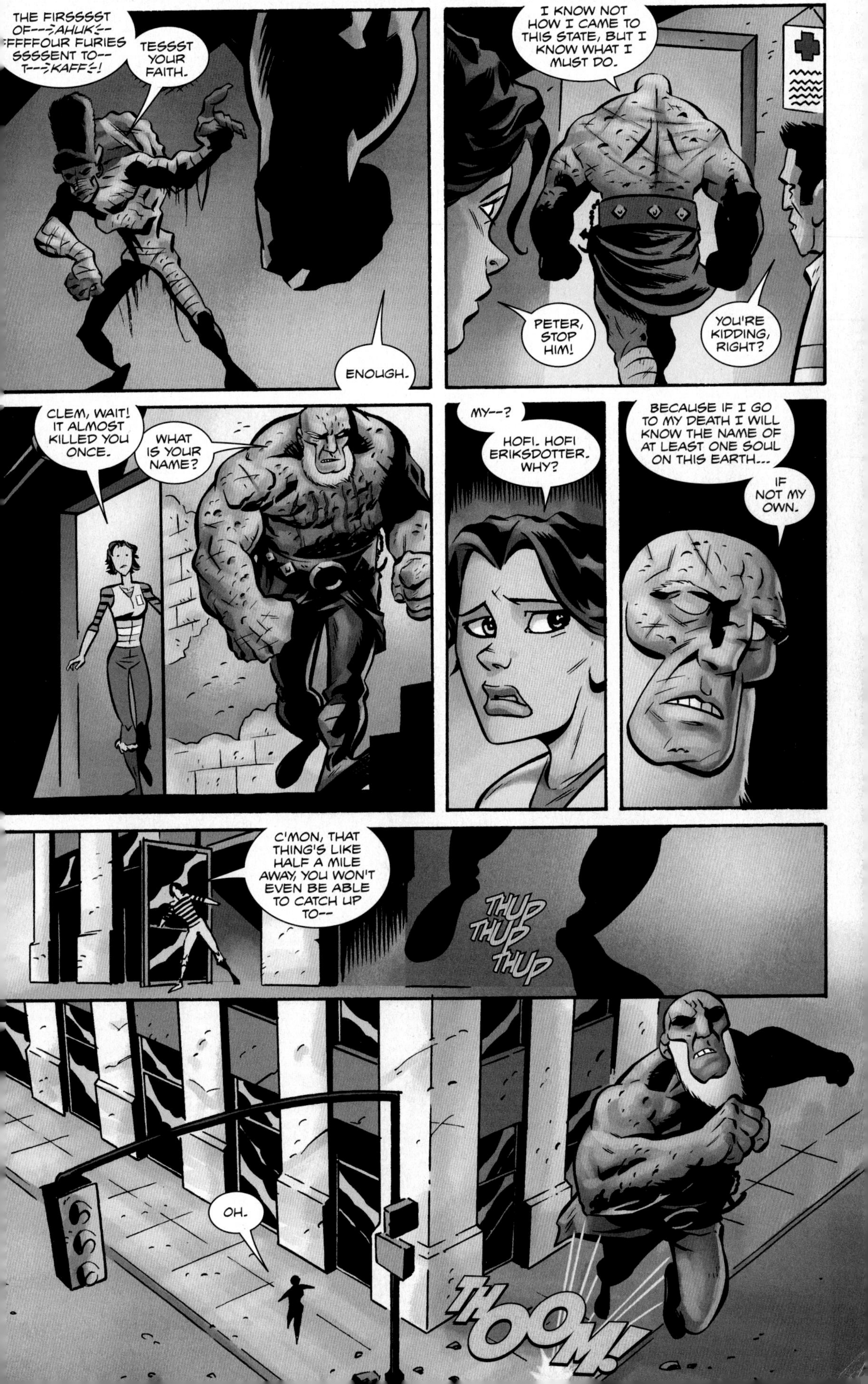

THE FIRSSSST OF--- AHUK --FFFFFOUR FURIES SSSSENT TO--T--- KAFF !
TESSST YOUR FAITH.
ENOUGH.
I KNOW NOT HOW I CAME TO THIS STATE, BUT I KNOW WHAT I MUST DO.
PETER, STOP HIM!
YOU'RE KIDDING, RIGHT?
CLEM, WAIT! IT ALMOST KILLED YOU ONCE.
WHAT IS YOUR NAME?
MY--?
HOFI. HOFI ERIKSDOTTER. WHY?
BECAUSE IF I GO TO MY DEATH I WILL KNOW THE NAME OF AT LEAST ONE SOUL ON THIS EARTH...
IF NOT MY OWN.
C'MON, THAT THING'S LIKE HALF A MILE AWAY, YOU WON'T EVEN BE ABLE TO CATCH UP TO--
THUP THUP THUP
OH.
THOOM!

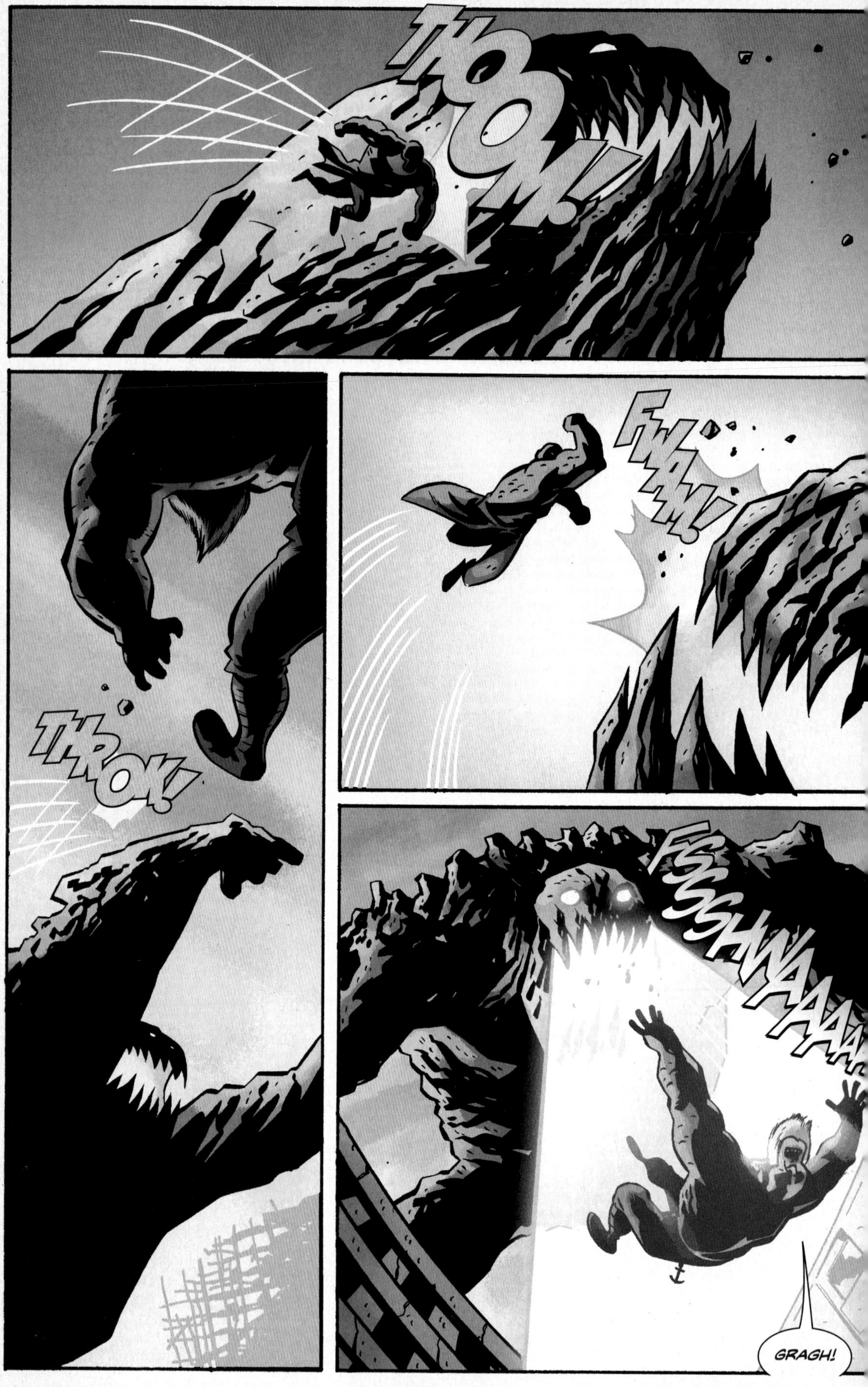
THOOM!
THROK!
FWAM!
FSSSHWAAAA
GRAGH!

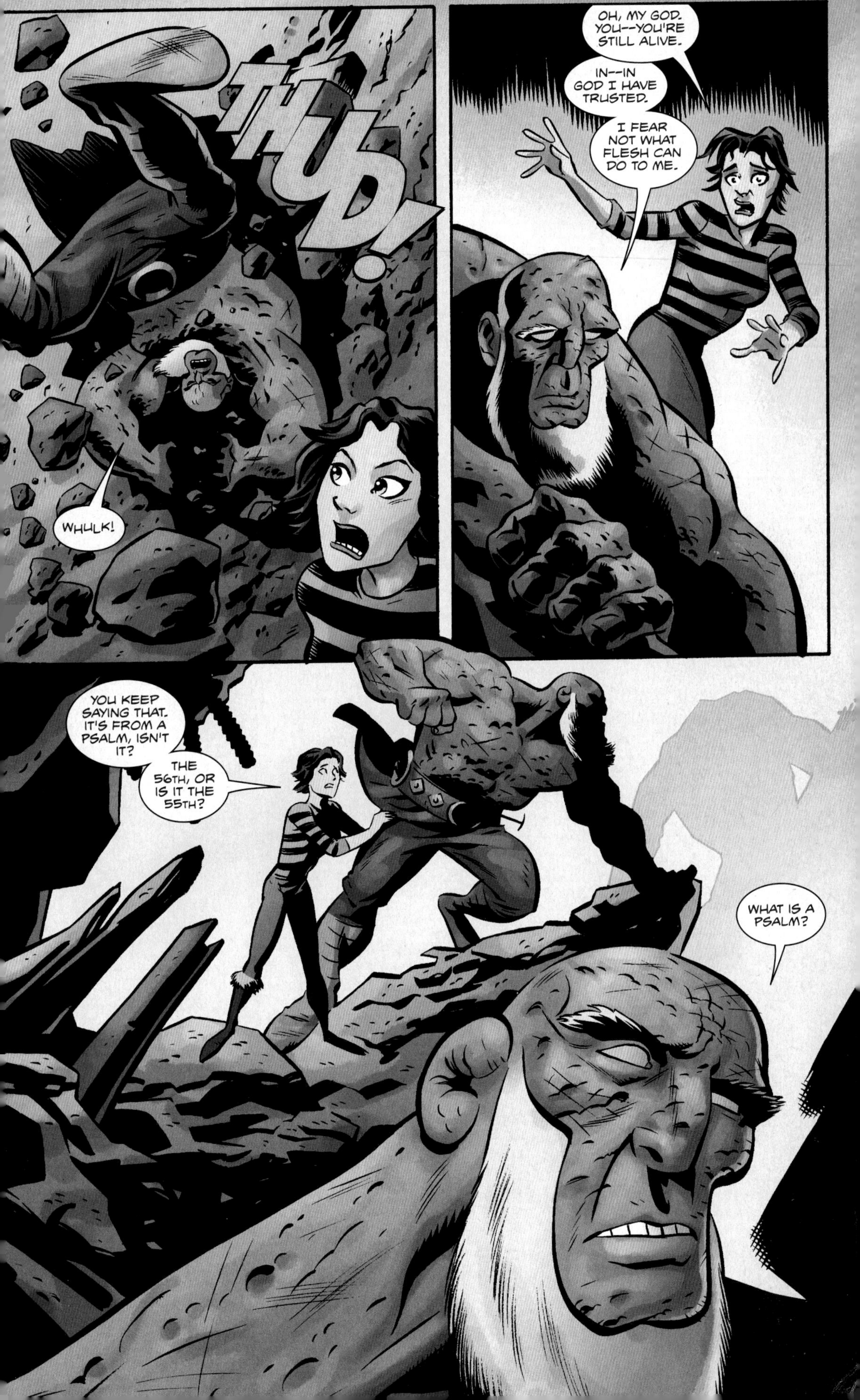
THUD!
WHULK!
OH, MY GOD. YOU--YOU'RE STILL ALIVE.
IN--IN GOD I HAVE TRUSTED.
I FEAR NOT WHAT FLESH CAN DO TO ME.
YOU KEEP SAYING THAT. IT'S FROM A PSALM, ISN'T IT?
THE 56TH, OR IS IT THE 55TH?
WHAT IS A PSALM?

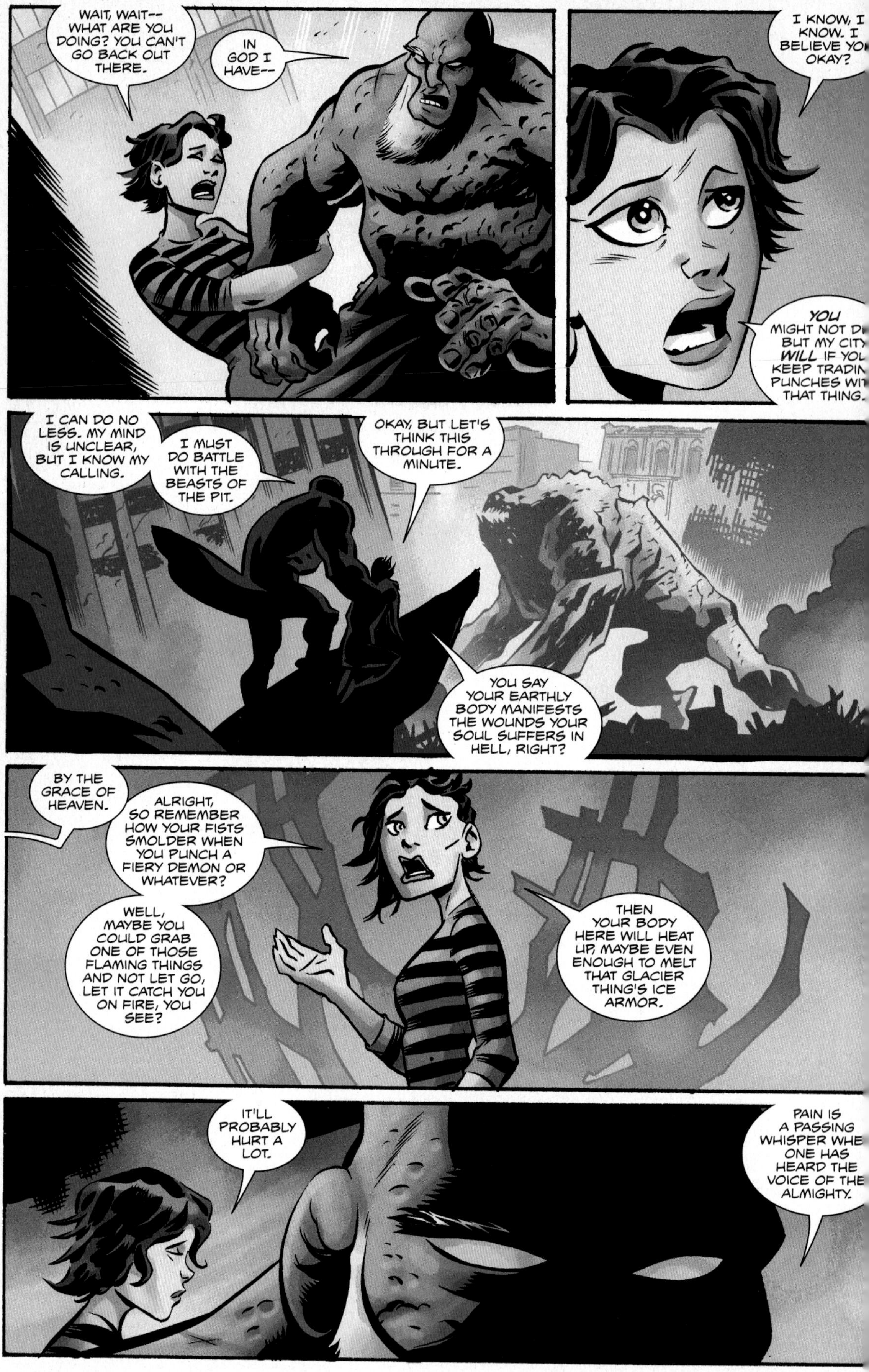

WAIT, WAIT-- WHAT ARE YOU DOING? YOU CAN'T GO BACK OUT THERE.
IN GOD I HAVE--
I KNOW, I KNOW. I BELIEVE YO OKAY?
YOU MIGHT NOT D BUT MY CITY WILL IF YOU KEEP TRADIN PUNCHES WIT THAT THING.
I CAN DO NO LESS. MY MIND IS UNCLEAR, BUT I KNOW MY CALLING.
I MUST DO BATTLE WITH THE BEASTS OF THE PIT.
OKAY, BUT LET'S THINK THIS THROUGH FOR A MINUTE.
YOU SAY YOUR EARTHLY BODY MANIFESTS THE WOUNDS YOUR SOUL SUFFERS IN HELL, RIGHT?
BY THE GRACE OF HEAVEN.
ALRIGHT, SO REMEMBER HOW YOUR FISTS SMOLDER WHEN YOU PUNCH A FIERY DEMON OR WHATEVER?
WELL, MAYBE YOU COULD GRAB ONE OF THOSE FLAMING THINGS AND NOT LET GO, LET IT CATCH YOU ON FIRE, YOU SEE?
THEN YOUR BODY HERE WILL HEAT UP, MAYBE EVEN ENOUGH TO MELT THAT GLACIER THING'S ICE ARMOR.
IT'LL PROBABLY HURT A LOT.
PAIN IS A PASSING WHISPER WHE ONE HAS HEARD THE VOICE OF THE ALMIGHTY.

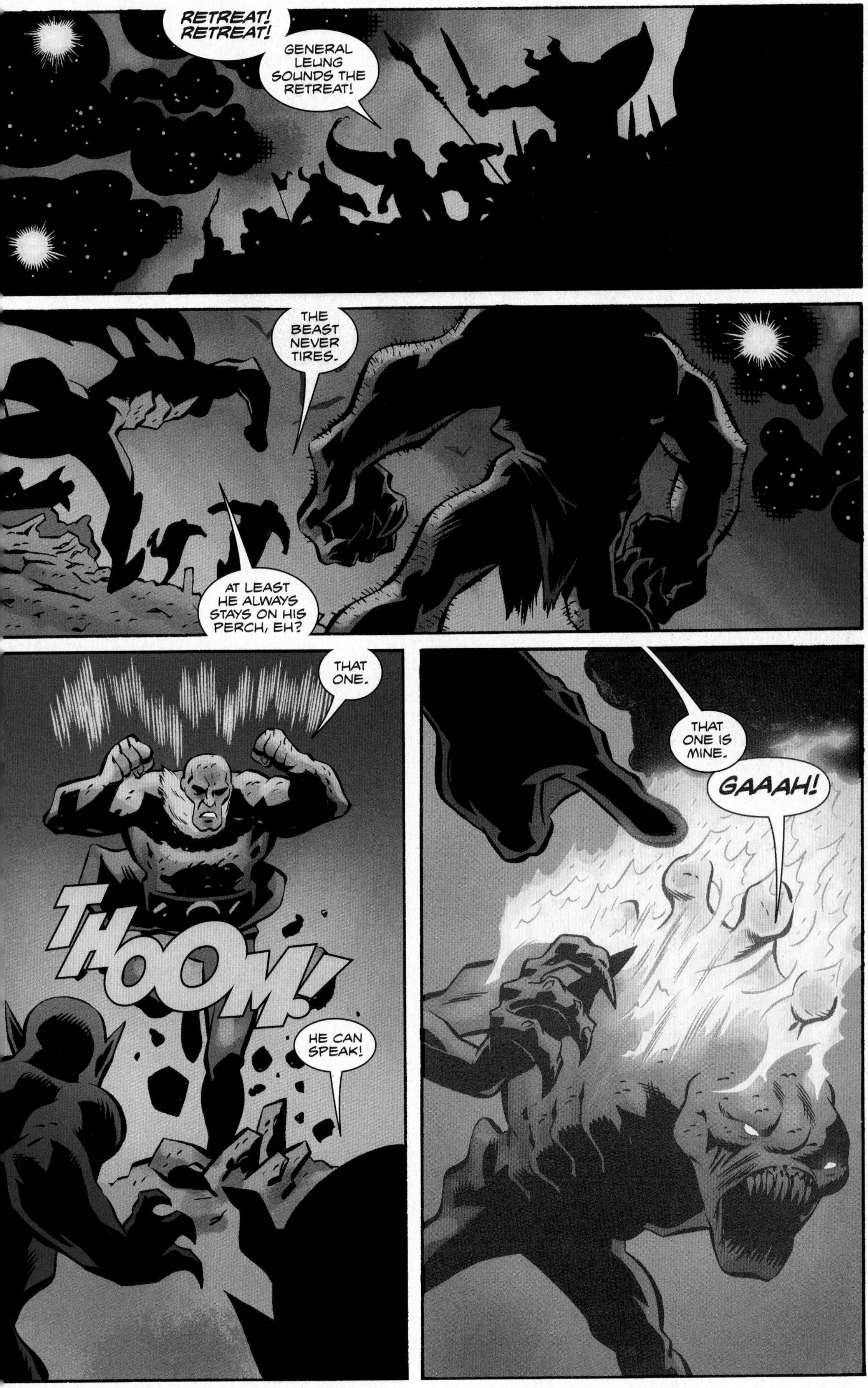

RETREAT! RETREAT!
GENERAL LEUNG SOUNDS THE RETREAT!
THE BEAST NEVER TIRES.
AT LEAST HE ALWAYS STAYS ON HIS PERCH, EH?
THAT ONE.
THOOM!
HE CAN SPEAK!
THAT ONE IS MINE.
GAAAH!

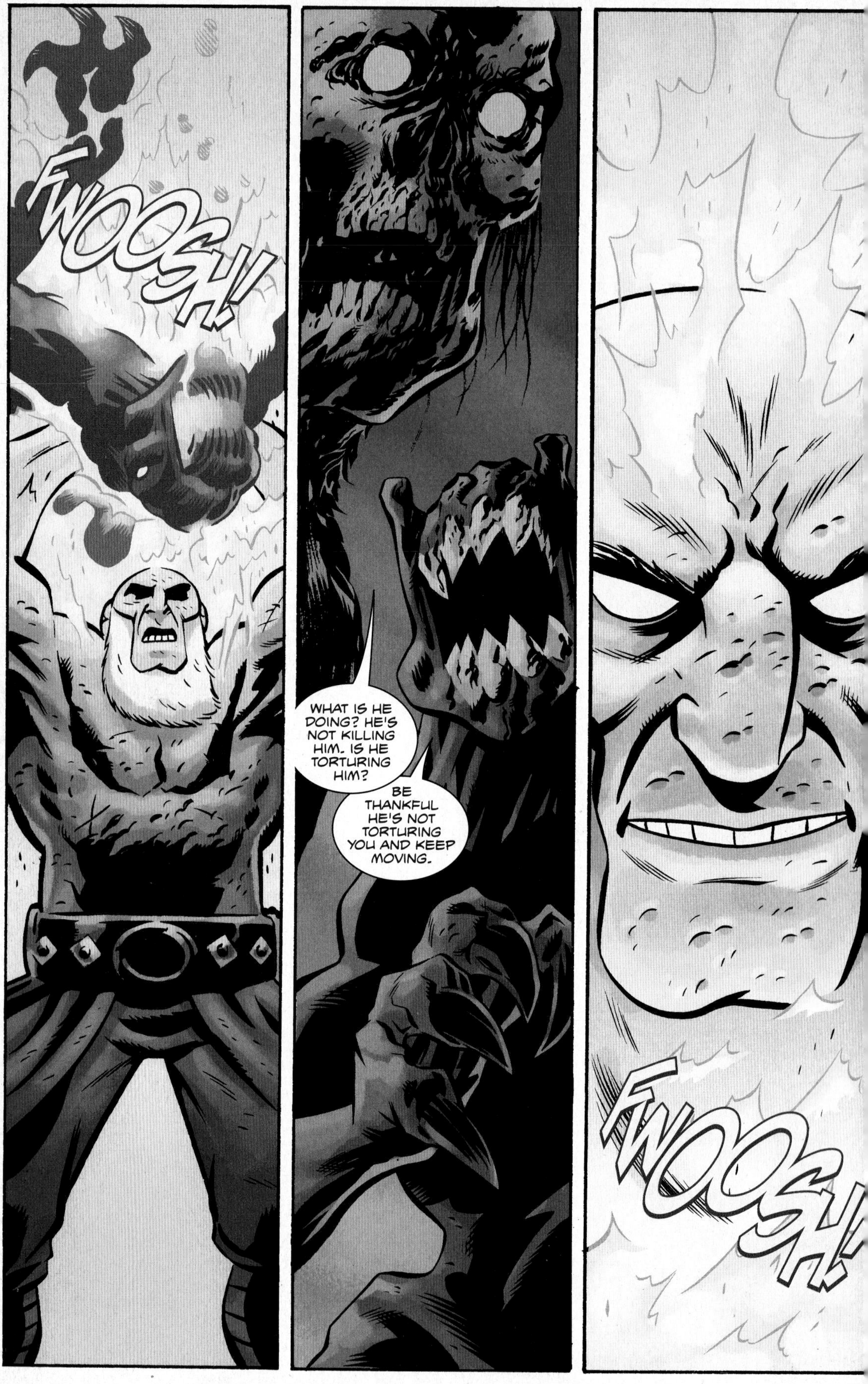
FWOOSH!
WHAT IS HE DOING? HE'S NOT KILLING HIM. IS HE TORTURING HIM?
BE THANKFUL HE'S NOT TORTURING YOU AND KEEP MOVING.
FWOOSH!

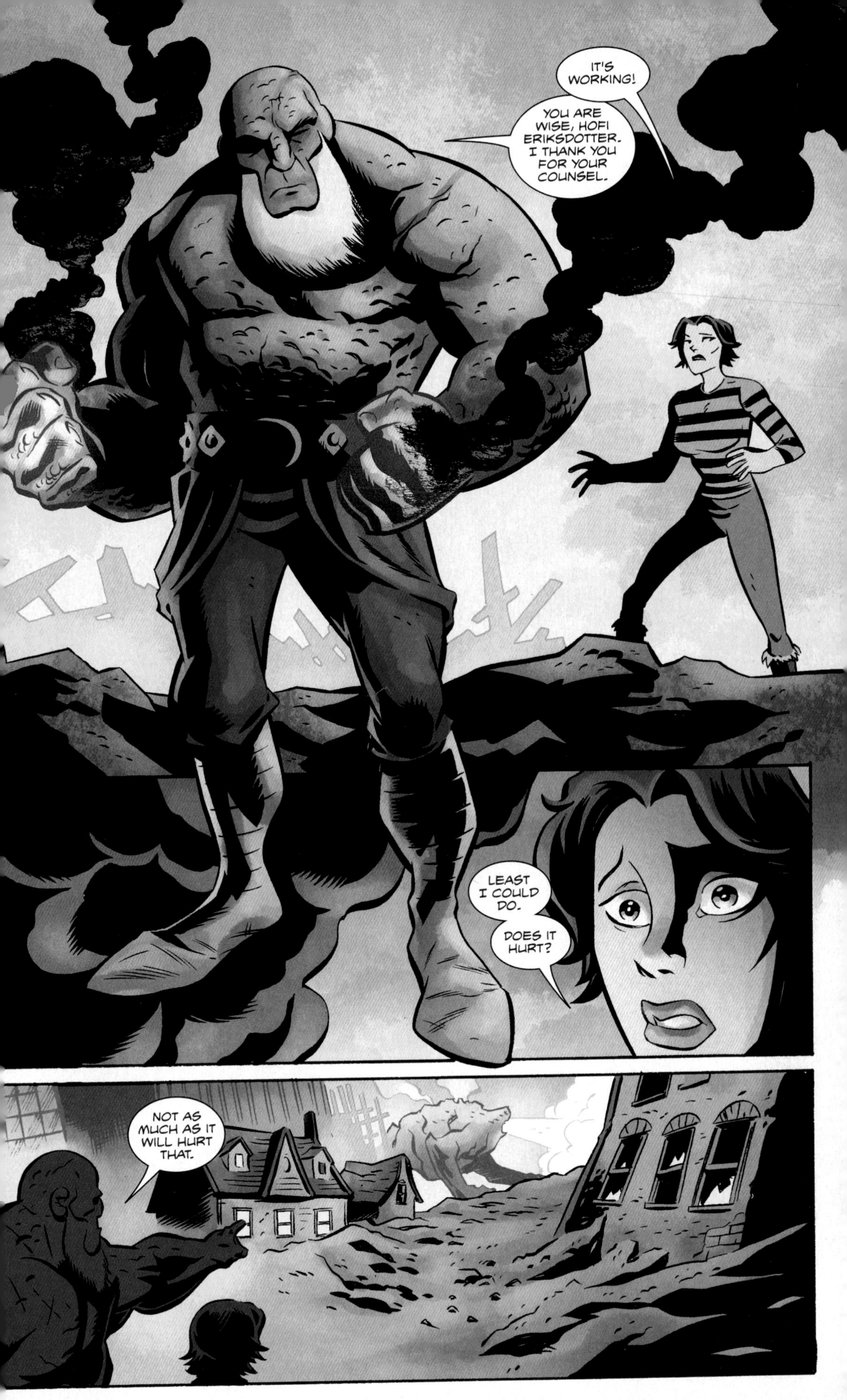
IT'S WORKING!
YOU ARE WISE, HOFI ERIKSDOTTER. I THANK YOU FOR YOUR COUNSEL.
LEAST I COULD DO.
DOES IT HURT?
NOT AS MUCH AS IT WILL HURT THAT.

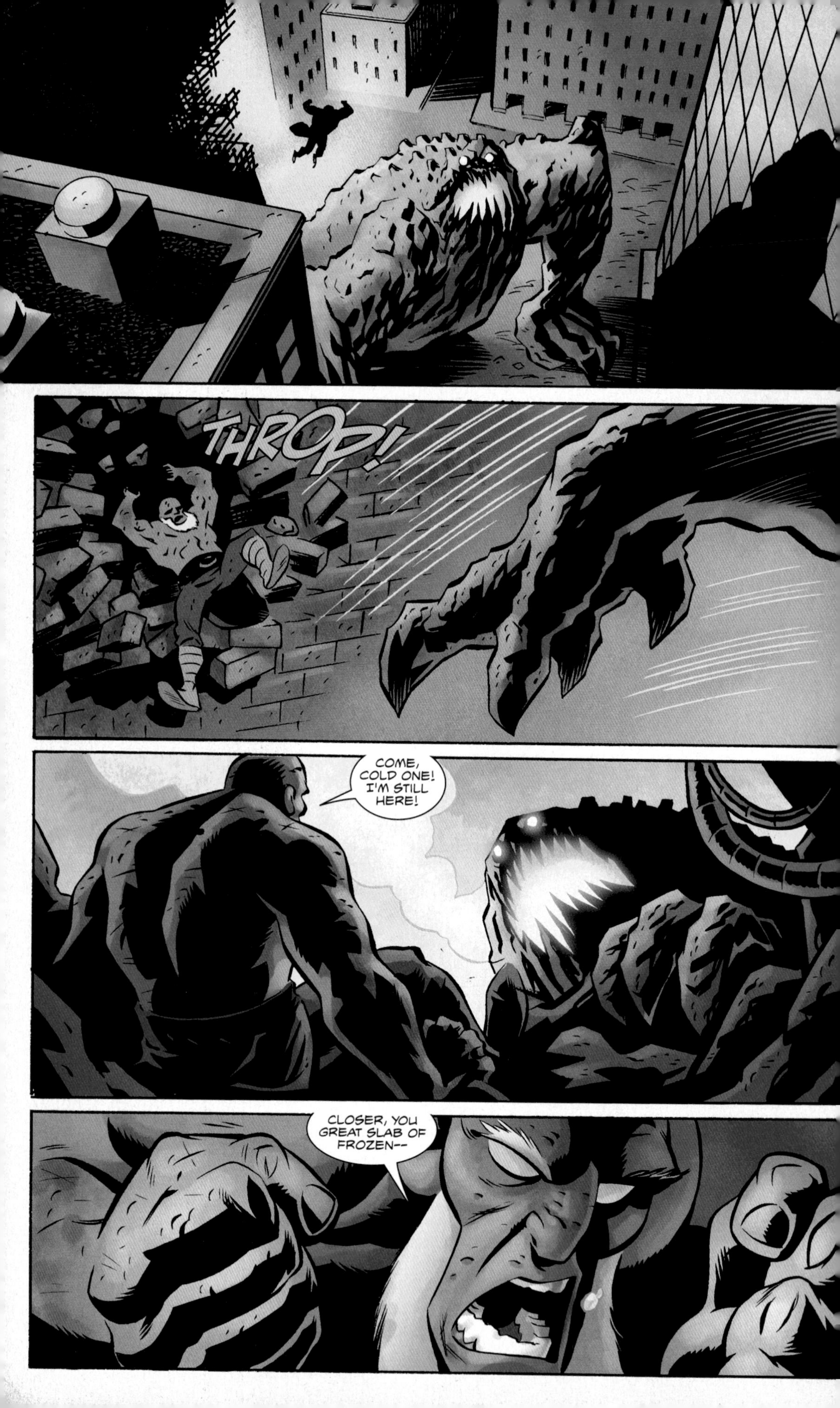
THROP!
COME, COLD ONE! I'M STILL HERE!
CLOSER, YOU GREAT SLAB OF FROZEN--

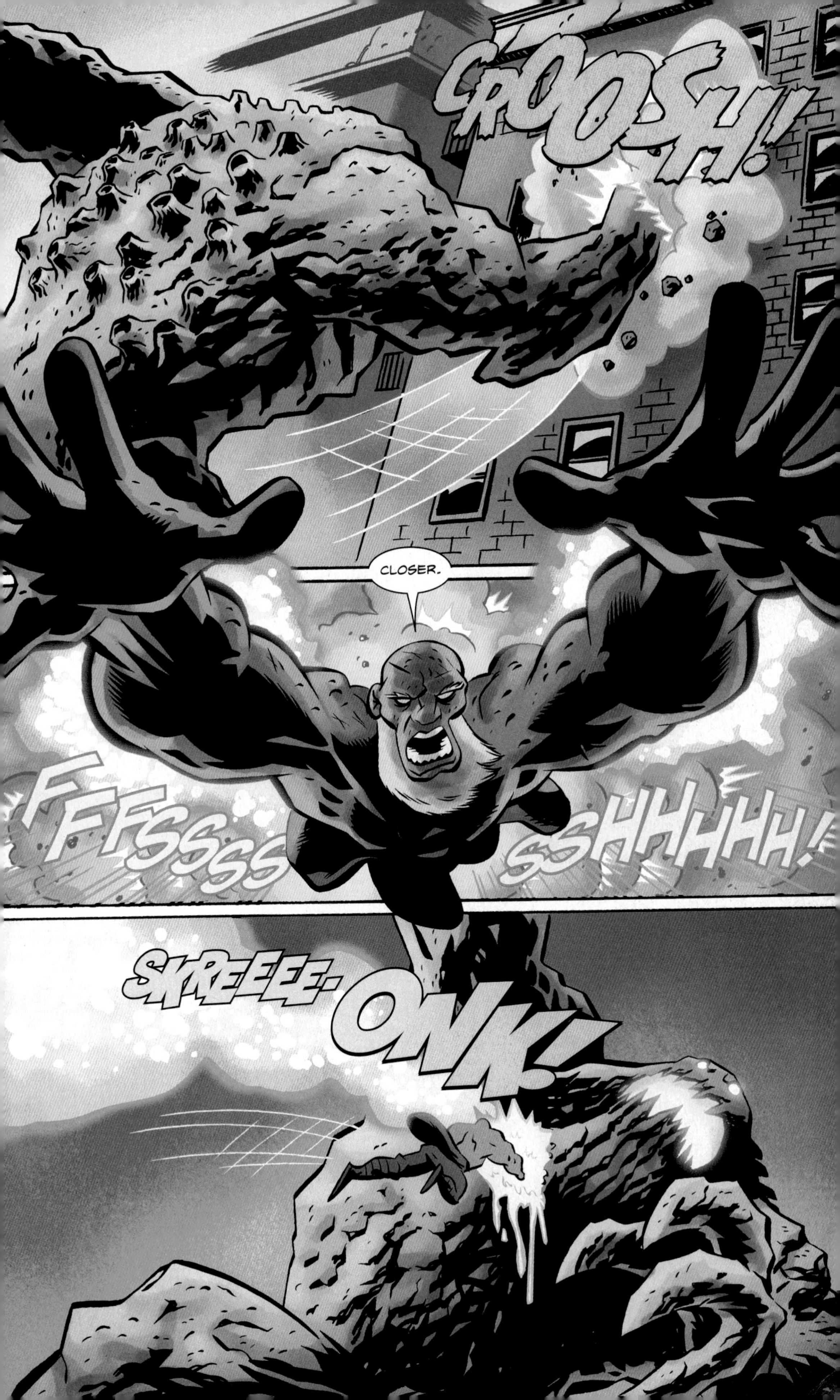
CROOOSH!!
CLOSER.
FFFSSSSS SSHHHHHH!
SKREEEE-ONK!

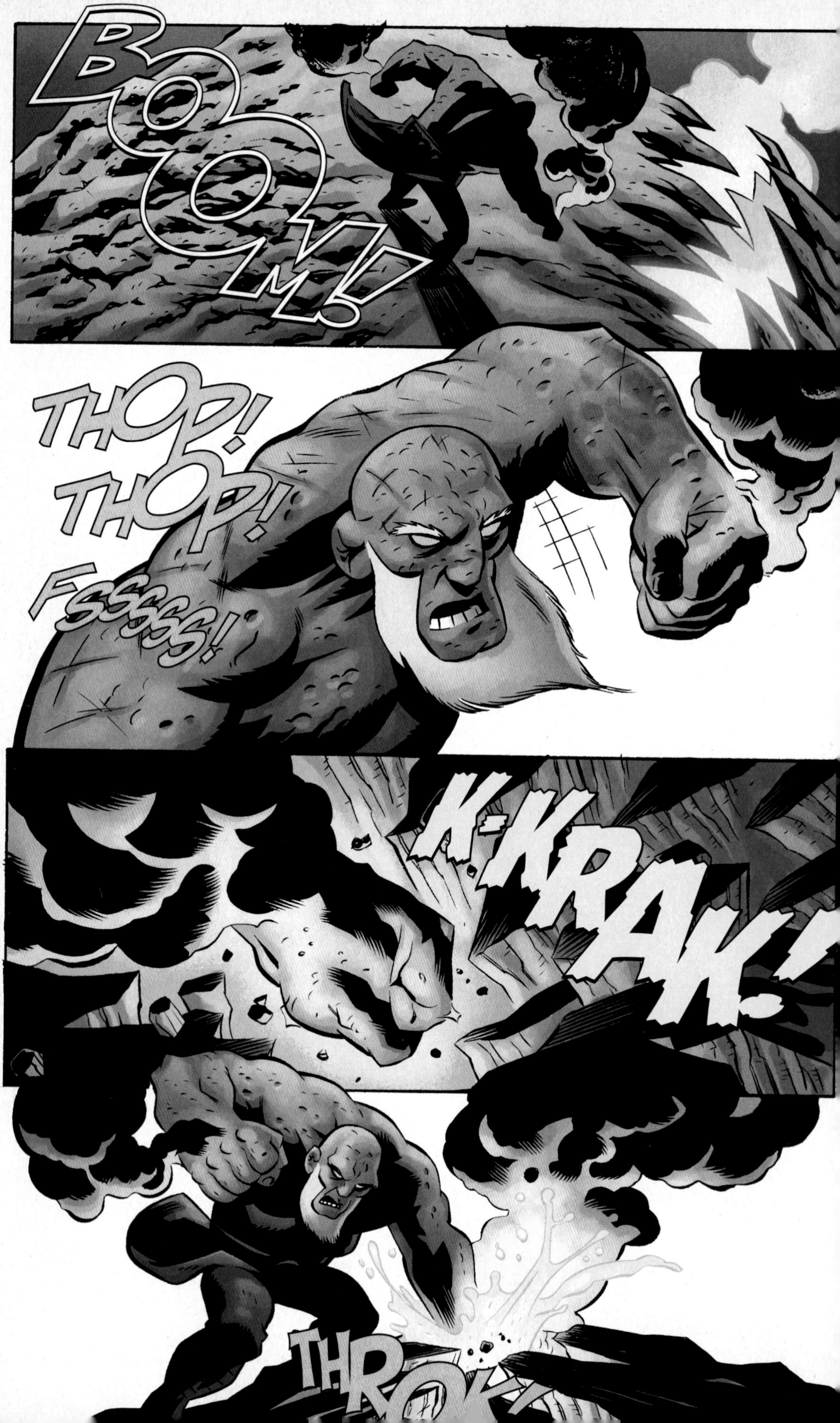
BOOOM!
THOP! THOP!
FSSSSS!
K-KRAK!
THROK!

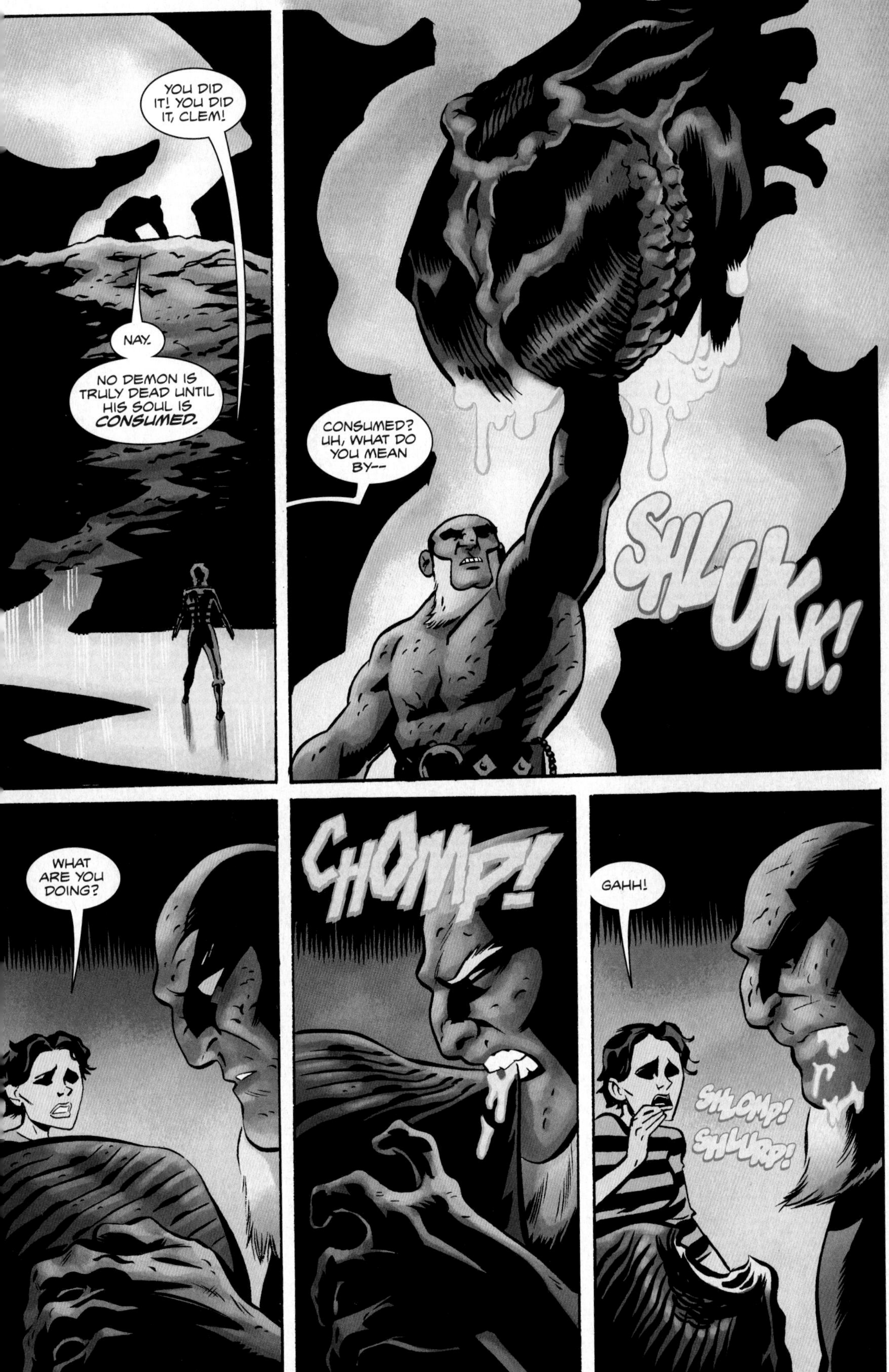

YOU DID IT! YOU DID IT, CLEM!
NAY.
NO DEMON IS TRULY DEAD UNTIL HIS SOUL IS CONSUMED.
CONSUMED? UH, WHAT DO YOU MEAN BY--
SHLUKK!
WHAT ARE YOU DOING?
CHOMP!
GAHH!
SHLOMP! SHLURP!

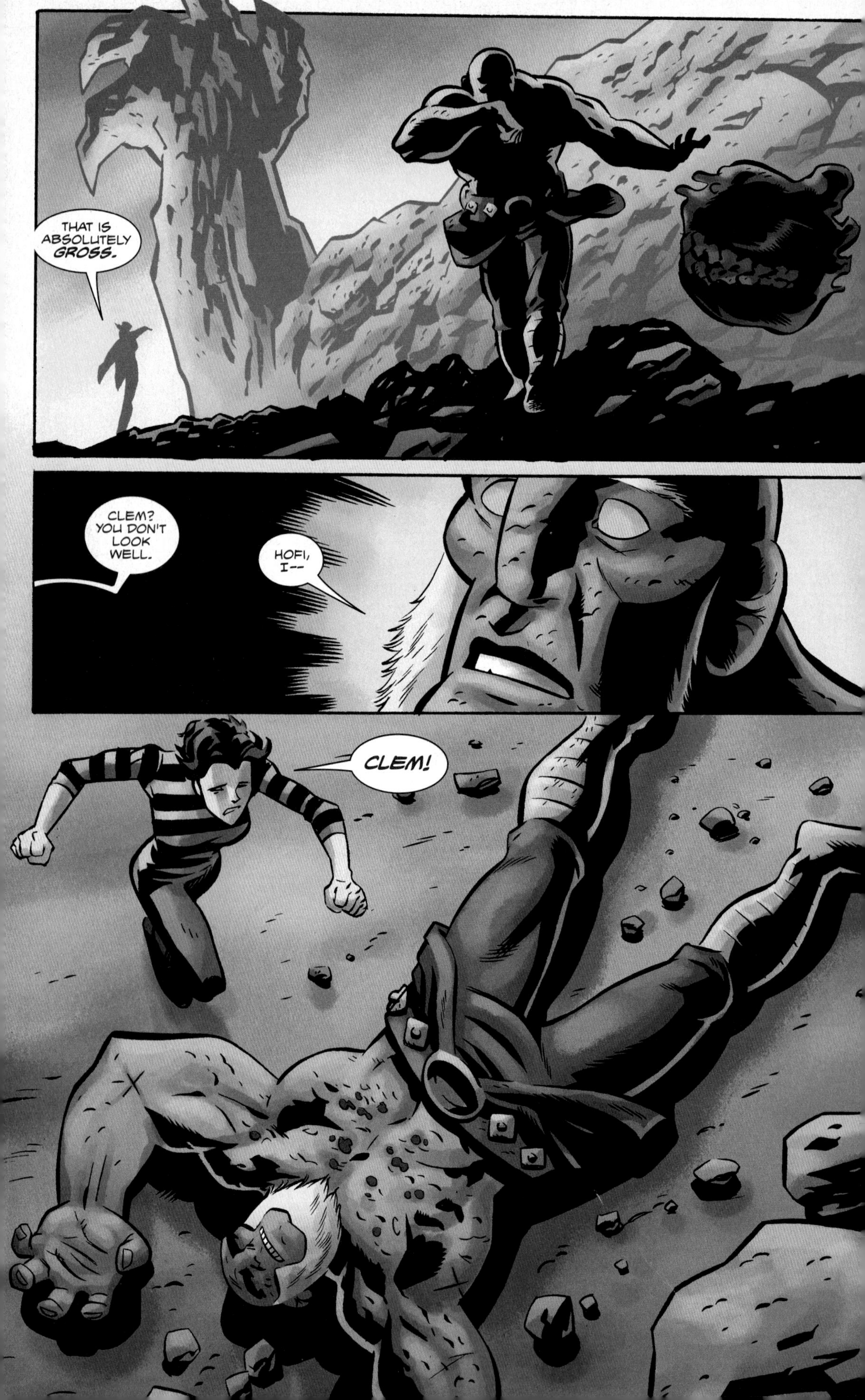
THAT IS ABSOLUTELY GROSS.
CLEM? YOU DON'T LOOK WELL.
HOFI, I--
CLEM!

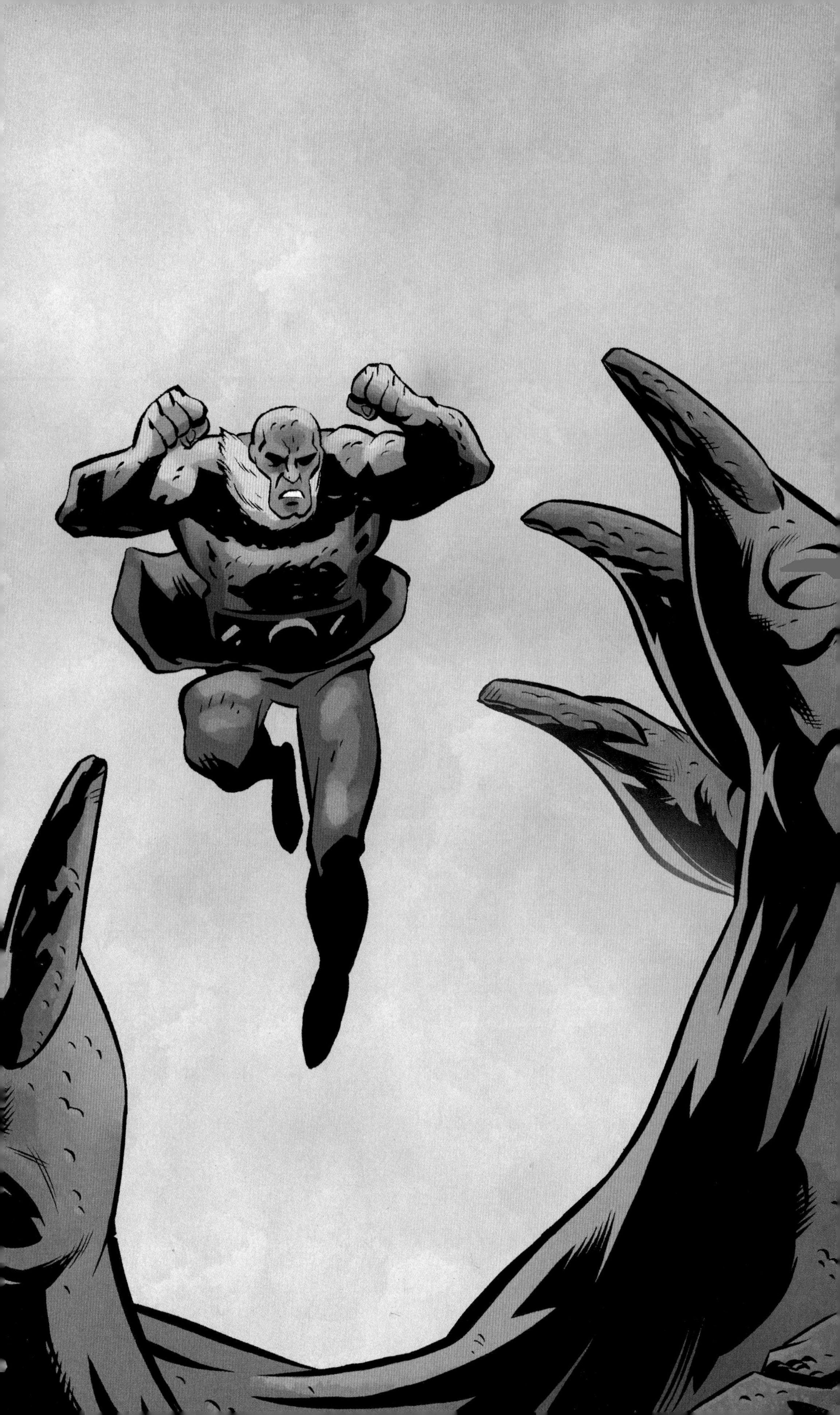

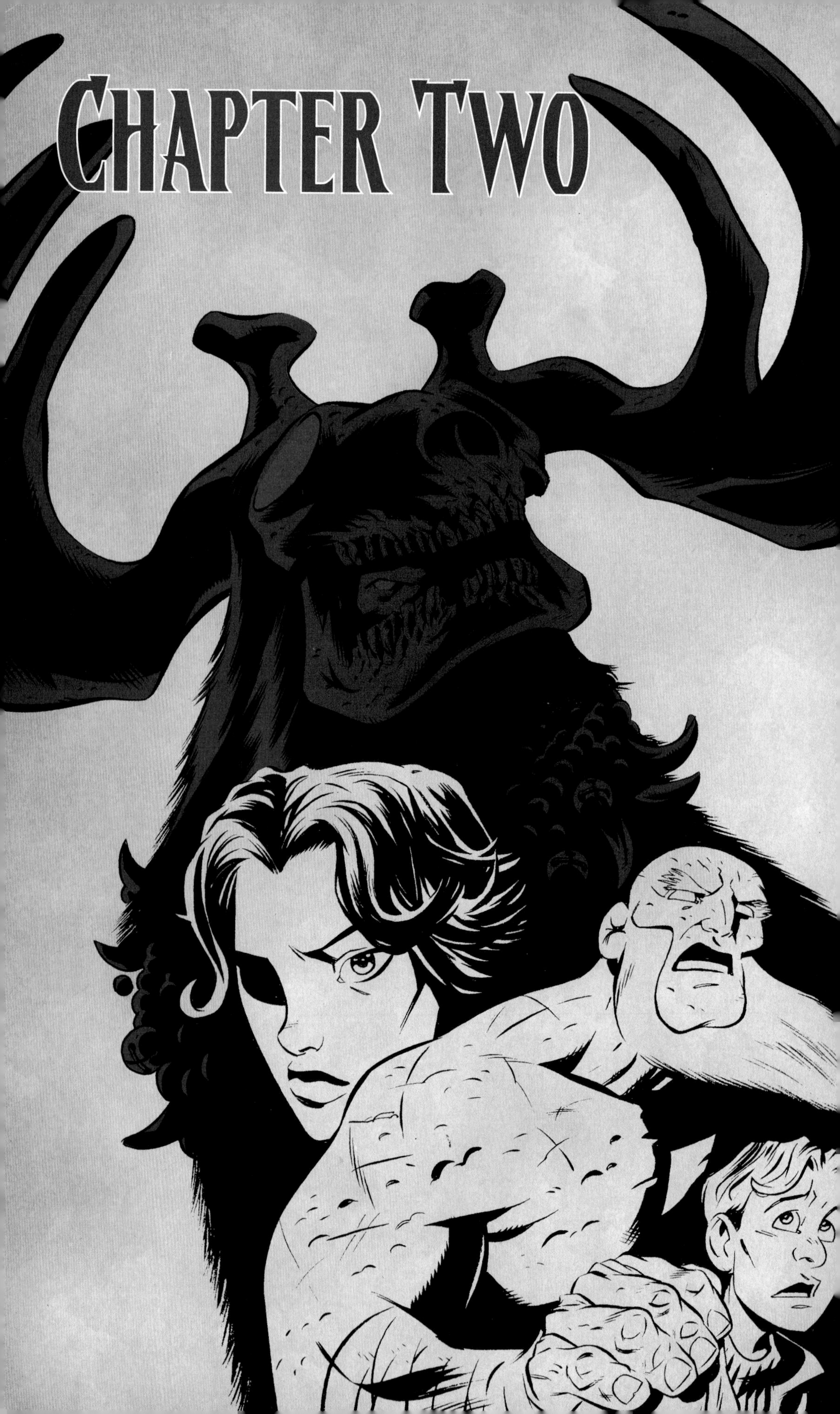
CHAPTER TWO

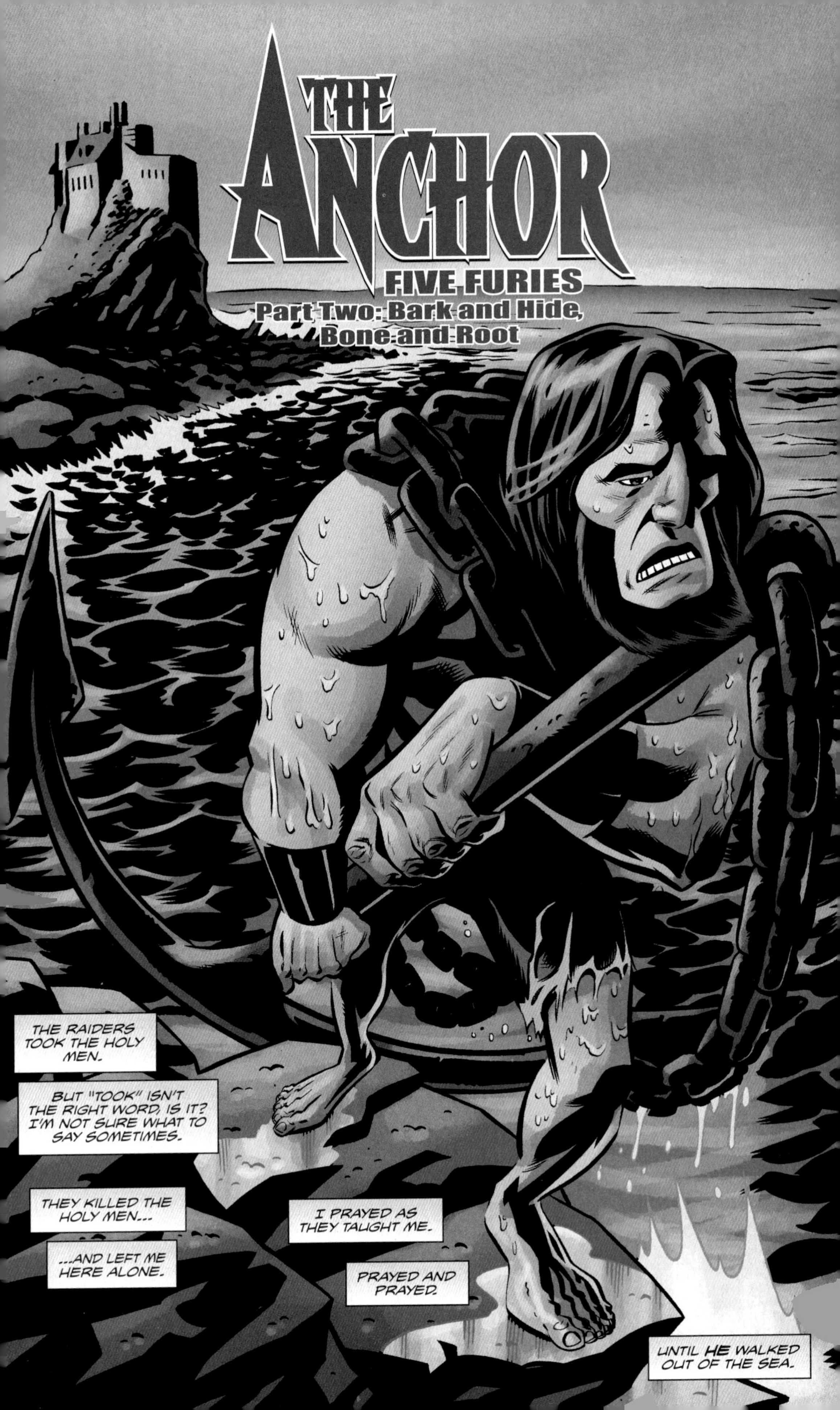
THE ANCHOR
FIVE FURIES
Part Two: Bark and Hide, Bone and Root
THE RAIDERS TOOK THE HOLY MEN.
BUT "TOOK" ISN'T THE RIGHT WORD, IS IT? I'M NOT SURE WHAT TO SAY SOMETIMES.
THEY KILLED THE HOLY MEN...
...AND LEFT ME HERE ALONE.
I PRAYED AS THEY TAUGHT ME.
PRAYED AND PRAYED.
UNTIL HE WALKED OUT OF THE SEA.

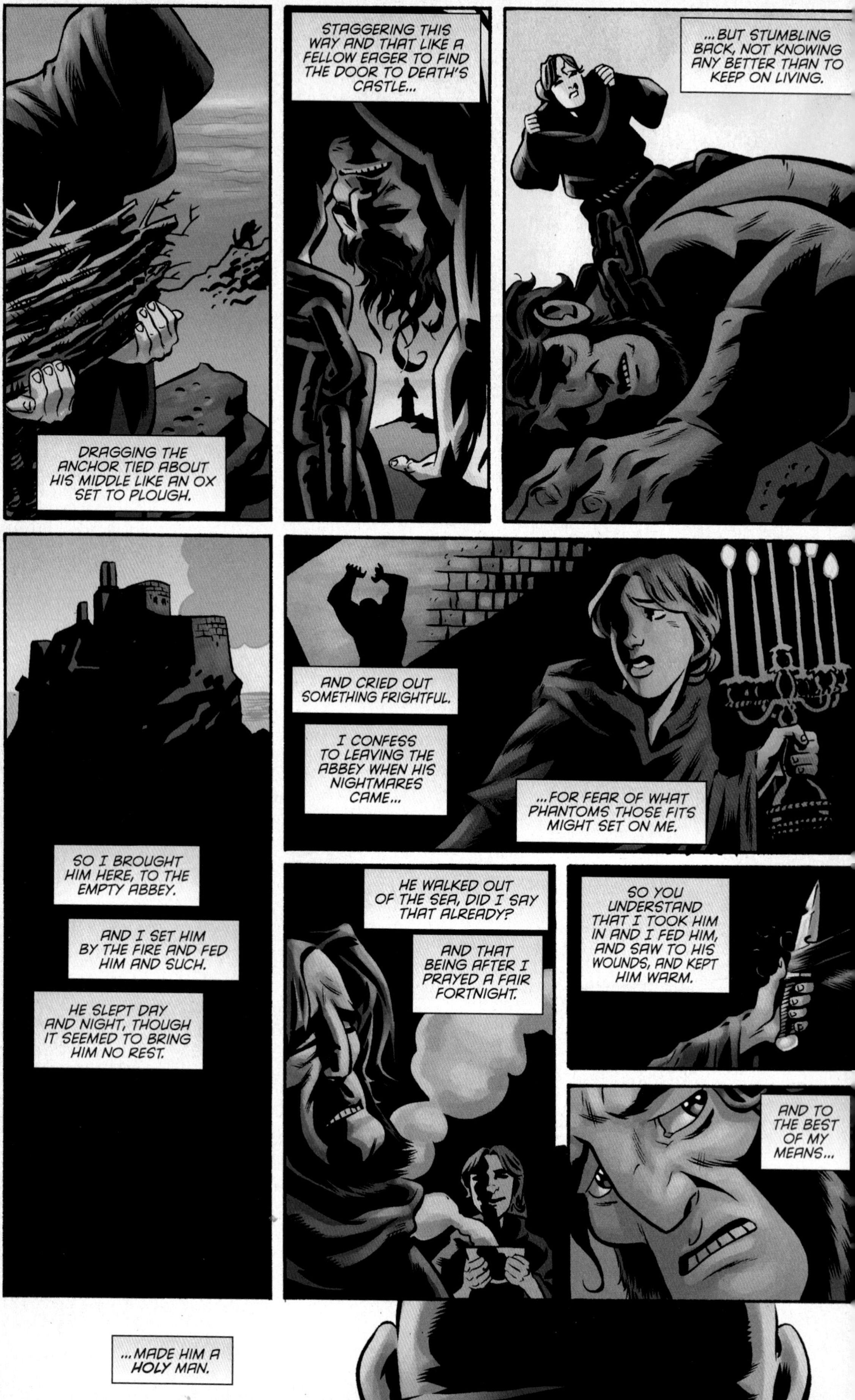
DRAGGING THE ANCHOR TIED ABOUT HIS MIDDLE LIKE AN OX SET TO PLOUGH.
STAGGERING THIS WAY AND THAT LIKE A FELLOW EAGER TO FIND THE DOOR TO DEATH'S CASTLE...
...BUT STUMBLING BACK, NOT KNOWING ANY BETTER THAN TO KEEP ON LIVING.
AND CRIED OUT SOMETHING FRIGHTFUL.
I CONFESS TO LEAVING THE ABBEY WHEN HIS NIGHTMARES CAME...
...FOR FEAR OF WHAT PHANTOMS THOSE FITS MIGHT SET ON ME.
SO I BROUGHT HIM HERE, TO THE EMPTY ABBEY.
AND I SET HIM BY THE FIRE AND FED HIM AND SUCH.
HE SLEPT DAY AND NIGHT, THOUGH IT SEEMED TO BRING HIM NO REST.
HE WALKED OUT OF THE SEA, DID I SAY THAT ALREADY?
AND THAT BEING AFTER I PRAYED A FAIR FORTNIGHT.
SO YOU UNDERSTAND THAT I TOOK HIM IN AND I FED HIM, AND SAW TO HIS WOUNDS, AND KEPT HIM WARM.
AND TO THE BEST OF MY MEANS...
...MADE HIM A **HOLY** MAN.

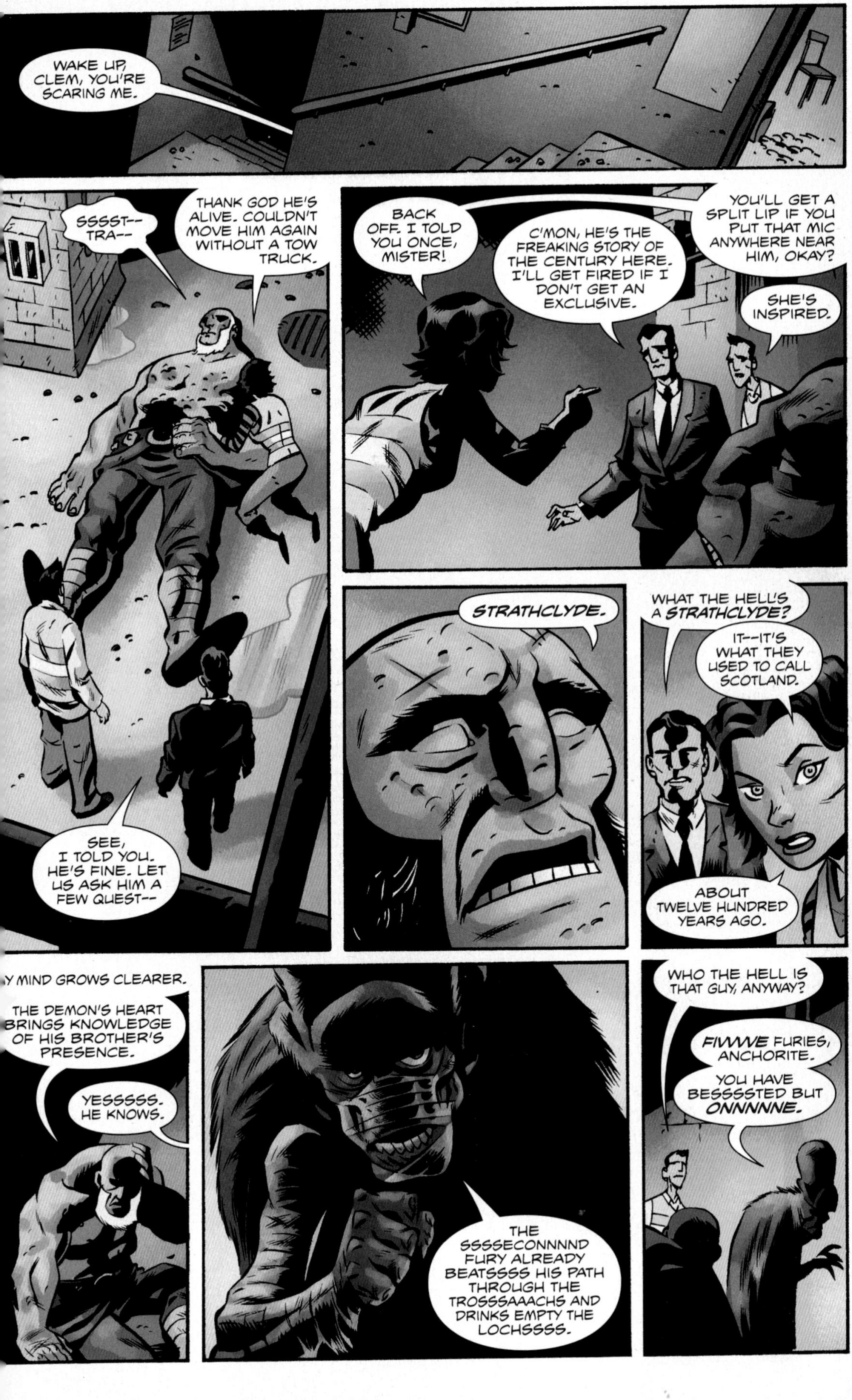
WAKE UP, CLEM, YOU'RE SCARING ME.
SSSST-- TRA--
THANK GOD HE'S ALIVE. COULDN'T MOVE HIM AGAIN WITHOUT A TOW TRUCK.
SEE, I TOLD YOU. HE'S FINE. LET US ASK HIM A FEW QUEST--
BACK OFF. I TOLD YOU ONCE, MISTER!
C'MON, HE'S THE FREAKING STORY OF THE CENTURY HERE. I'LL GET FIRED IF I DON'T GET AN EXCLUSIVE.
YOU'LL GET A SPLIT LIP IF YOU PUT THAT MIC ANYWHERE NEAR HIM, OKAY?
SHE'S INSPIRED.
STRATHCLYDE.
WHAT THE HELL'S A STRATHCLYDE?
IT--IT'S WHAT THEY USED TO CALL SCOTLAND.
ABOUT TWELVE HUNDRED YEARS AGO.
Y MIND GROWS CLEARER.
THE DEMON'S HEART BRINGS KNOWLEDGE OF HIS BROTHER'S PRESENCE.
YESSSSS. HE KNOWS.
THE SSSSECONNNND FURY ALREADY BEATSSSS HIS PATH THROUGH THE TROSSSAAACHS AND DRINKS EMPTY THE LOCHSSSS.
WHO THE HELL IS THAT GUY, ANYWAY?
FIVVVVE FURIES, ANCHORITE.
YOU HAVE BESSSSTED BUT ONNNNNE.

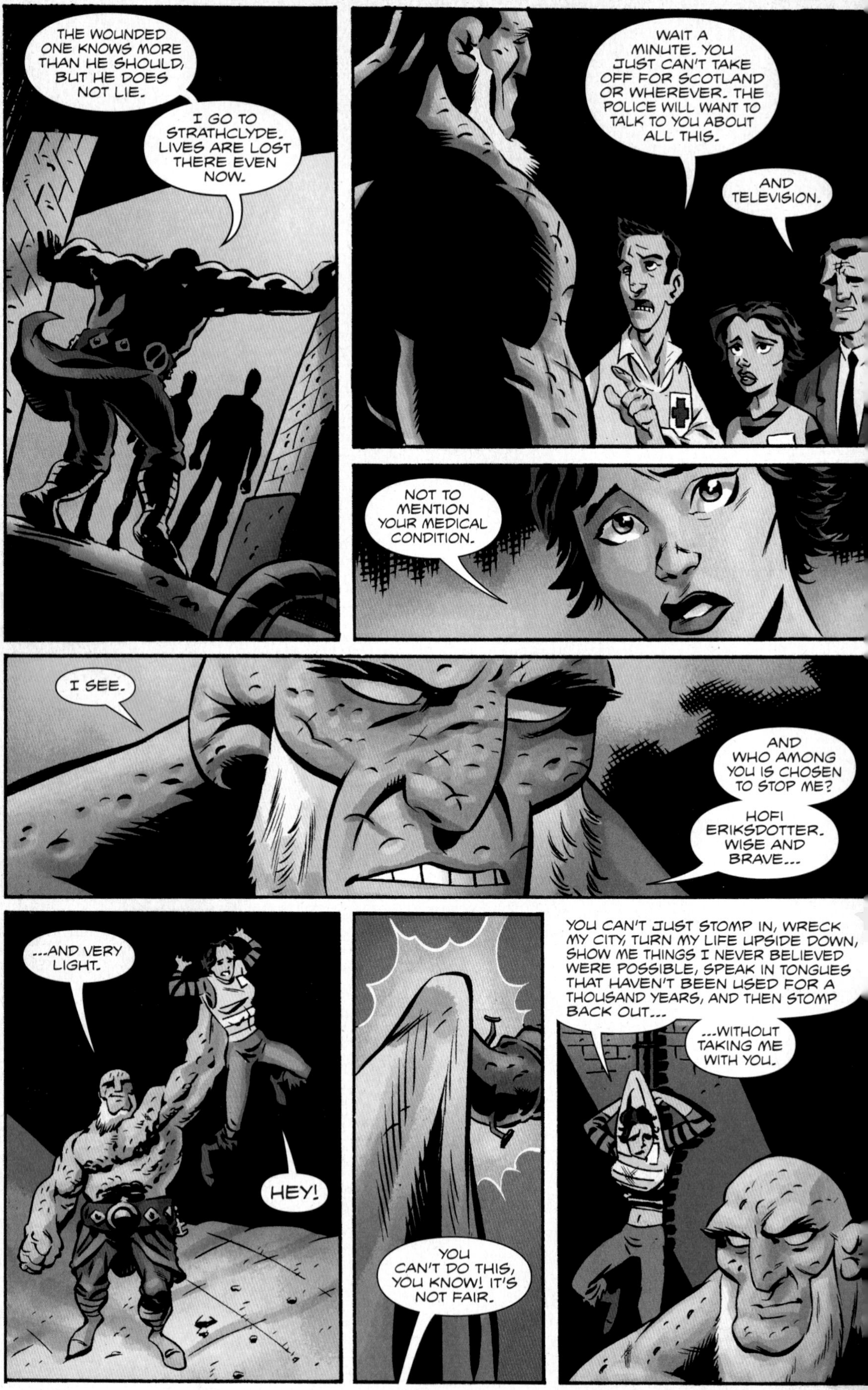
THE WOUNDED ONE KNOWS MORE THAN HE SHOULD, BUT HE DOES NOT LIE.
I GO TO STRATHCLYDE. LIVES ARE LOST THERE EVEN NOW.
WAIT A MINUTE. YOU JUST CAN'T TAKE OFF FOR SCOTLAND OR WHEREVER. THE POLICE WILL WANT TO TALK TO YOU ABOUT ALL THIS.
AND TELEVISION.
NOT TO MENTION YOUR MEDICAL CONDITION.
I SEE.
AND WHO AMONG YOU IS CHOSEN TO STOP ME?
HOFI ERIKSDOTTER. WISE AND BRAVE...
...AND VERY LIGHT.
HEY!
YOU CAN'T DO THIS, YOU KNOW! IT'S NOT FAIR.
YOU CAN'T JUST STOMP IN, WRECK MY CITY, TURN MY LIFE UPSIDE DOWN, SHOW ME THINGS I NEVER BELIEVED WERE POSSIBLE, SPEAK IN TONGUES THAT HAVEN'T BEEN USED FOR A THOUSAND YEARS, AND THEN STOMP BACK OUT...
...WITHOUT TAKING ME WITH YOU.

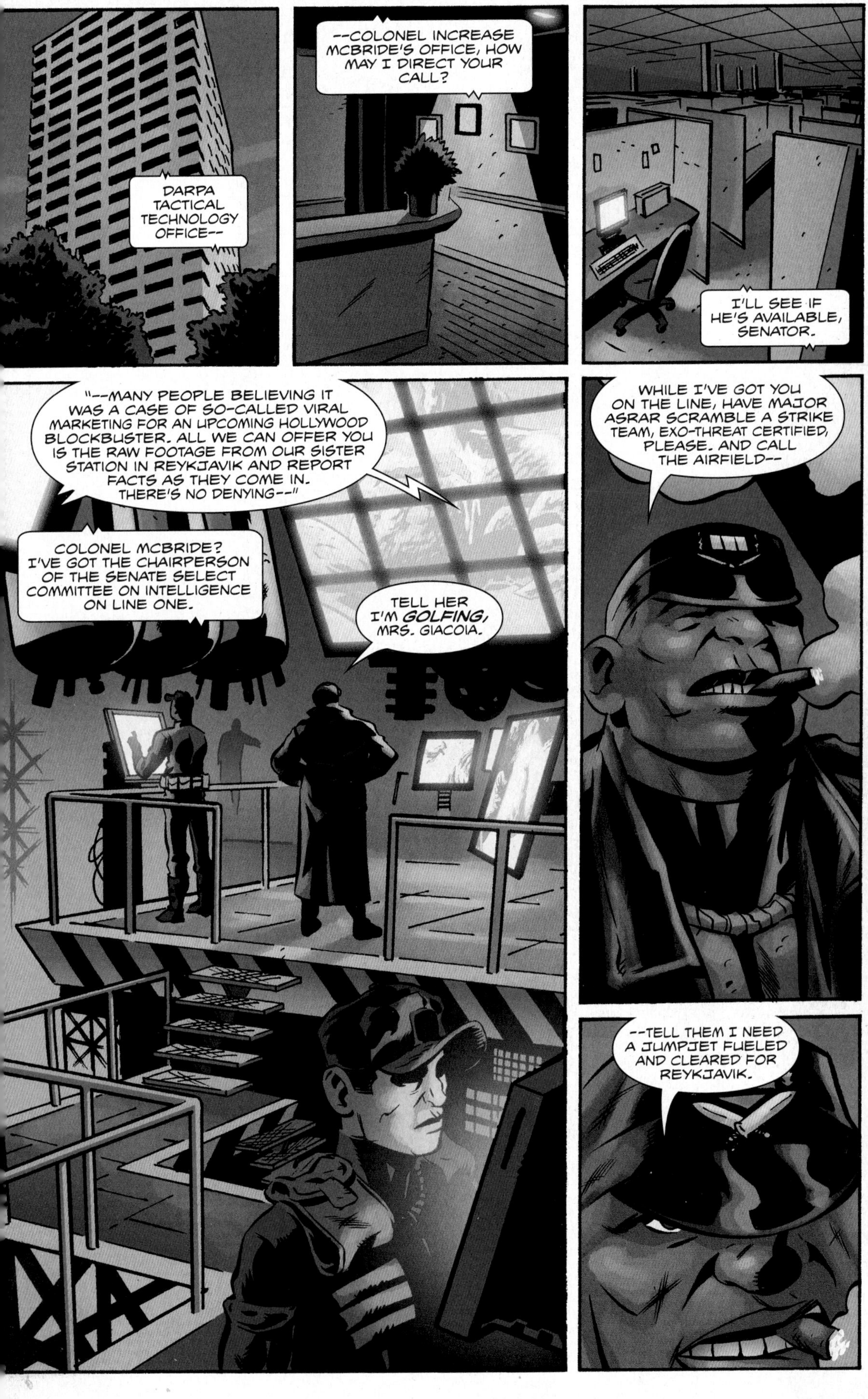
DARPA TACTICAL TECHNOLOGY OFFICE--
--COLONEL INCREASE MCBRIDE'S OFFICE, HOW MAY I DIRECT YOUR CALL?
I'LL SEE IF HE'S AVAILABLE, SENATOR.
"--MANY PEOPLE BELIEVING IT WAS A CASE OF SO-CALLED VIRAL MARKETING FOR AN UPCOMING HOLLYWOOD BLOCKBUSTER. ALL WE CAN OFFER YOU IS THE RAW FOOTAGE FROM OUR SISTER STATION IN REYKJAVIK AND REPORT FACTS AS THEY COME IN. THERE'S NO DENYING--"
COLONEL MCBRIDE? I'VE GOT THE CHAIRPERSON OF THE SENATE SELECT COMMITTEE ON INTELLIGENCE ON LINE ONE.
TELL HER I'M *GOLFING,* MRS. GIACOIA.
WHILE I'VE GOT YOU ON THE LINE, HAVE MAJOR ASRAR SCRAMBLE A STRIKE TEAM, EXO-THREAT CERTIFIED, PLEASE. AND CALL THE AIRFIELD--
--TELL THEM I NEED A JUMPJET FUELED AND CLEARED FOR REYKJAVIK.

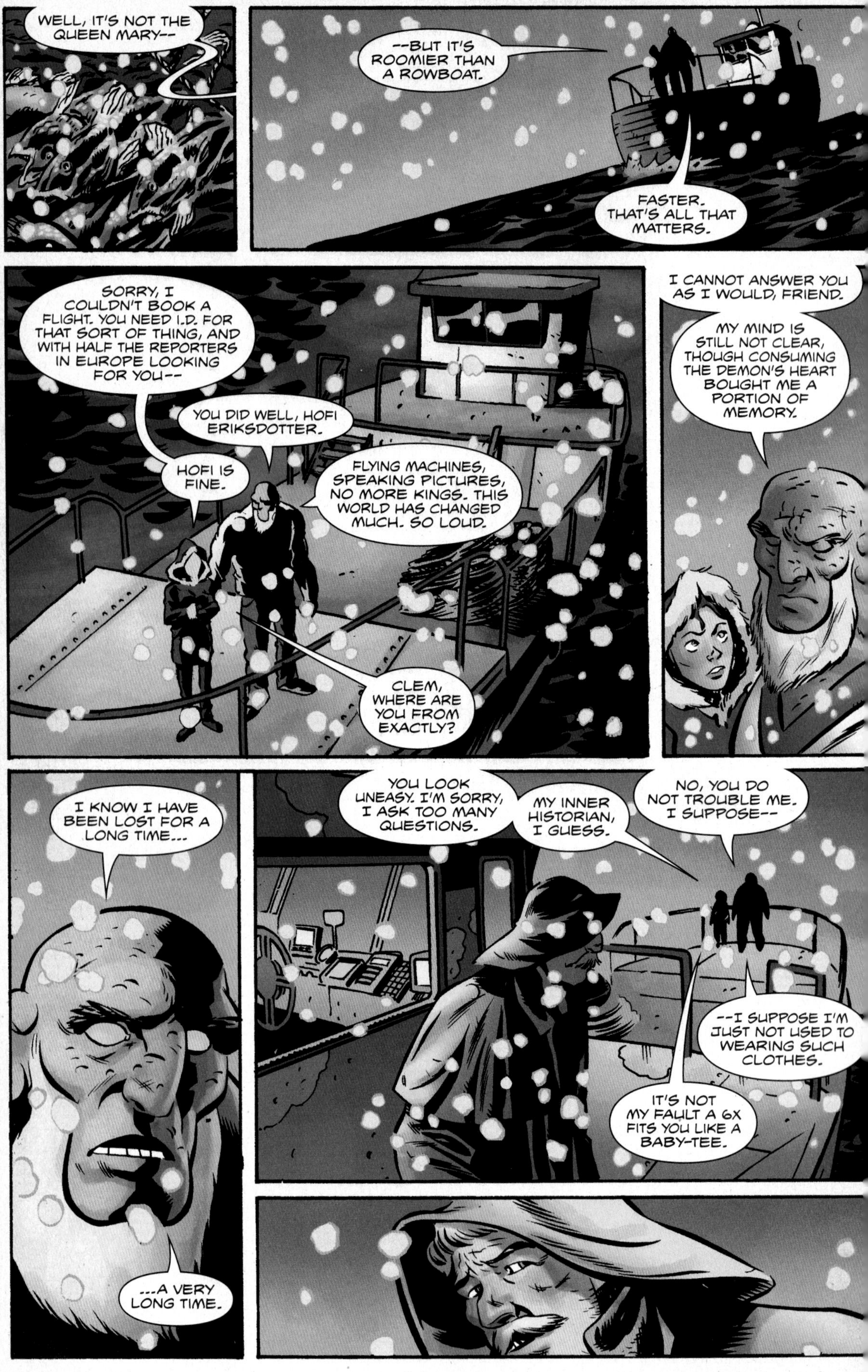
WELL, IT'S NOT THE QUEEN MARY--
--BUT IT'S ROOMIER THAN A ROWBOAT.
FASTER. THAT'S ALL THAT MATTERS.
SORRY, I COULDN'T BOOK A FLIGHT. YOU NEED I.D. FOR THAT SORT OF THING, AND WITH HALF THE REPORTERS IN EUROPE LOOKING FOR YOU--
YOU DID WELL, HOFI ERIKSDOTTER.
HOFI IS FINE.
FLYING MACHINES, SPEAKING PICTURES, NO MORE KINGS. THIS WORLD HAS CHANGED MUCH. SO LOUD.
CLEM, WHERE ARE YOU FROM EXACTLY?
I CANNOT ANSWER YOU AS I WOULD, FRIEND.
MY MIND IS STILL NOT CLEAR, THOUGH CONSUMING THE DEMON'S HEART BOUGHT ME A PORTION OF MEMORY.
I KNOW I HAVE BEEN LOST FOR A LONG TIME...
...A VERY LONG TIME.
YOU LOOK UNEASY. I'M SORRY, I ASK TOO MANY QUESTIONS.
MY INNER HISTORIAN, I GUESS.
NO, YOU DO NOT TROUBLE ME. I SUPPOSE--
--I SUPPOSE I'M JUST NOT USED TO WEARING SUCH CLOTHES.
IT'S NOT MY FAULT A 6X FITS YOU LIKE A BABY-TEE.

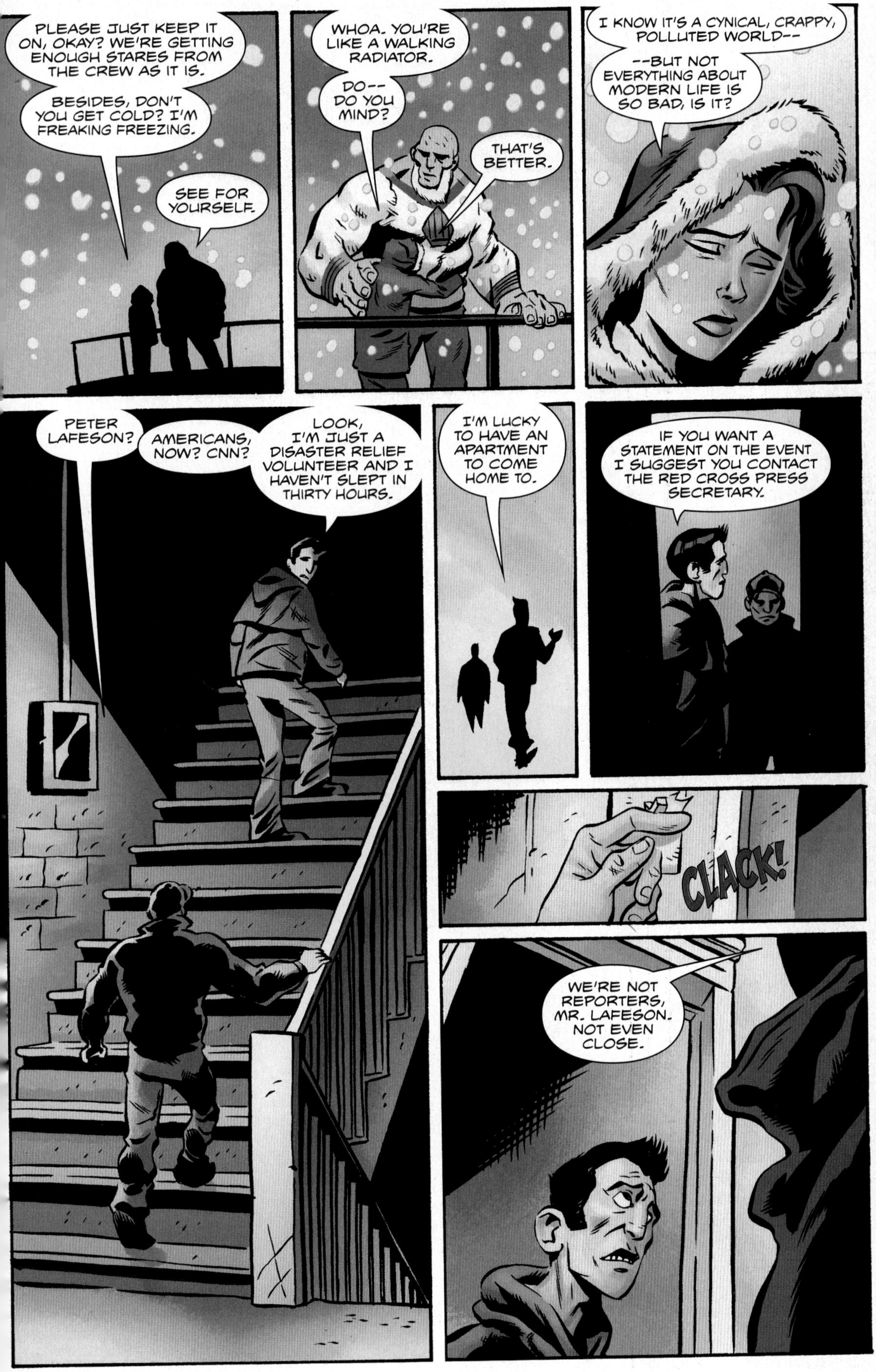
PLEASE JUST KEEP IT ON, OKAY? WE'RE GETTING ENOUGH STARES FROM THE CREW AS IT IS.
BESIDES, DON'T YOU GET COLD? I'M FREAKING FREEZING.
SEE FOR YOURSELF.
WHOA. YOU'RE LIKE A WALKING RADIATOR.
DO-- DO YOU MIND?
THAT'S BETTER.
I KNOW IT'S A CYNICAL, CRAPPY, POLLUTED WORLD--
--BUT NOT EVERYTHING ABOUT MODERN LIFE IS SO BAD, IS IT?
PETER LAFESON?
AMERICANS, NOW? CNN?
LOOK, I'M JUST A DISASTER RELIEF VOLUNTEER AND I HAVEN'T SLEPT IN THIRTY HOURS.
I'M LUCKY TO HAVE AN APARTMENT TO COME HOME TO.
IF YOU WANT A STATEMENT ON THE EVENT I SUGGEST YOU CONTACT THE RED CROSS PRESS SECRETARY.
CLACK!
WE'RE NOT REPORTERS, MR. LAFESON. NOT EVEN CLOSE.

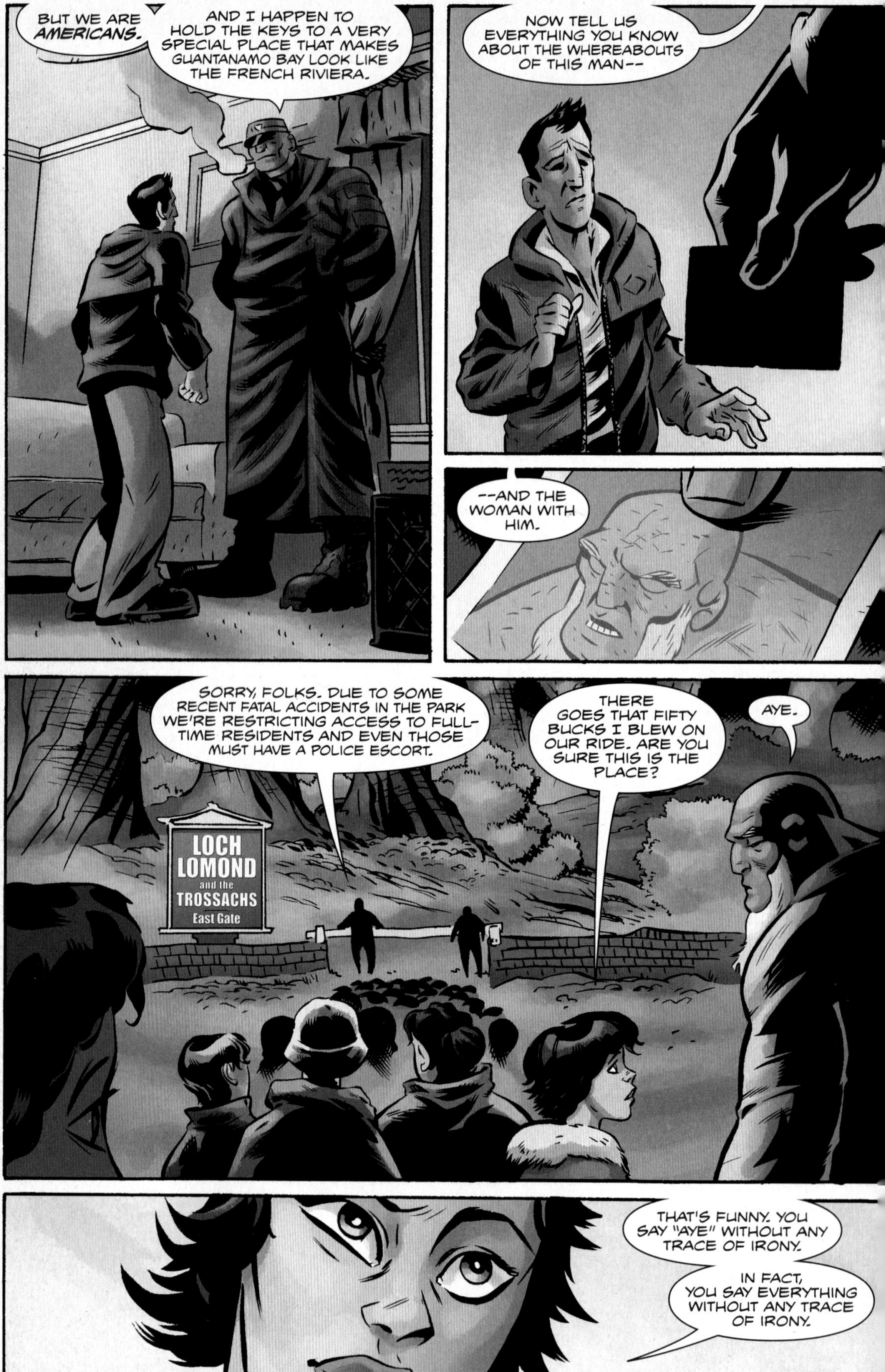

BUT WE ARE *AMERICANS.*
AND I HAPPEN TO HOLD THE KEYS TO A VERY SPECIAL PLACE THAT MAKES GUANTANAMO BAY LOOK LIKE THE FRENCH RIVIERA.
NOW TELL US EVERYTHING YOU KNOW ABOUT THE WHEREABOUTS OF THIS MAN--
--AND THE WOMAN WITH HIM.
SORRY, FOLKS. DUE TO SOME RECENT FATAL ACCIDENTS IN THE PARK WE'RE RESTRICTING ACCESS TO FULL-TIME RESIDENTS AND EVEN THOSE MUST HAVE A POLICE ESCORT.
LOCH LOMOND and the TROSSACHS East Gate
THERE GOES THAT FIFTY BUCKS I BLEW ON OUR RIDE. ARE YOU SURE THIS IS THE PLACE?
AYE.
THAT'S FUNNY. YOU SAY "AYE" WITHOUT ANY TRACE OF IRONY.
IN FACT, YOU SAY EVERYTHING WITHOUT ANY TRACE OF IRONY.

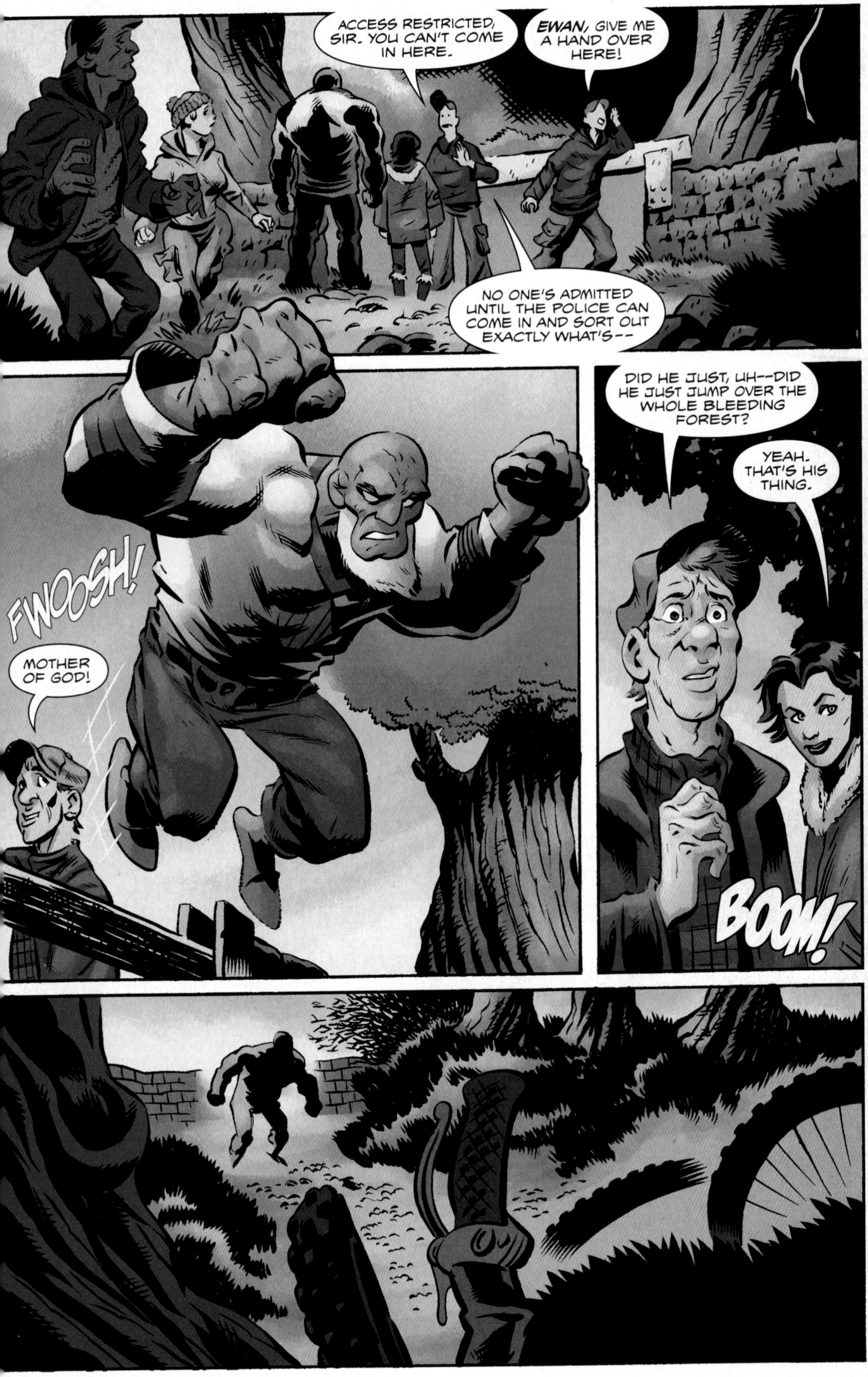
ACCESS RESTRICTED, SIR. YOU CAN'T COME IN HERE.
EWAN, GIVE ME A HAND OVER HERE!
NO ONE'S ADMITTED UNTIL THE POLICE CAN COME IN AND SORT OUT EXACTLY WHAT'S--
FWOOSH!
MOTHER OF GOD!
DID HE JUST, UH--DID HE JUST JUMP OVER THE WHOLE BLEEDING FOREST?
YEAH. THAT'S HIS THING.
BOOM!

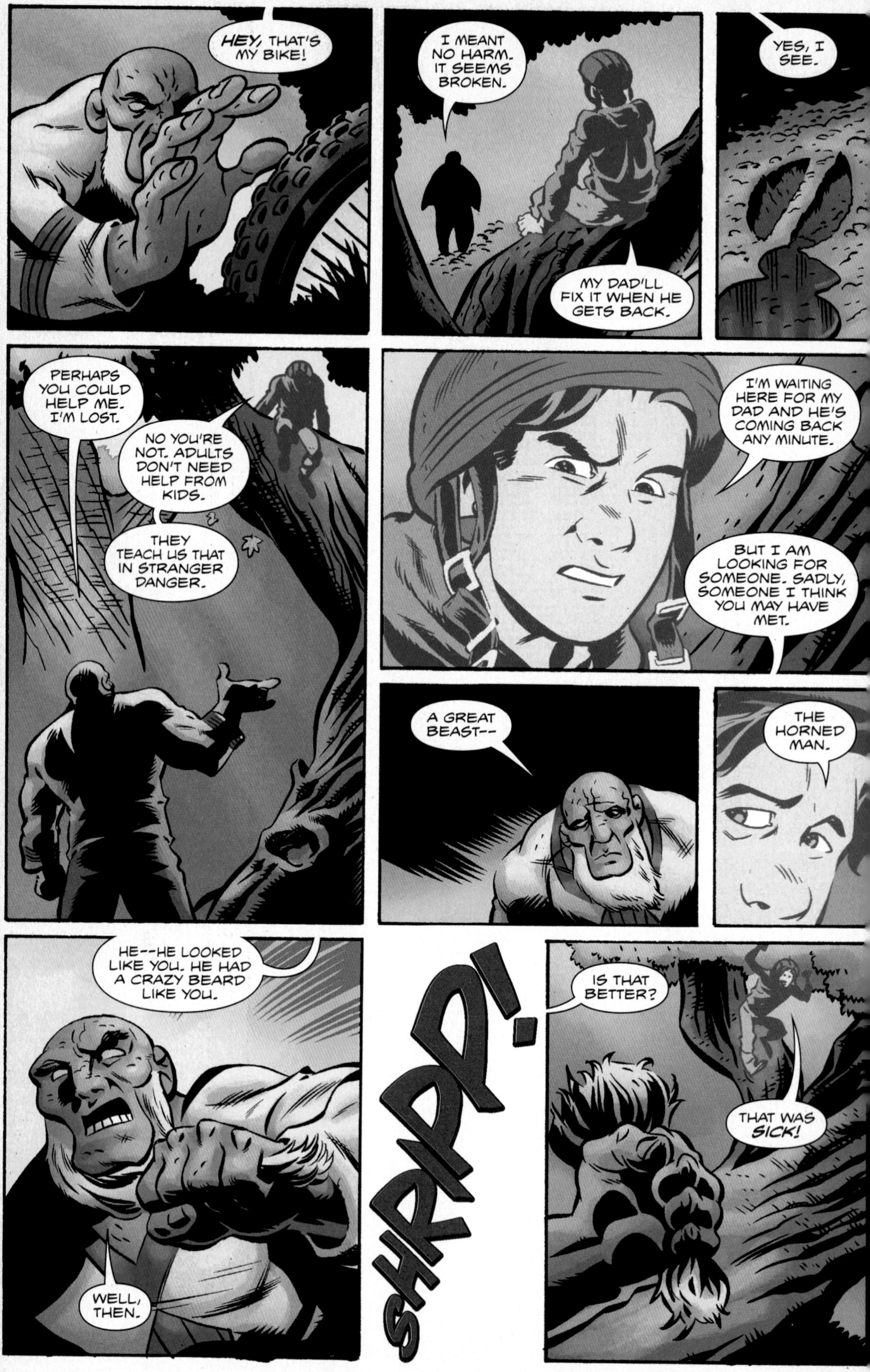
HEY, THAT'S MY BIKE!
I MEANT NO HARM. IT SEEMS BROKEN.
MY DAD'LL FIX IT WHEN HE GETS BACK.
YES, I SEE.
PERHAPS YOU COULD HELP ME. I'M LOST.
NO YOU'RE NOT. ADULTS DON'T NEED HELP FROM KIDS.
THEY TEACH US THAT IN STRANGER DANGER.
I'M WAITING HERE FOR MY DAD AND HE'S COMING BACK ANY MINUTE.
BUT I AM LOOKING FOR SOMEONE. SADLY, SOMEONE I THINK YOU MAY HAVE MET.
A GREAT BEAST--
THE HORNED MAN.
HE--HE LOOKED LIKE YOU. HE HAD A CRAZY BEARD LIKE YOU.
WELL, THEN.
SHRIP!
IS THAT BETTER?
THAT WAS SICK!

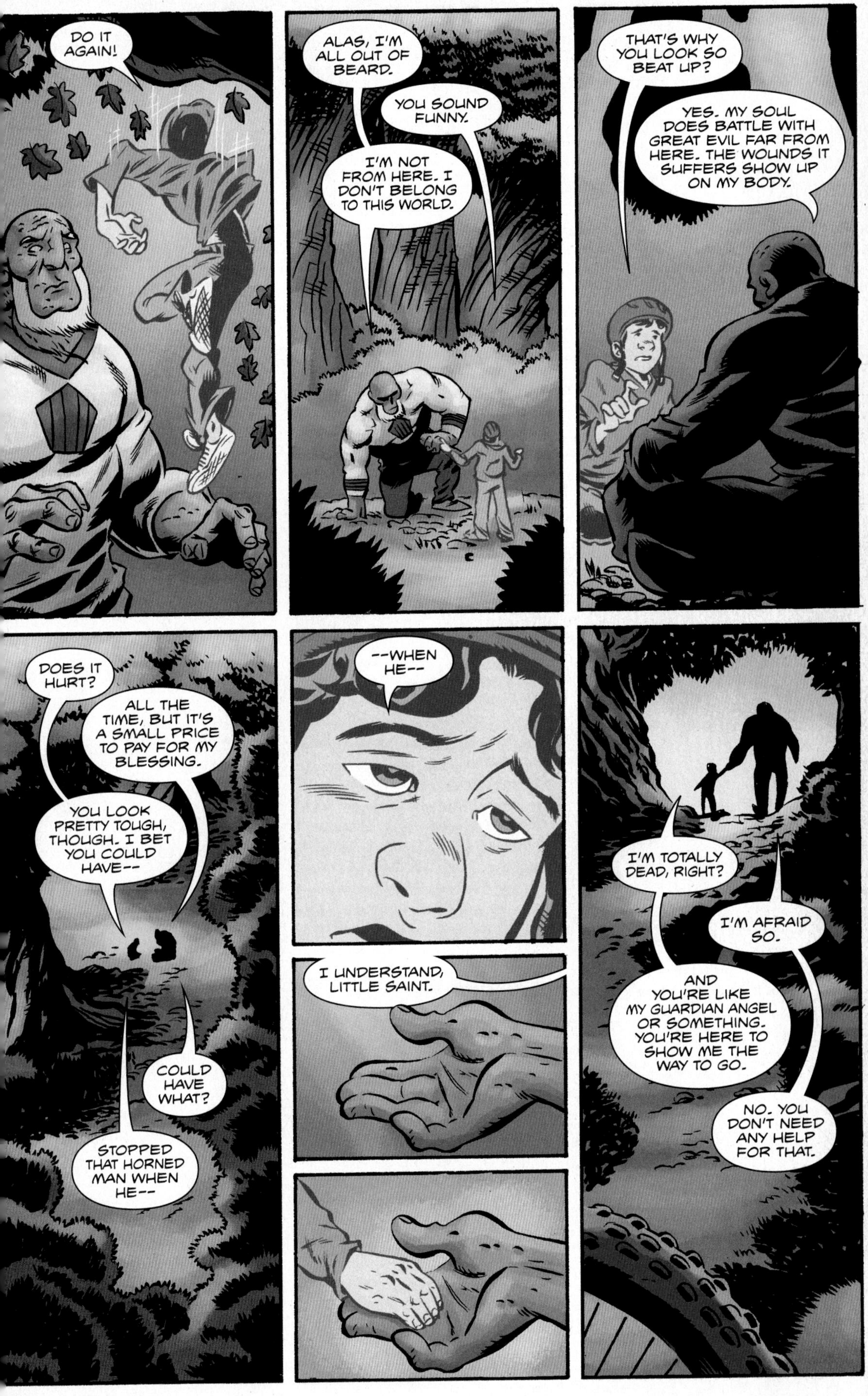
DO IT AGAIN!
ALAS, I'M ALL OUT OF BEARD.
YOU SOUND FUNNY.
I'M NOT FROM HERE. I DON'T BELONG TO THIS WORLD.
THAT'S WHY YOU LOOK SO BEAT UP?
YES. MY SOUL DOES BATTLE WITH GREAT EVIL FAR FROM HERE. THE WOUNDS IT SUFFERS SHOW UP ON MY BODY.
DOES IT HURT?
ALL THE TIME, BUT IT'S A SMALL PRICE TO PAY FOR MY BLESSING.
YOU LOOK PRETTY TOUGH, THOUGH. I BET YOU COULD HAVE--
COULD HAVE WHAT?
STOPPED THAT HORNED MAN WHEN HE--
--WHEN HE--
I UNDERSTAND, LITTLE SAINT.
I'M TOTALLY DEAD, RIGHT?
I'M AFRAID SO.
AND YOU'RE LIKE MY GUARDIAN ANGEL OR SOMETHING. YOU'RE HERE TO SHOW ME THE WAY TO GO.
NO. YOU DON'T NEED ANY HELP FOR THAT.

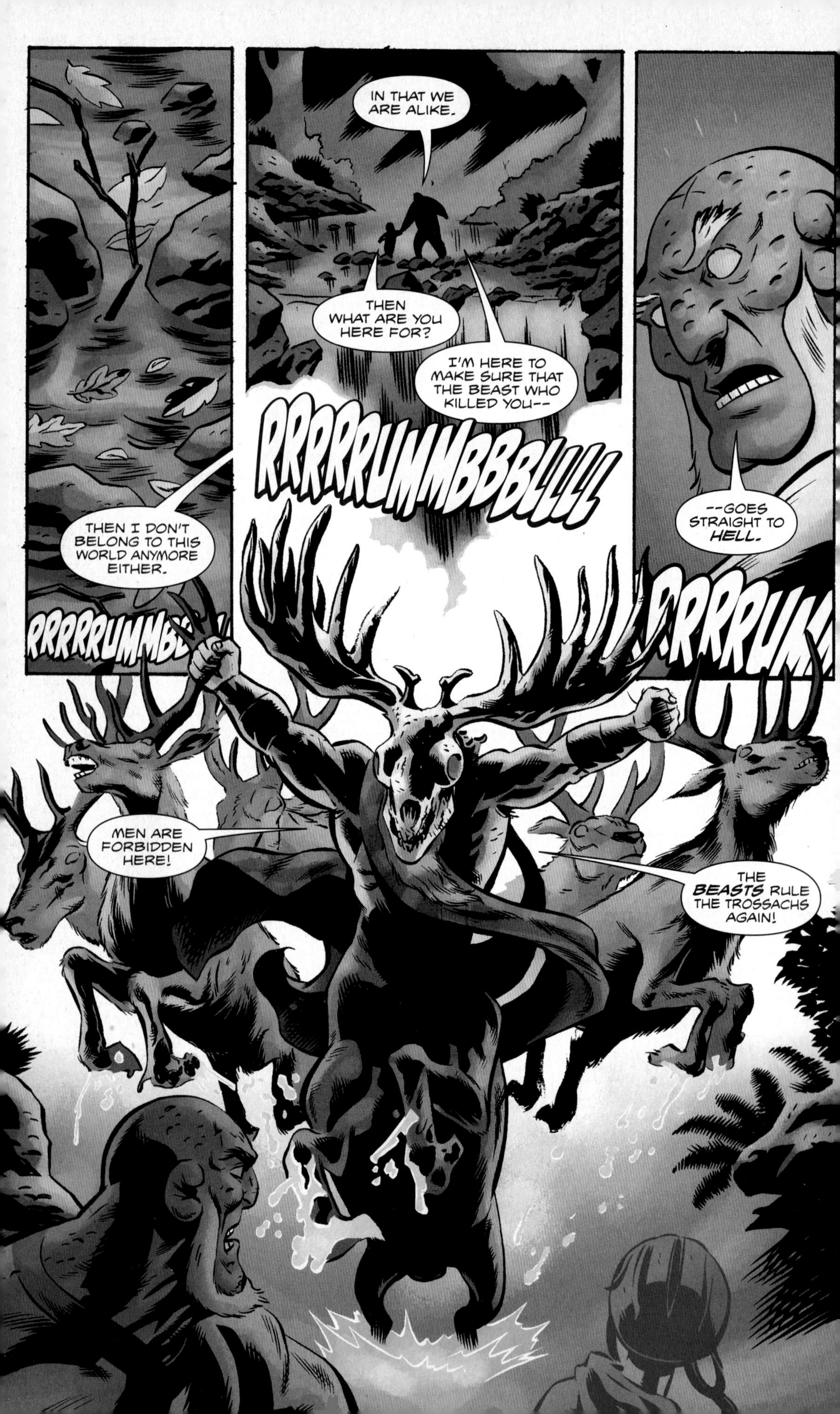

THEN I DON'T BELONG TO THIS WORLD ANYMORE EITHER.
RRRRRUMMBB
IN THAT WE ARE ALIKE.
THEN WHAT ARE YOU HERE FOR?
I'M HERE TO MAKE SURE THAT THE BEAST WHO KILLED YOU--
RRRRRUMMBBBLLLLL
--GOES STRAIGHT TO HELL.
RRRRUM
MEN ARE FORBIDDEN HERE!
THE BEASTS RULE THE TROSSACHS AGAIN!

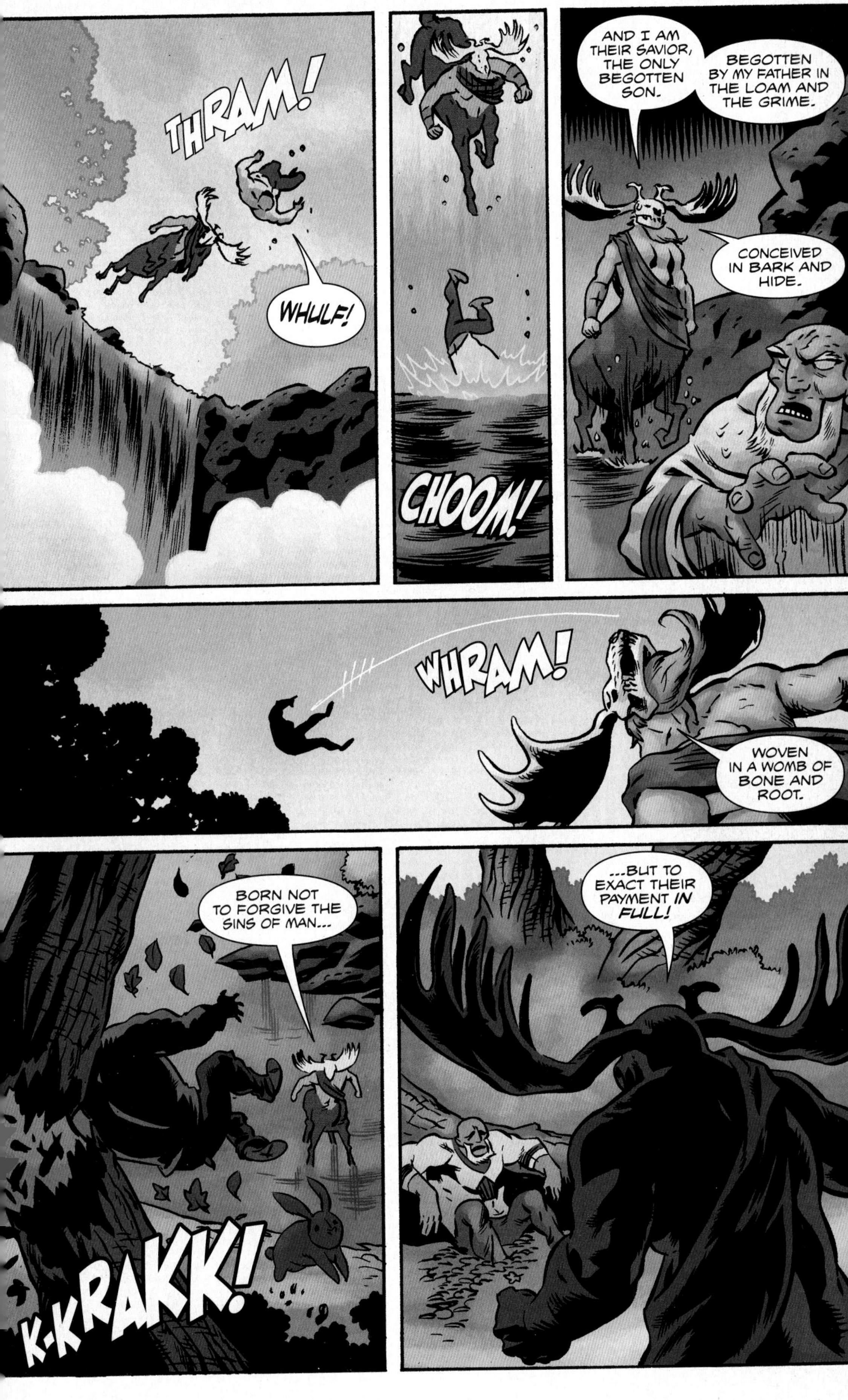
THRAM!
WHULF!
CHOOM!
AND I AM THEIR SAVIOR, THE ONLY BEGOTTEN SON.
BEGOTTEN BY MY FATHER IN THE LOAM AND THE GRIME.
CONCEIVED IN BARK AND HIDE.
WHRAM!
WOVEN IN A WOMB OF BONE AND ROOT.
BORN NOT TO FORGIVE THE SINS OF MAN...
K-KRAKK!
...BUT TO EXACT THEIR PAYMENT IN FULL!

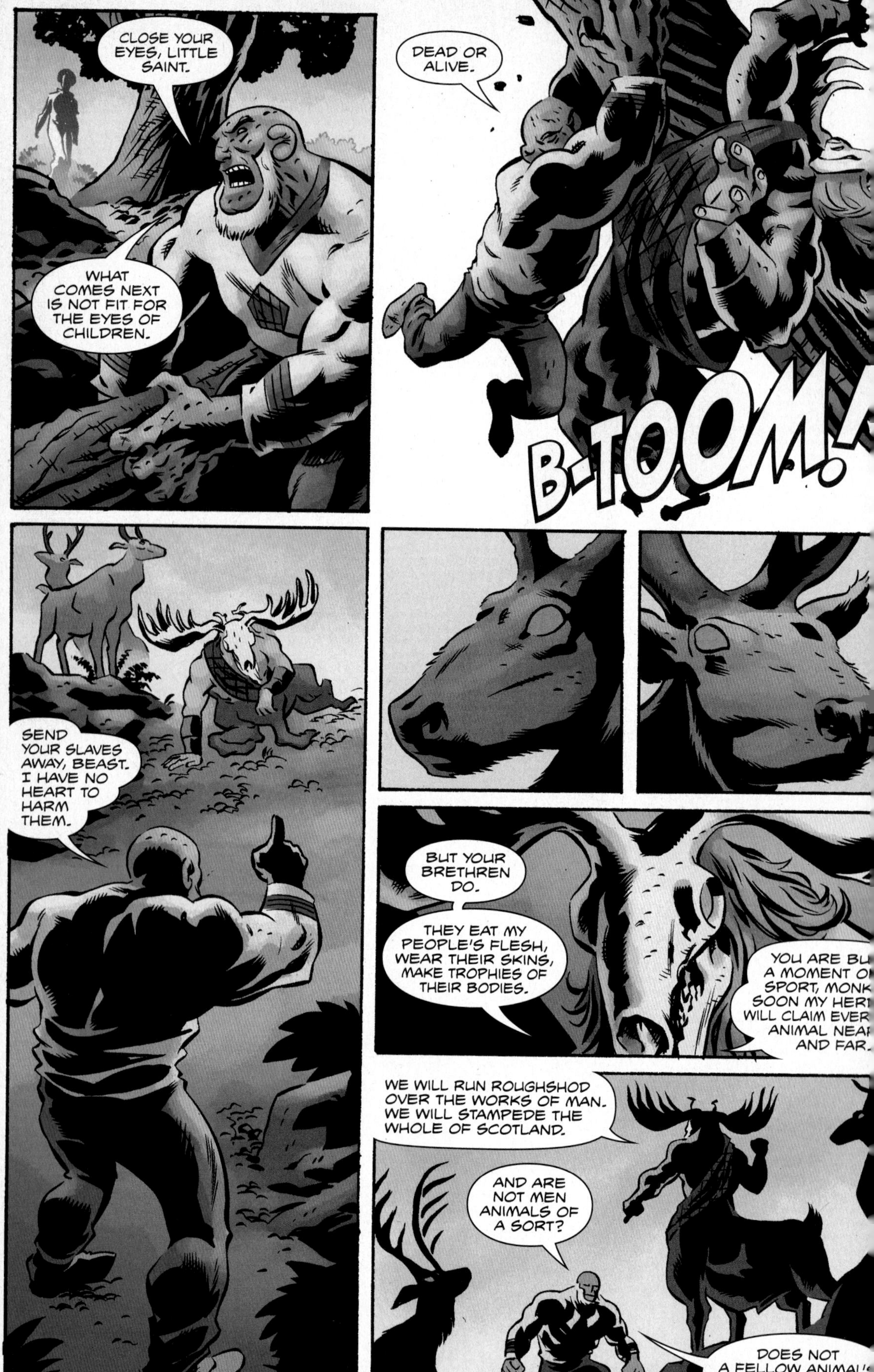

CLOSE YOUR EYES, LITTLE SAINT.
WHAT COMES NEXT IS NOT FIT FOR THE EYES OF CHILDREN.
DEAD OR ALIVE.
B-TOOM!
SEND YOUR SLAVES AWAY, BEAST. I HAVE NO HEART TO HARM THEM.
BUT YOUR BRETHREN DO.
THEY EAT MY PEOPLE'S FLESH, WEAR THEIR SKINS, MAKE TROPHIES OF THEIR BODIES.
YOU ARE BU A MOMENT O SPORT, MONK SOON MY HER WILL CLAIM EVER ANIMAL NEA AND FAR.
WE WILL RUN ROUGHSHOD OVER THE WORKS OF MAN. WE WILL STAMPEDE THE WHOLE OF SCOTLAND.
AND ARE NOT MEN ANIMALS OF A SORT?
DOES NOT A FELLOW ANIMAL'S BLOOD PAINT YOUR HOOVES?

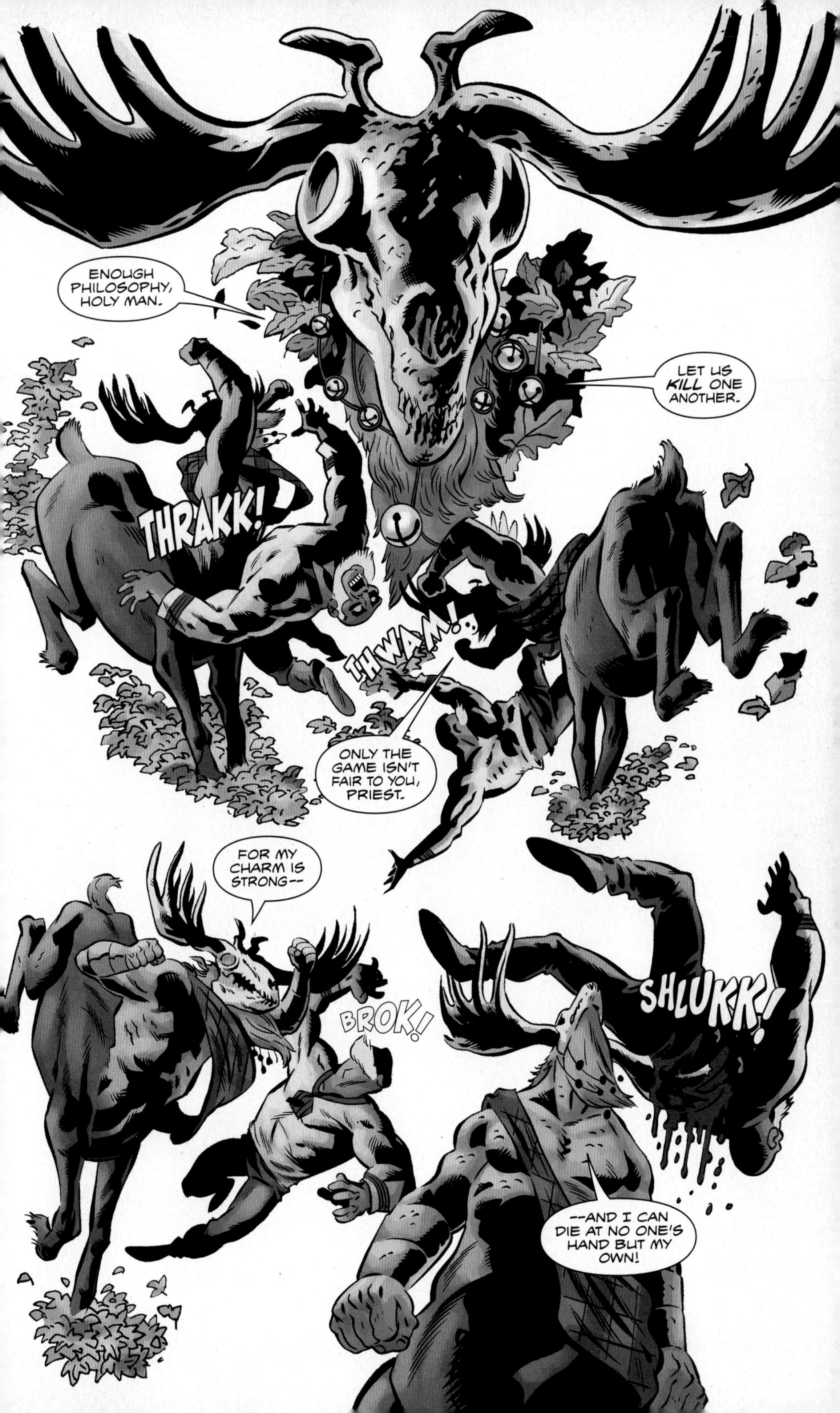
ENOUGH PHILOSOPHY, HOLY MAN.
LET US KILL ONE ANOTHER.
THRAKK!
THWAM!
ONLY THE GAME ISN'T FAIR TO YOU, PRIEST.
FOR MY CHARM IS STRONG--
BROK!
SHLUKK!
--AND I CAN DIE AT NO ONE'S HAND BUT MY OWN!

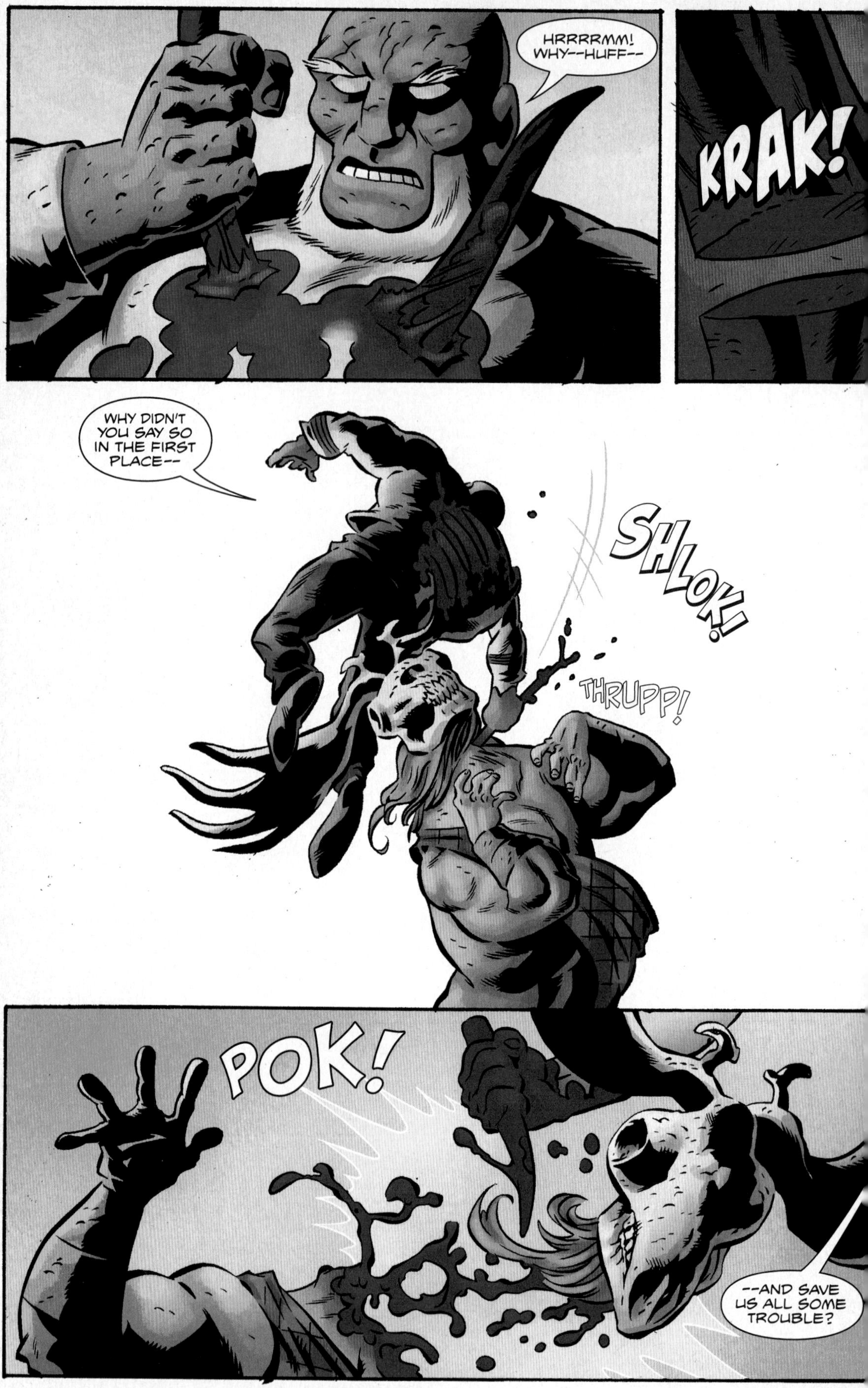
HRRRRMM! WHY--HUFF--
KRAK!
WHY DIDN'T YOU SAY SO IN THE FIRST PLACE--
SHLOK!
THRUPP!
POK!
--AND SAVE US ALL SOME TROUBLE?

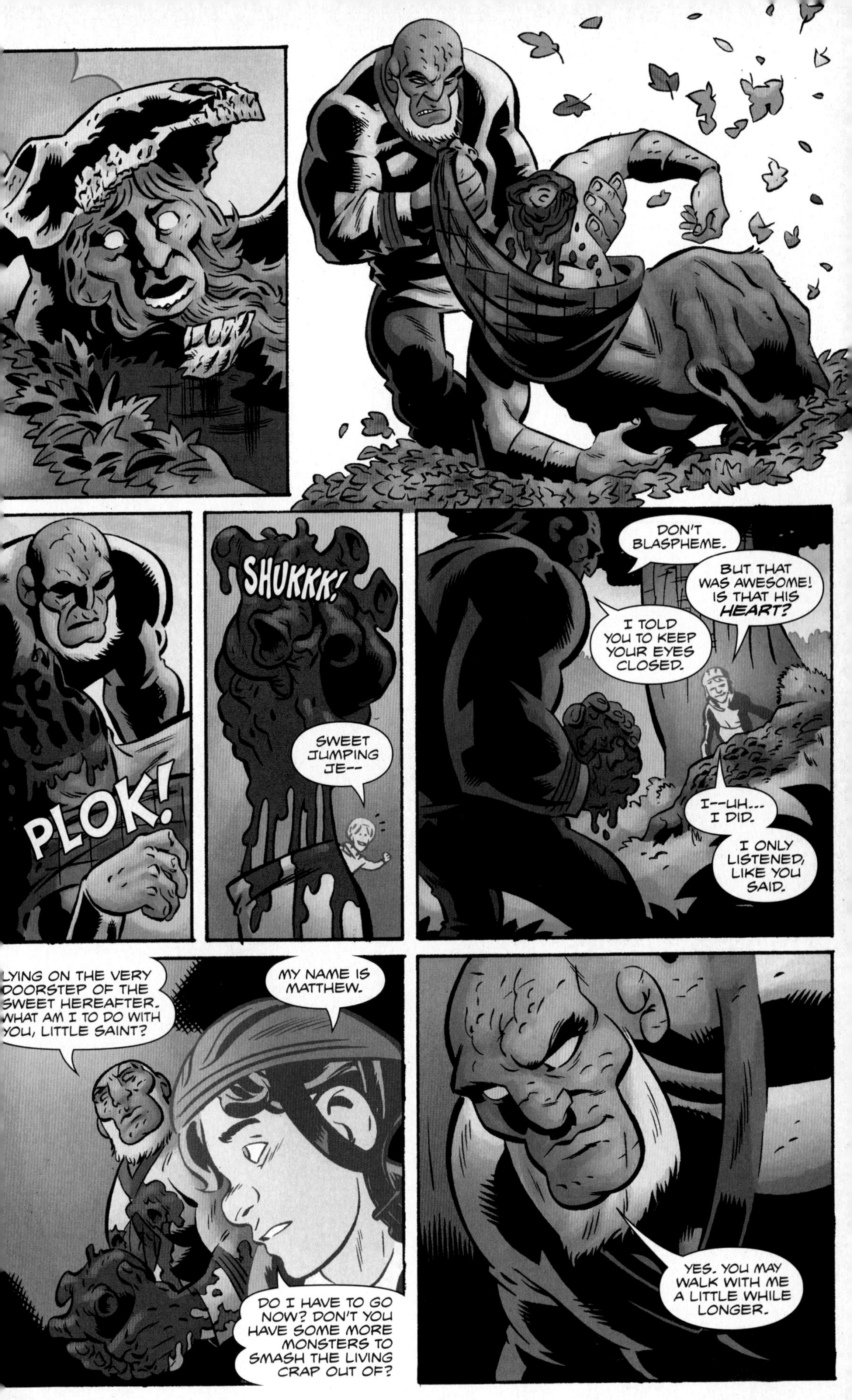
SHUKKK!
SWEET JUMPING JE--
PLOK!
DON'T BLASPHEME.
BUT THAT WAS AWESOME! IS THAT HIS *HEART?*
I TOLD YOU TO KEEP YOUR EYES CLOSED.
I--UH... I DID.
I ONLY LISTENED, LIKE YOU SAID.
LYING ON THE VERY DOORSTEP OF THE SWEET HEREAFTER. WHAT AM I TO DO WITH YOU, LITTLE SAINT?
MY NAME IS MATTHEW.
DO I HAVE TO GO NOW? DON'T YOU HAVE SOME MORE MONSTERS TO SMASH THE LIVING CRAP OUT OF?
YES. YOU MAY WALK WITH ME A LITTLE WHILE LONGER.

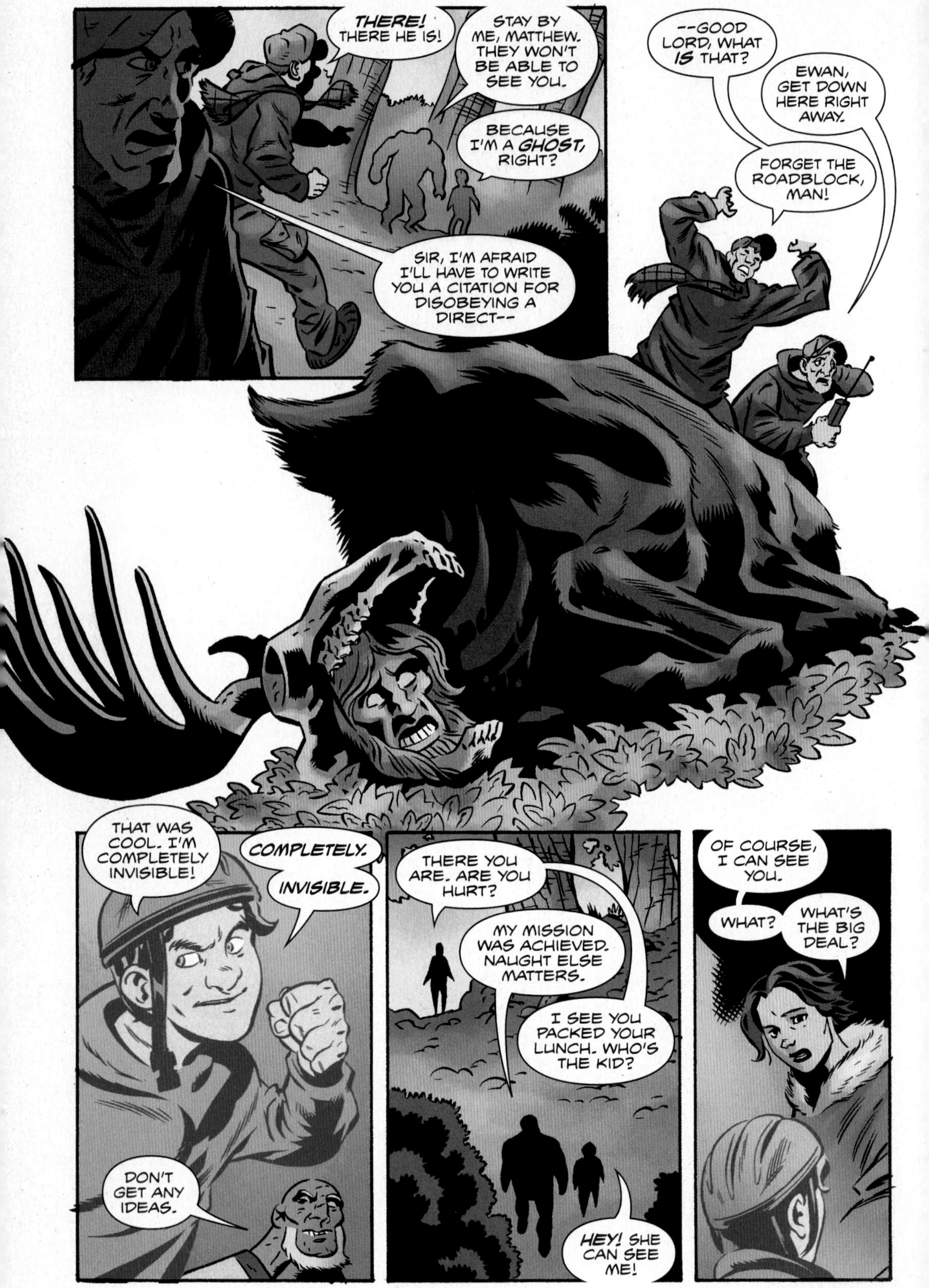
THERE! THERE HE IS!
STAY BY ME, MATTHEW. THEY WON'T BE ABLE TO SEE YOU.
BECAUSE I'M A GHOST, RIGHT?
SIR, I'M AFRAID I'LL HAVE TO WRITE YOU A CITATION FOR DISOBEYING A DIRECT--
--GOOD LORD, WHAT IS THAT?
EWAN, GET DOWN HERE RIGHT AWAY.
FORGET THE ROADBLOCK, MAN!
THAT WAS COOL. I'M COMPLETELY INVISIBLE!
COMPLETELY.
INVISIBLE.
DON'T GET ANY IDEAS.
THERE YOU ARE. ARE YOU HURT?
MY MISSION WAS ACHIEVED. NAUGHT ELSE MATTERS.
I SEE YOU PACKED YOUR LUNCH. WHO'S THE KID?
HEY! SHE CAN SEE ME!
OF COURSE, I CAN SEE YOU.
WHAT?
WHAT'S THE BIG DEAL?

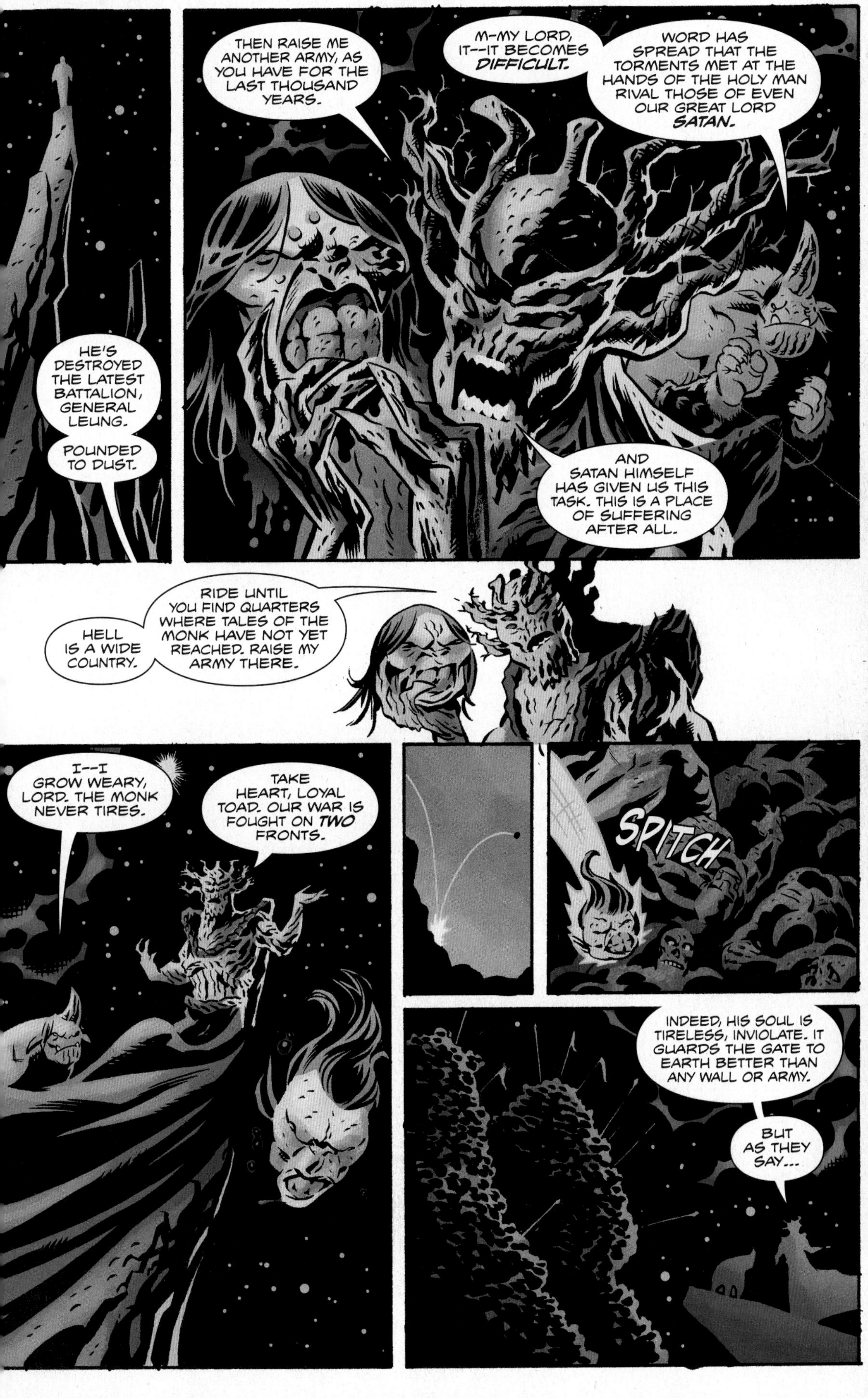

HE'S DESTROYED THE LATEST BATTALION, GENERAL LEUNG.
POUNDED TO DUST.
THEN RAISE ME ANOTHER ARMY, AS YOU HAVE FOR THE LAST THOUSAND YEARS.
M-MY LORD, IT--IT BECOMES DIFFICULT.
WORD HAS SPREAD THAT THE TORMENTS MET AT THE HANDS OF THE HOLY MAN RIVAL THOSE OF EVEN OUR GREAT LORD SATAN.
AND SATAN HIMSELF HAS GIVEN US THIS TASK. THIS IS A PLACE OF SUFFERING AFTER ALL.
HELL IS A WIDE COUNTRY.
RIDE UNTIL YOU FIND QUARTERS WHERE TALES OF THE MONK HAVE NOT YET REACHED. RAISE MY ARMY THERE.
I--I GROW WEARY, LORD. THE MONK NEVER TIRES.
TAKE HEART, LOYAL TOAD. OUR WAR IS FOUGHT ON TWO FRONTS.
SPITCH
INDEED, HIS SOUL IS TIRELESS, INVIOLATE. IT GUARDS THE GATE TO EARTH BETTER THAN ANY WALL OR ARMY.
BUT AS THEY SAY...

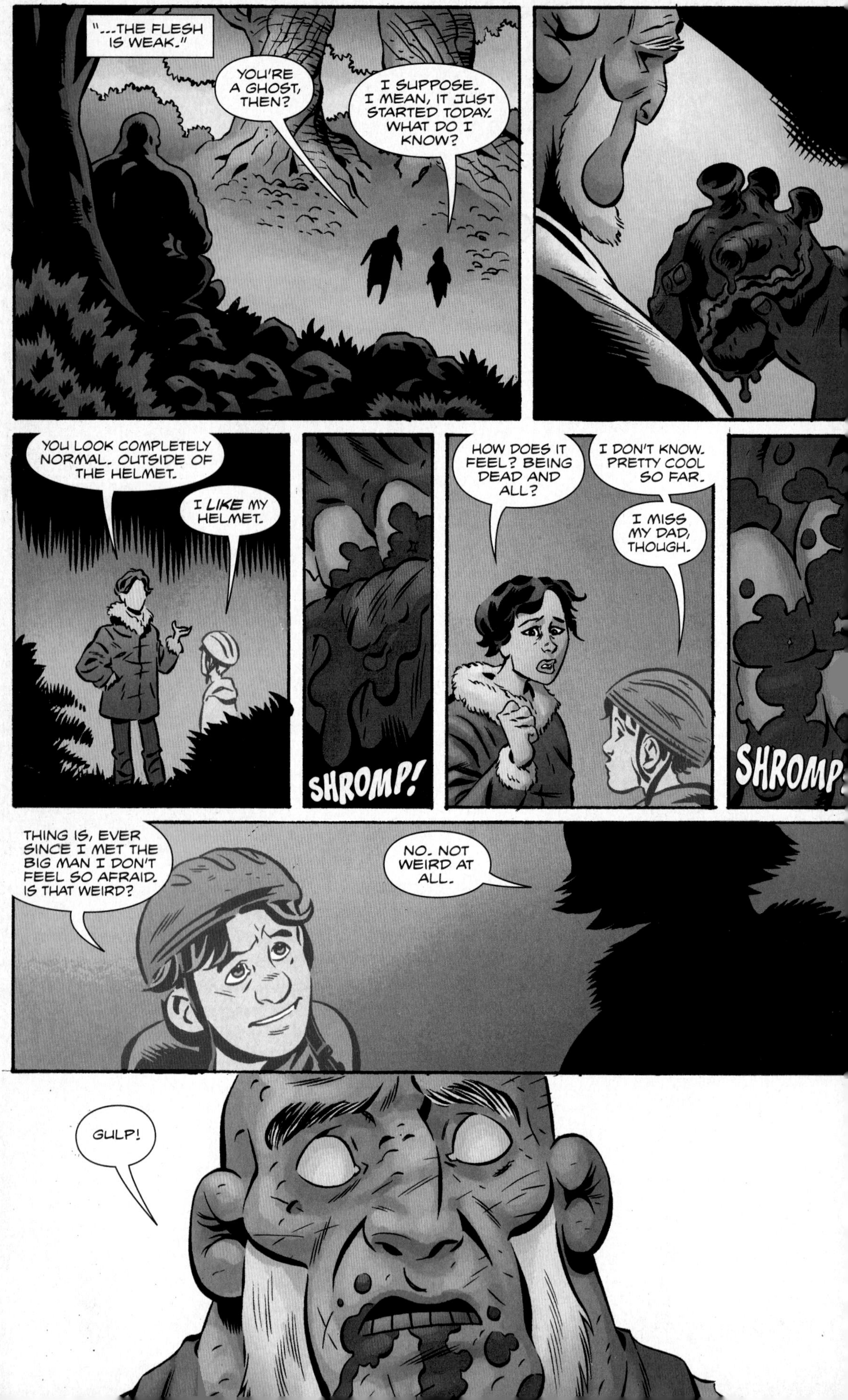
"...THE FLESH IS WEAK."
YOU'RE A GHOST, THEN?
I SUPPOSE. I MEAN, IT JUST STARTED TODAY. WHAT DO I KNOW?
YOU LOOK COMPLETELY NORMAL. OUTSIDE OF THE HELMET.
I LIKE MY HELMET.
SHROMP!
HOW DOES IT FEEL? BEING DEAD AND ALL?
I DON'T KNOW. PRETTY COOL SO FAR.
I MISS MY DAD, THOUGH.
SHROMP
THING IS, EVER SINCE I MET THE BIG MAN I DON'T FEEL SO AFRAID. IS THAT WEIRD?
NO. NOT WEIRD AT ALL.
GULP!

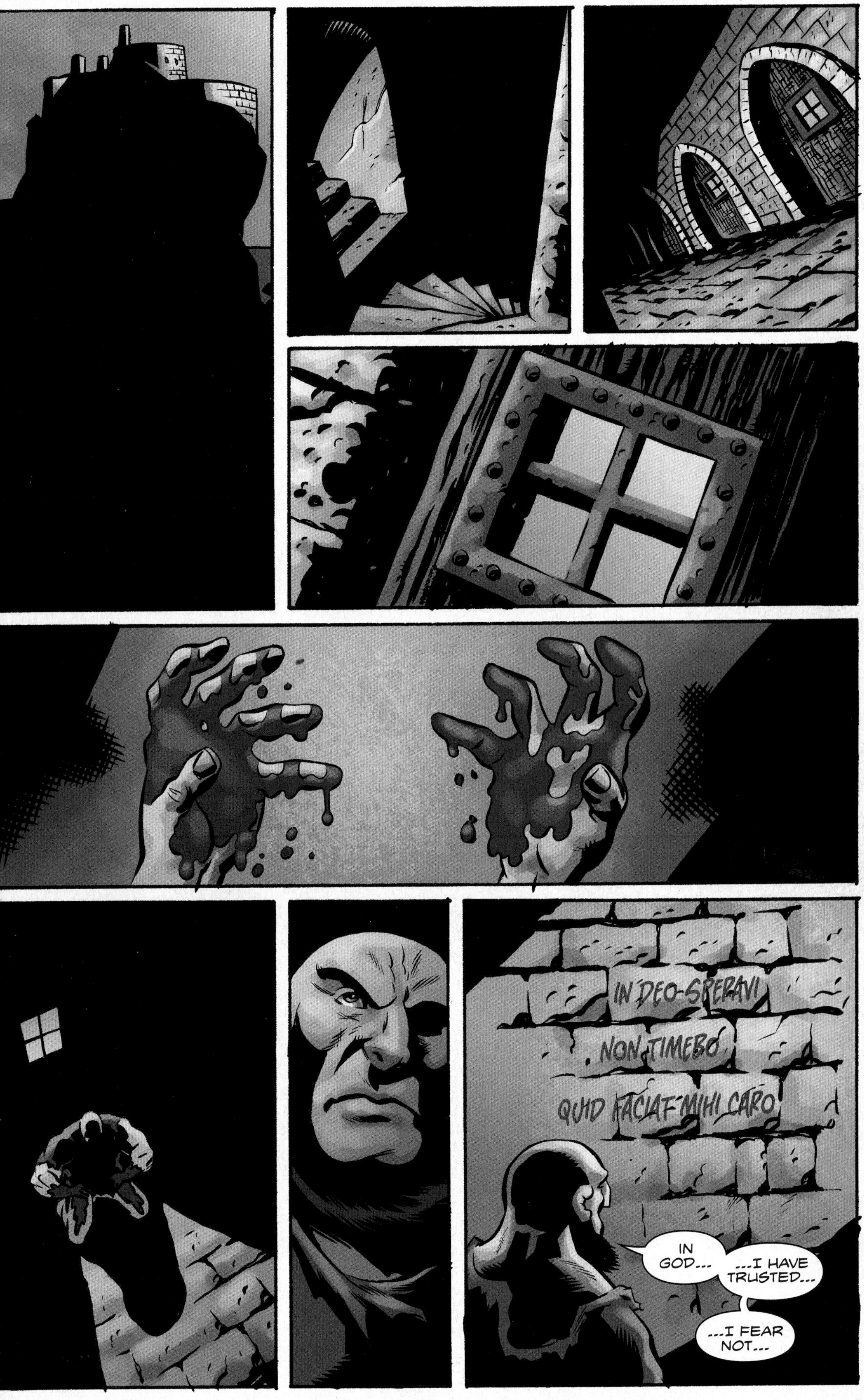
IN DEO SPERAVI
NON TIMEBO
QUID FACIAT MIHI CARO
IN GOD...
...I HAVE TRUSTED...
...I FEAR NOT...

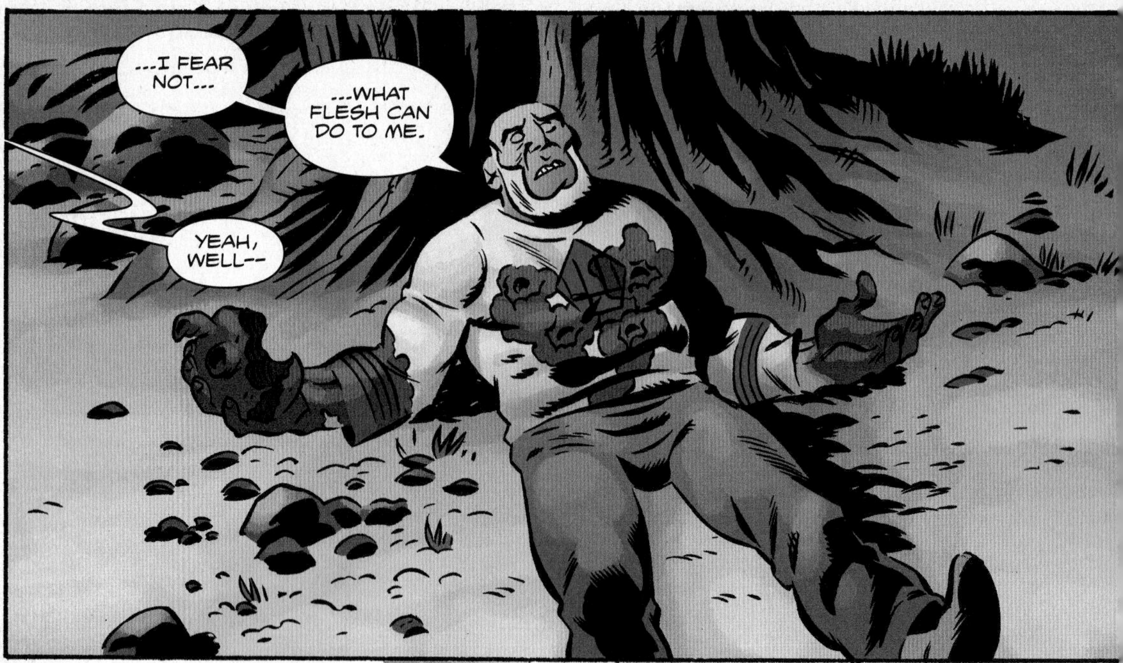
...I FEAR NOT...
...WHAT FLESH CAN DO TO ME.
YEAH, WELL--
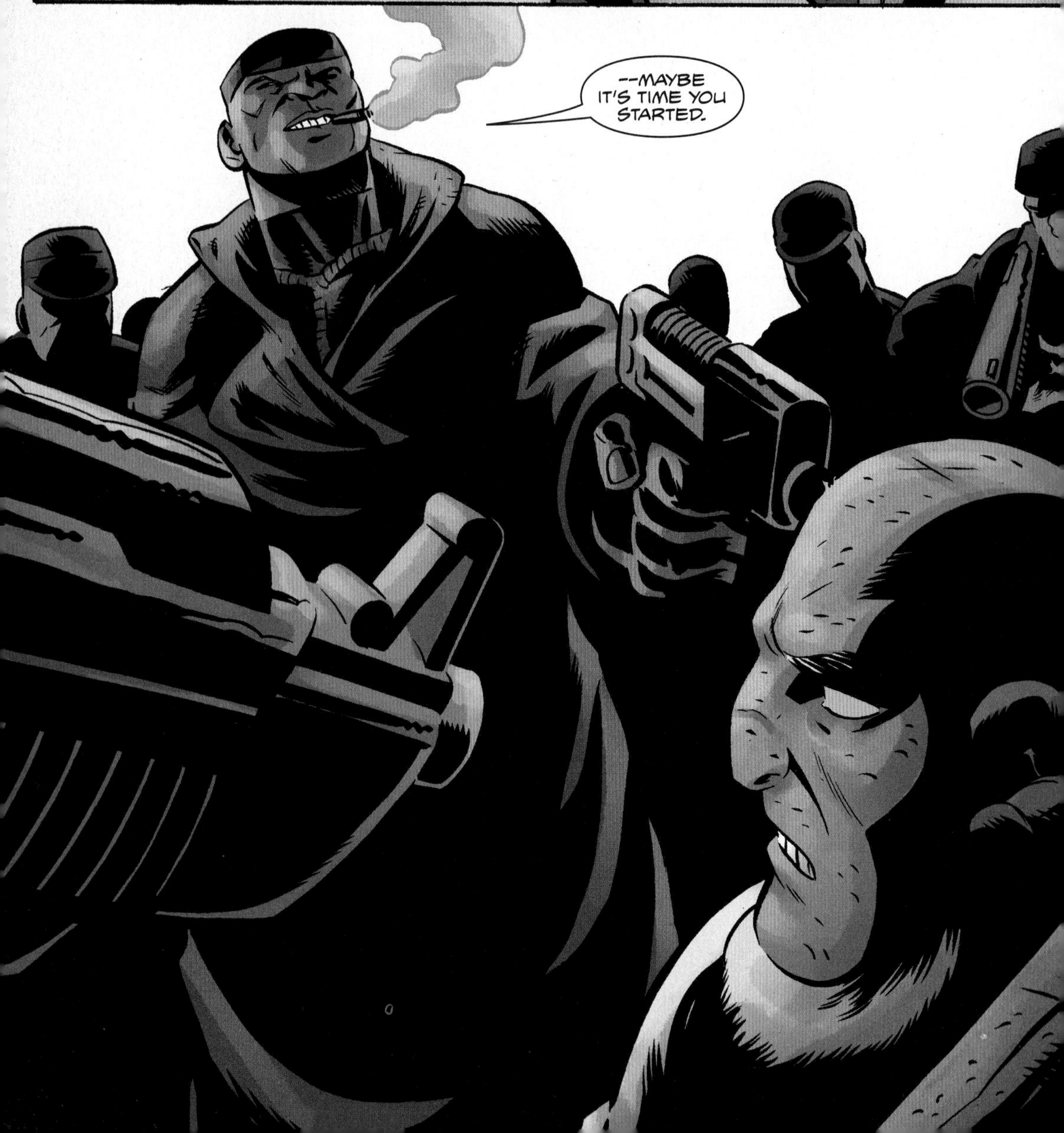
--MAYBE IT'S TIME YOU STARTED.

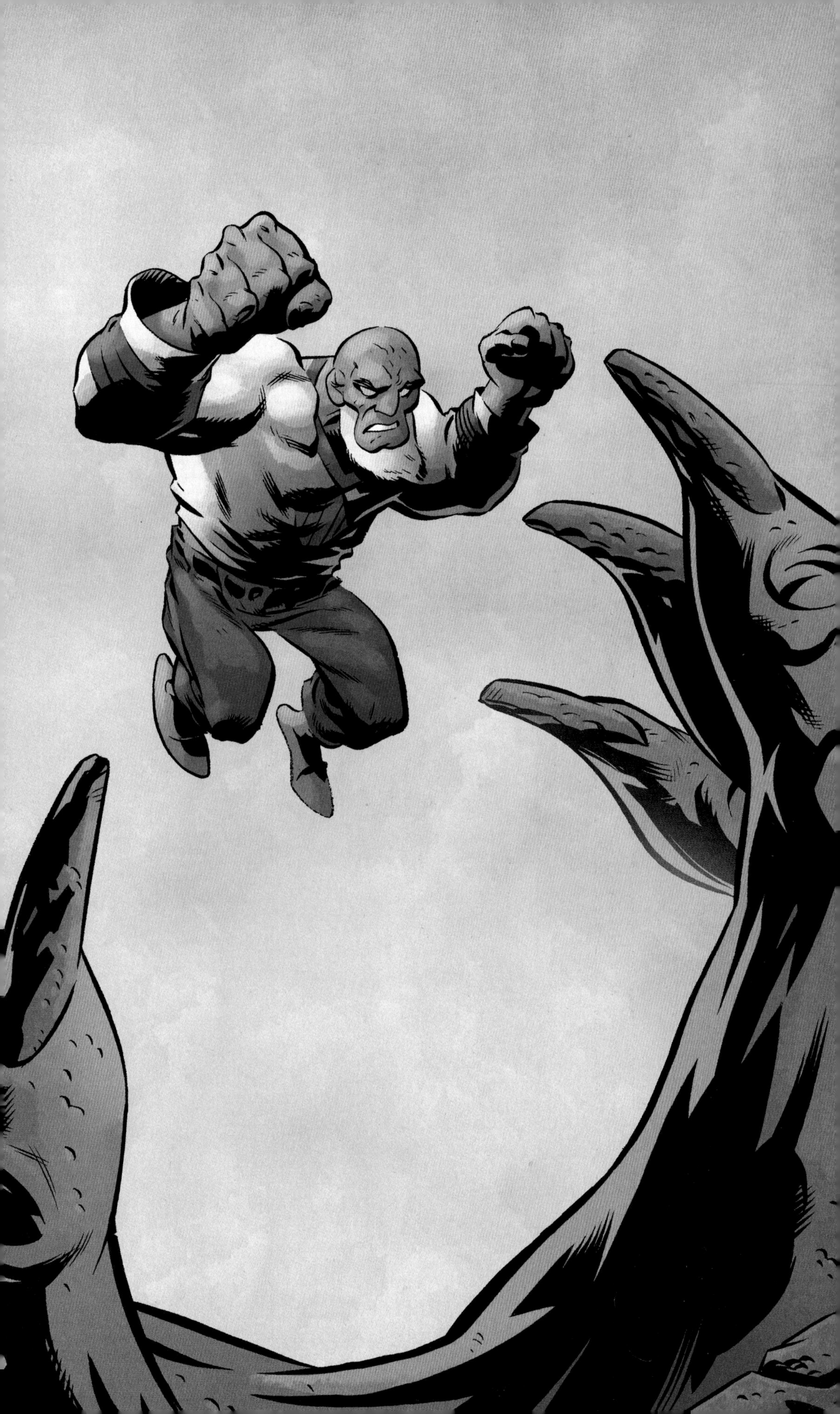

CHAPTER THREE

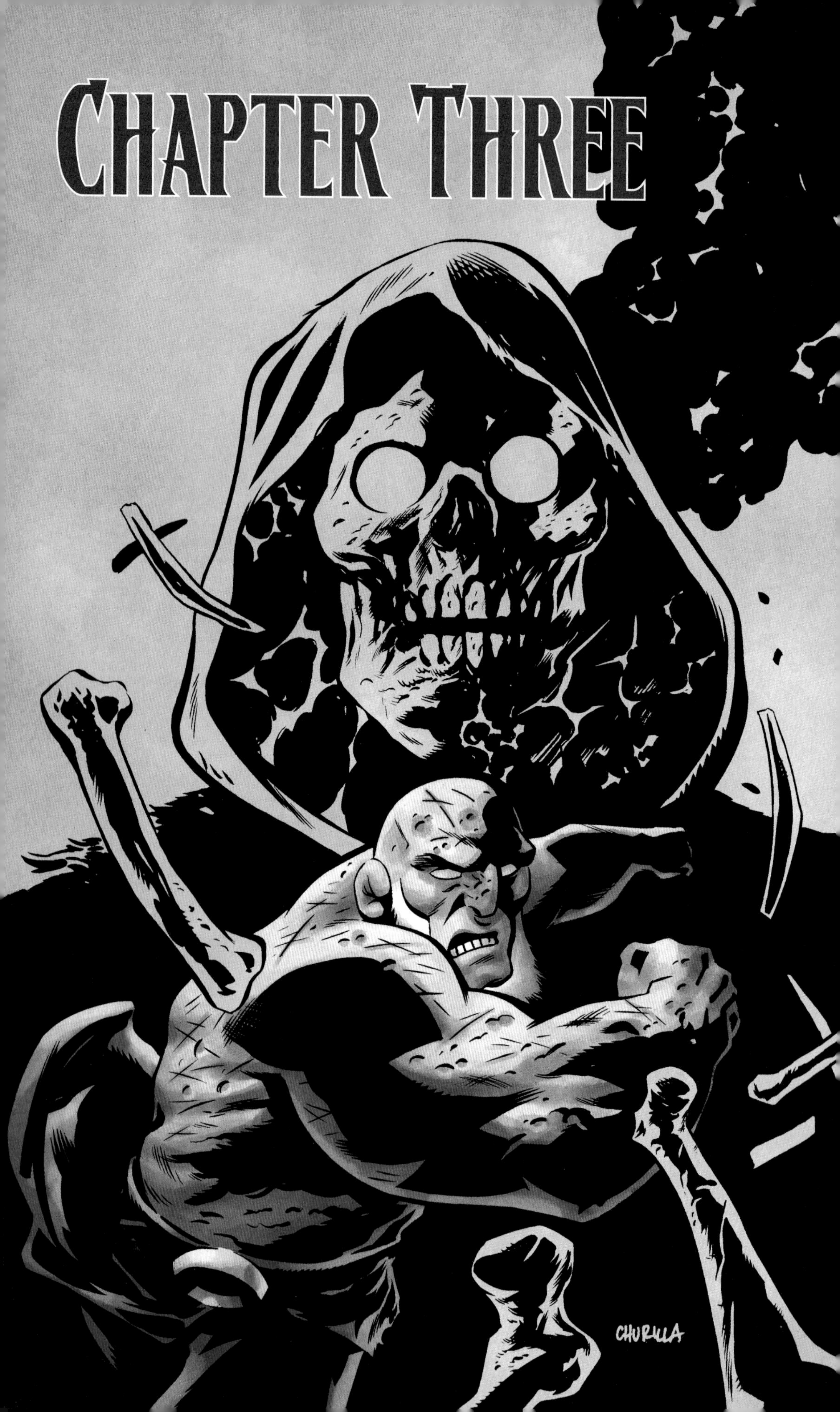
CHURILLA

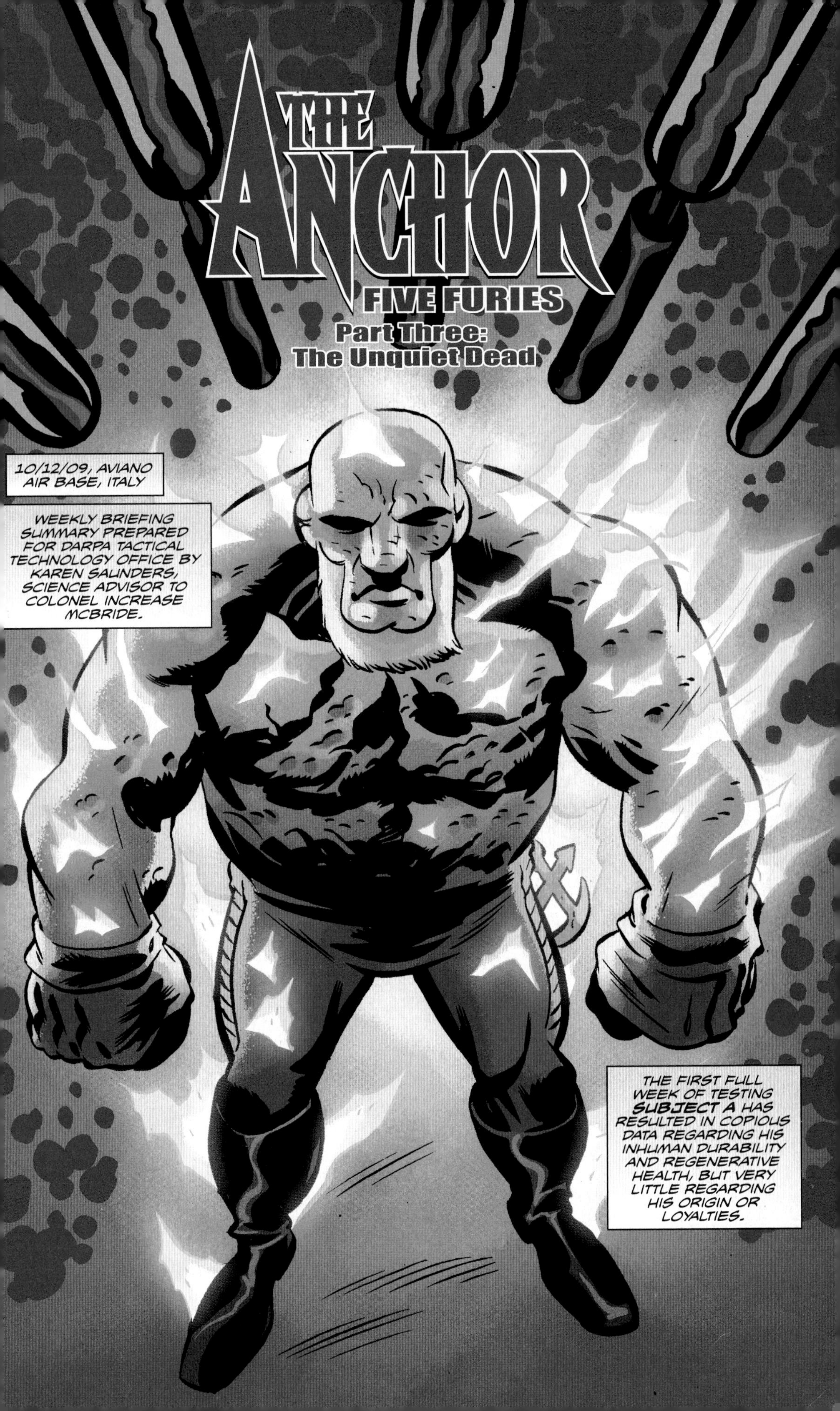
THE ANCHOR
FIVE FURIES
Part Three: The Unquiet Dead
10/12/09, AVIANO AIR BASE, ITALY
WEEKLY BRIEFING SUMMARY PREPARED FOR DARPA TACTICAL TECHNOLOGY OFFICE BY KAREN SAUNDERS, SCIENCE ADVISOR TO COLONEL INCREASE MCBRIDE.
THE FIRST FULL WEEK OF TESTING SUBJECT A HAS RESULTED IN COPIOUS DATA REGARDING HIS INHUMAN DURABILITY AND REGENERATIVE HEALTH, BUT VERY LITTLE REGARDING HIS ORIGIN OR LOYALTIES.

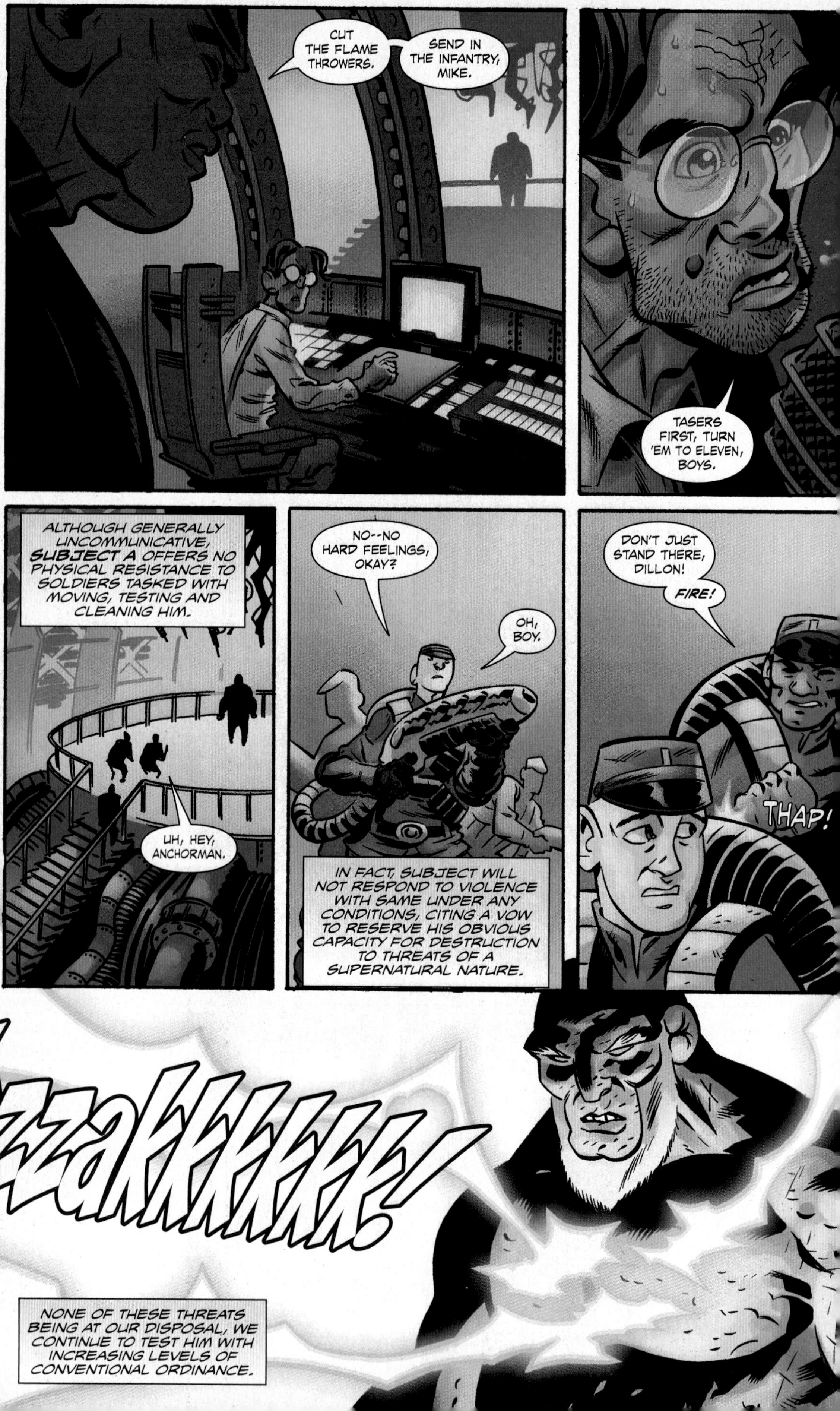
CUT THE FLAME THROWERS.
SEND IN THE INFANTRY, MIKE.
TASERS FIRST; TURN 'EM TO ELEVEN, BOYS.
ALTHOUGH GENERALLY UNCOMMUNICATIVE, SUBJECT A OFFERS NO PHYSICAL RESISTANCE TO SOLDIERS TASKED WITH MOVING, TESTING AND CLEANING HIM.
UH, HEY, ANCHORMAN.
NO--NO HARD FEELINGS, OKAY?
OH, BOY.
IN FACT, SUBJECT WILL NOT RESPOND TO VIOLENCE WITH SAME UNDER ANY CONDITIONS, CITING A VOW TO RESERVE HIS OBVIOUS CAPACITY FOR DESTRUCTION TO THREATS OF A SUPERNATURAL NATURE.
DON'T JUST STAND THERE, DILLON! FIRE!
THAP!
ZZAKKKKKK!
NONE OF THESE THREATS BEING AT OUR DISPOSAL, WE CONTINUE TO TEST HIM WITH INCREASING LEVELS OF CONVENTIONAL ORDINANCE.

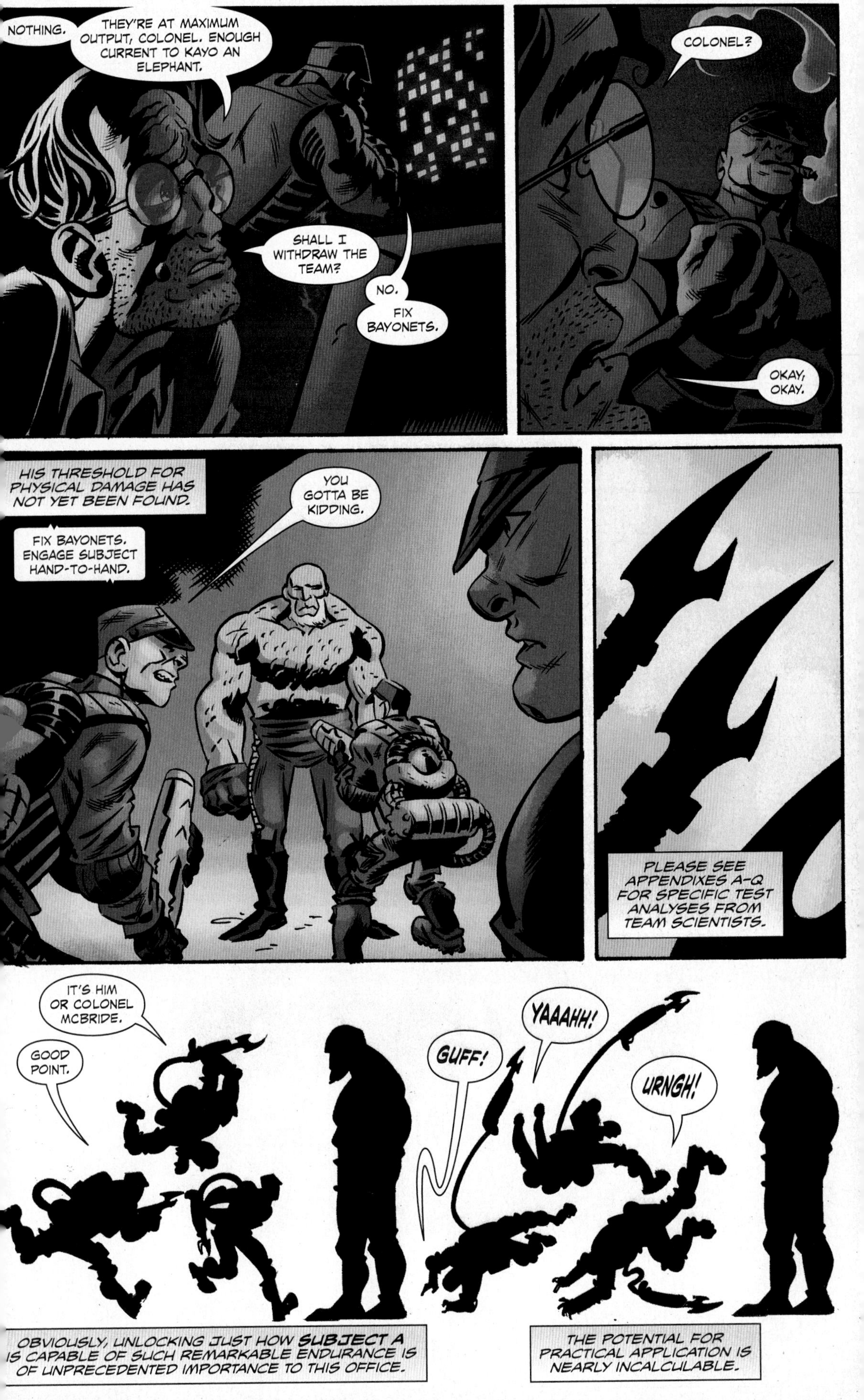

NOTHING.
THEY'RE AT MAXIMUM OUTPUT, COLONEL. ENOUGH CURRENT TO KAYO AN ELEPHANT.
SHALL I WITHDRAW THE TEAM?
NO.
FIX BAYONETS.
COLONEL?
OKAY, OKAY.
HIS THRESHOLD FOR PHYSICAL DAMAGE HAS NOT YET BEEN FOUND.
YOU GOTTA BE KIDDING.
FIX BAYONETS. ENGAGE SUBJECT HAND-TO-HAND.
PLEASE SEE APPENDIXES A-Q FOR SPECIFIC TEST ANALYSES FROM TEAM SCIENTISTS.
IT'S HIM OR COLONEL MCBRIDE.
GOOD POINT.
GUFF!
YAAAHH!
URNGH!
OBVIOUSLY, UNLOCKING JUST HOW SUBJECT A IS CAPABLE OF SUCH REMARKABLE ENDURANCE IS OF UNPRECEDENTED IMPORTANCE TO THIS OFFICE.
THE POTENTIAL FOR PRACTICAL APPLICATION IS NEARLY INCALCULABLE.

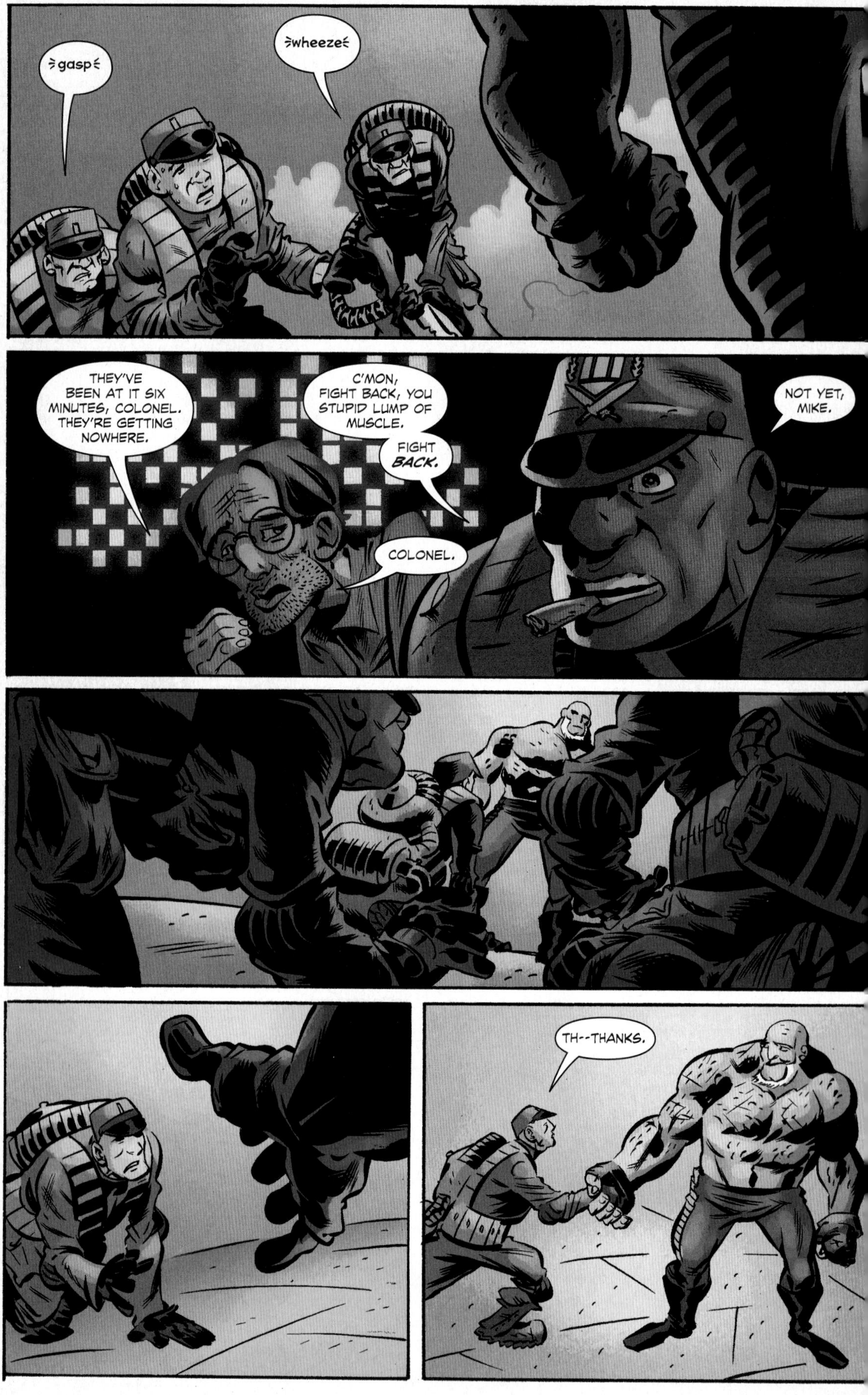
gasp
wheeze
THEY'VE BEEN AT IT SIX MINUTES, COLONEL. THEY'RE GETTING NOWHERE.
C'MON, FIGHT BACK, YOU STUPID LUMP OF MUSCLE.
FIGHT *BACK.*
COLONEL.
NOT YET, MIKE.
TH--THANKS.

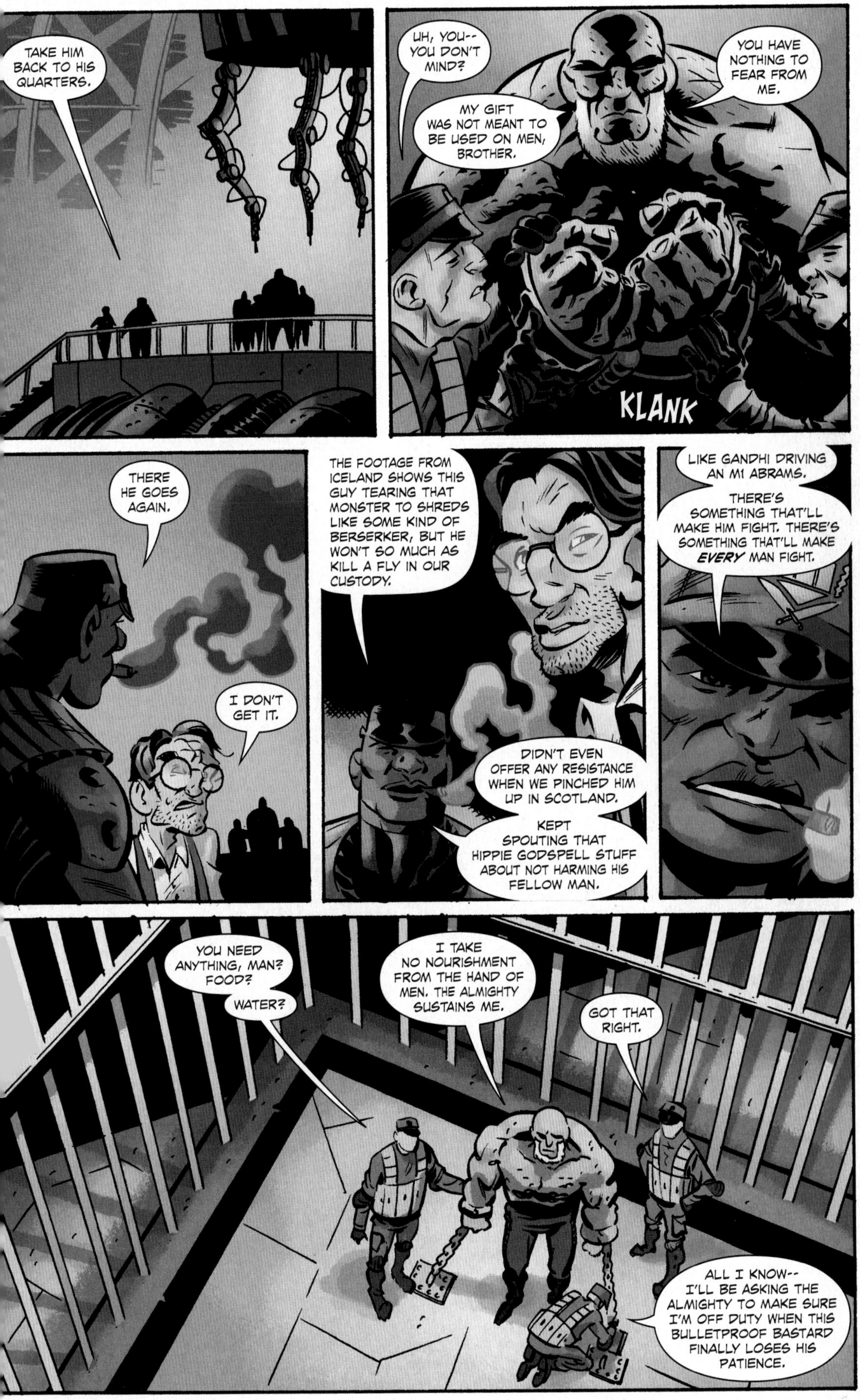
TAKE HIM BACK TO HIS QUARTERS.
UH, YOU-- YOU DON'T MIND?
MY GIFT WAS NOT MEANT TO BE USED ON MEN, BROTHER.
YOU HAVE NOTHING TO FEAR FROM ME.
KLANK
THERE HE GOES AGAIN.
I DON'T GET IT.
THE FOOTAGE FROM ICELAND SHOWS THIS GUY TEARING THAT MONSTER TO SHREDS LIKE SOME KIND OF BERSERKER, BUT HE WON'T SO MUCH AS KILL A FLY IN OUR CUSTODY.
DIDN'T EVEN OFFER ANY RESISTANCE WHEN WE PINCHED HIM UP IN SCOTLAND.
KEPT SPOUTING THAT HIPPIE GODSPELL STUFF ABOUT NOT HARMING HIS FELLOW MAN.
LIKE GANDHI DRIVING AN M1 ABRAMS.
THERE'S SOMETHING THAT'LL MAKE HIM FIGHT. THERE'S SOMETHING THAT'LL MAKE *EVERY* MAN FIGHT.
YOU NEED ANYTHING, MAN? FOOD?
WATER?
I TAKE NO NOURISHMENT FROM THE HAND OF MEN. THE ALMIGHTY SUSTAINS ME.
GOT THAT RIGHT.
ALL I KNOW-- I'LL BE ASKING THE ALMIGHTY TO MAKE SURE I'M OFF DUTY WHEN THIS BULLETPROOF BASTARD FINALLY LOSES HIS PATIENCE.

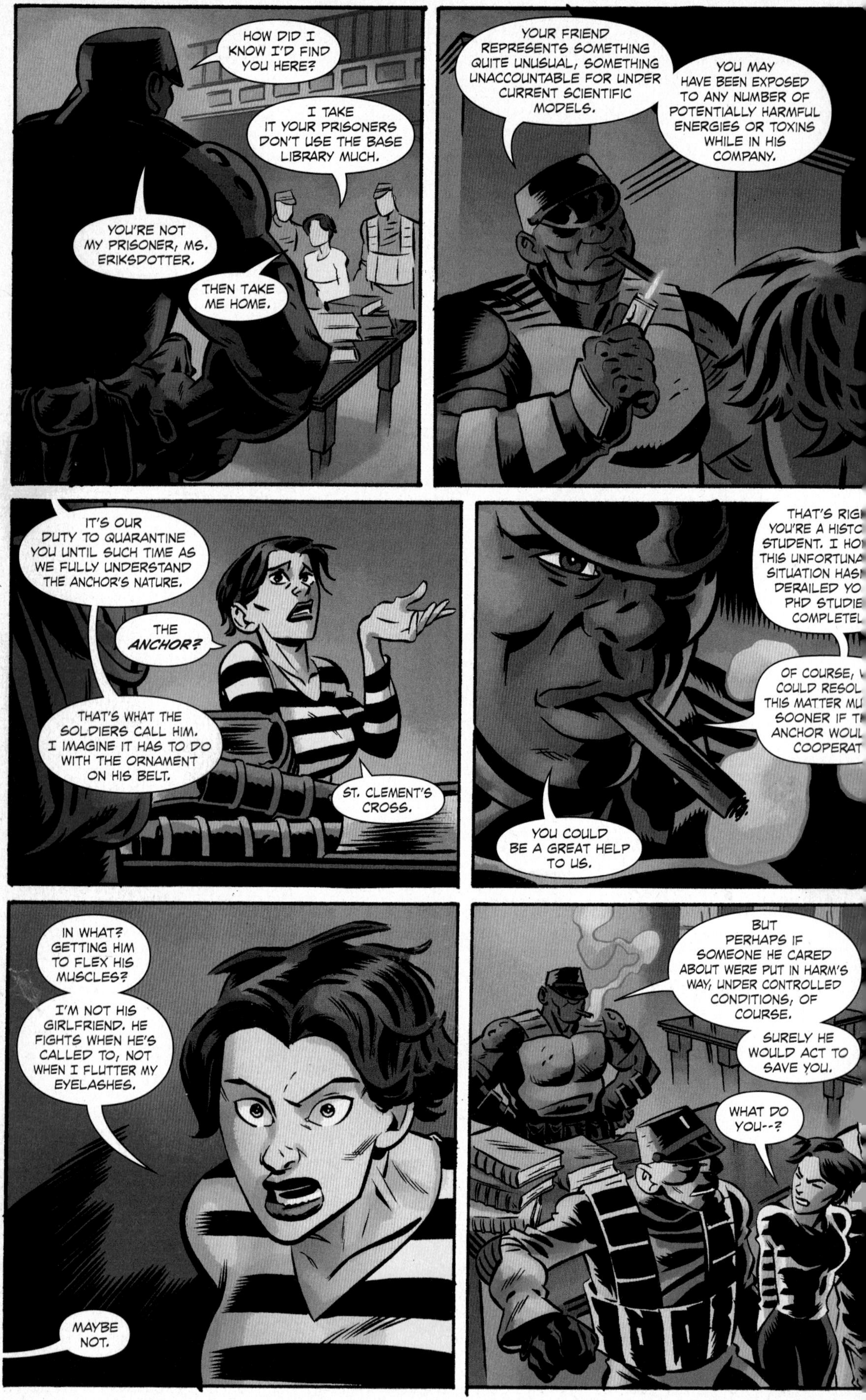
HOW DID I KNOW I'D FIND YOU HERE?
I TAKE IT YOUR PRISONERS DON'T USE THE BASE LIBRARY MUCH.
YOU'RE NOT MY PRISONER, MS. ERIKSDOTTER.
THEN TAKE ME HOME.
YOUR FRIEND REPRESENTS SOMETHING QUITE UNUSUAL, SOMETHING UNACCOUNTABLE FOR UNDER CURRENT SCIENTIFIC MODELS.
YOU MAY HAVE BEEN EXPOSED TO ANY NUMBER OF POTENTIALLY HARMFUL ENERGIES OR TOXINS WHILE IN HIS COMPANY.
IT'S OUR DUTY TO QUARANTINE YOU UNTIL SUCH TIME AS WE FULLY UNDERSTAND THE ANCHOR'S NATURE.
THE *ANCHOR?*
THAT'S WHAT THE SOLDIERS CALL HIM. I IMAGINE IT HAS TO DO WITH THE ORNAMENT ON HIS BELT.
ST. CLEMENT'S CROSS.
THAT'S RIG YOU'RE A HISTO STUDENT. I HO THIS UNFORTUNA SITUATION HAS DERAILED YO PHD STUDIE COMPLETEL
OF COURSE, COULD RESOL THIS MATTER MU SOONER IF T ANCHOR WOUL COOPERAT
YOU COULD BE A GREAT HELP TO US.
IN WHAT? GETTING HIM TO FLEX HIS MUSCLES?
I'M NOT HIS GIRLFRIEND. HE FIGHTS WHEN HE'S CALLED TO, NOT WHEN I FLUTTER MY EYELASHES.
MAYBE NOT.
BUT PERHAPS IF SOMEONE HE CARED ABOUT WERE PUT IN HARM'S WAY, UNDER CONTROLLED CONDITIONS, OF COURSE.
SURELY HE WOULD ACT TO SAVE YOU.
WHAT DO YOU--?

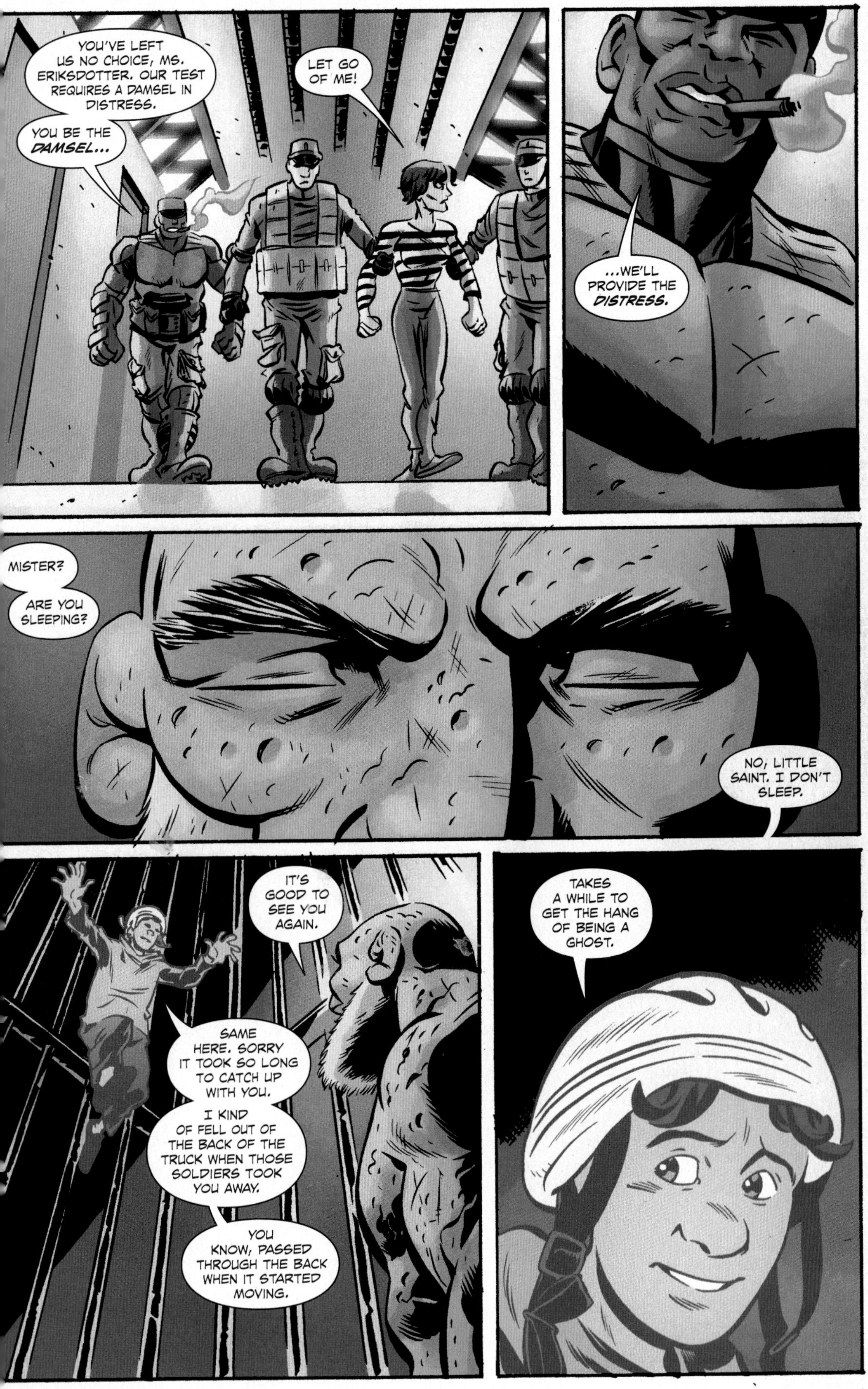

YOU'VE LEFT US NO CHOICE, MS. ERIKSDOTTER. OUR TEST REQUIRES A DAMSEL IN DISTRESS.
YOU BE THE *DAMSEL...*
LET GO OF ME!
...WE'LL PROVIDE THE *DISTRESS.*
MISTER?
ARE YOU SLEEPING?
NO, LITTLE SAINT. I DON'T SLEEP.
IT'S GOOD TO SEE YOU AGAIN.
SAME HERE. SORRY IT TOOK SO LONG TO CATCH UP WITH YOU.
I KIND OF FELL OUT OF THE BACK OF THE TRUCK WHEN THOSE SOLDIERS TOOK YOU AWAY.
YOU KNOW, PASSED THROUGH THE BACK WHEN IT STARTED MOVING.
TAKES A WHILE TO GET THE HANG OF BEING A GHOST.

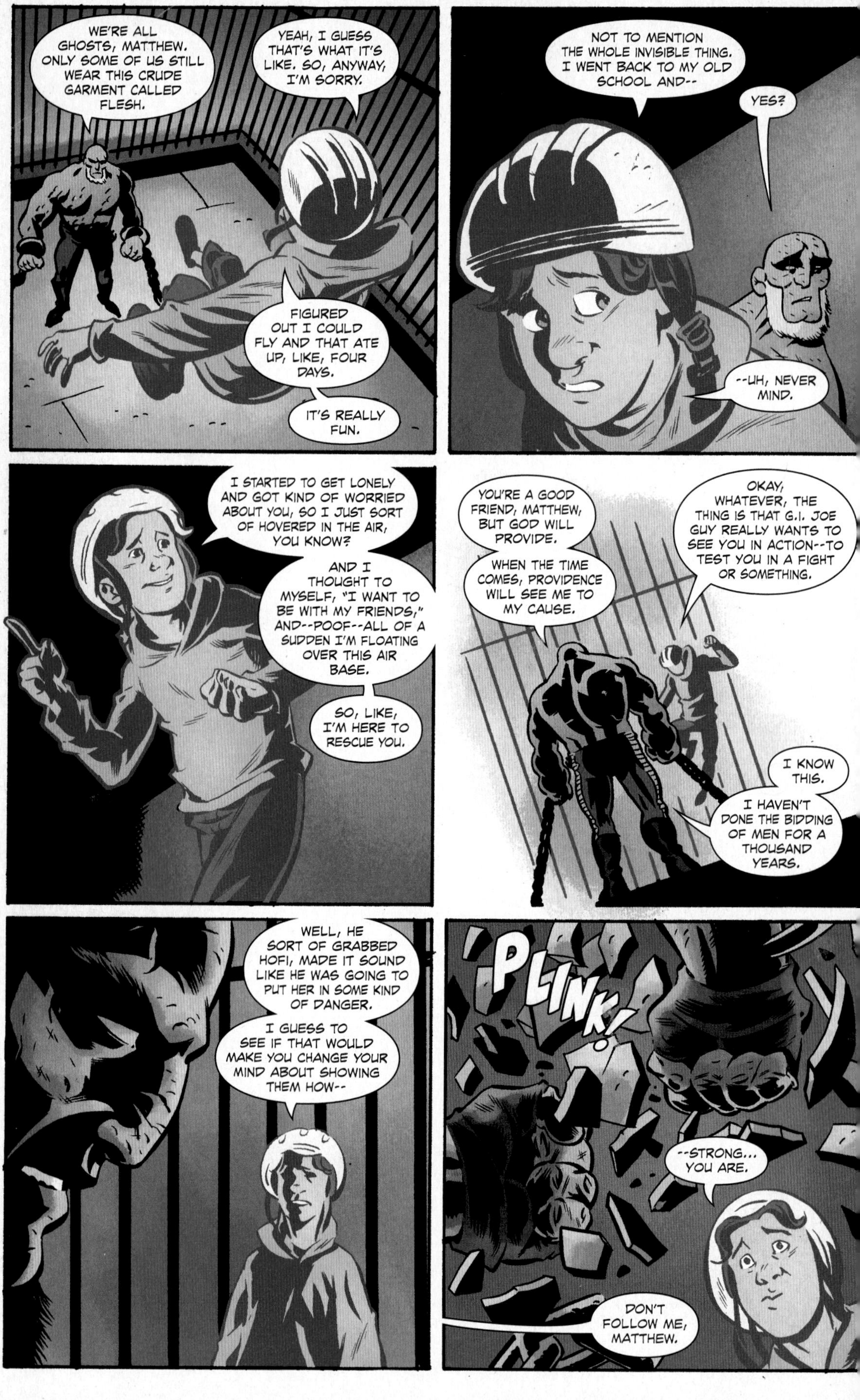
WE'RE ALL GHOSTS, MATTHEW. ONLY SOME OF US STILL WEAR THIS CRUDE GARMENT CALLED FLESH.
YEAH, I GUESS THAT'S WHAT IT'S LIKE. SO, ANYWAY, I'M SORRY.
FIGURED OUT I COULD FLY AND THAT ATE UP, LIKE, FOUR DAYS.
IT'S REALLY FUN.
NOT TO MENTION THE WHOLE INVISIBLE THING. I WENT BACK TO MY OLD SCHOOL AND--
YES?
--UH, NEVER MIND.
I STARTED TO GET LONELY AND GOT KIND OF WORRIED ABOUT YOU, SO I JUST SORT OF HOVERED IN THE AIR, YOU KNOW?
AND I THOUGHT TO MYSELF, "I WANT TO BE WITH MY FRIENDS," AND--POOF--ALL OF A SUDDEN I'M FLOATING OVER THIS AIR BASE.
SO, LIKE, I'M HERE TO RESCUE YOU.
YOU'RE A GOOD FRIEND, MATTHEW, BUT GOD WILL PROVIDE.
WHEN THE TIME COMES, PROVIDENCE WILL SEE ME TO MY CAUSE.
OKAY, WHATEVER, THE THING IS THAT G.I. JOE GUY REALLY WANTS TO SEE YOU IN ACTION--TO TEST YOU IN A FIGHT OR SOMETHING.
I KNOW THIS.
I HAVEN'T DONE THE BIDDING OF MEN FOR A THOUSAND YEARS.
WELL, HE SORT OF GRABBED HOFI, MADE IT SOUND LIKE HE WAS GOING TO PUT HER IN SOME KIND OF DANGER.
I GUESS TO SEE IF THAT WOULD MAKE YOU CHANGE YOUR MIND ABOUT SHOWING THEM HOW--
PLINK!
--STRONG... YOU ARE.
DON'T FOLLOW ME, MATTHEW.

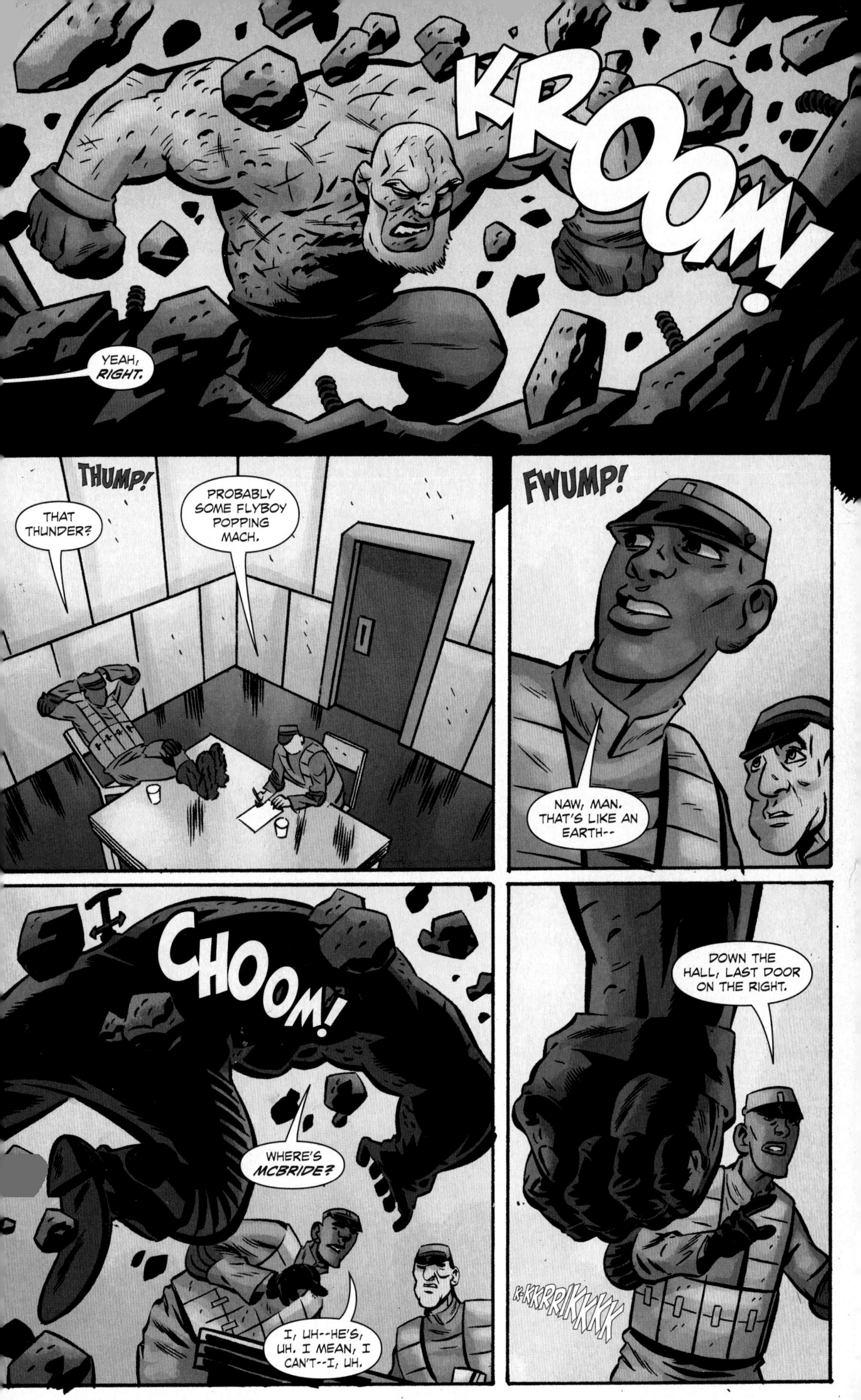
KROOOM!
YEAH, *RIGHT.*
THUMP!
THAT THUNDER?
PROBABLY SOME FLYBOY POPPING MACH.
FWUMP!
NAW, MAN. THAT'S LIKE AN EARTH--
CHOOM!
WHERE'S *MCBRIDE?*
I, UH--HE'S, UH. I MEAN, I CAN'T--I, UH.
DOWN THE HALL, LAST DOOR ON THE RIGHT.
K-KKRRIKKKK

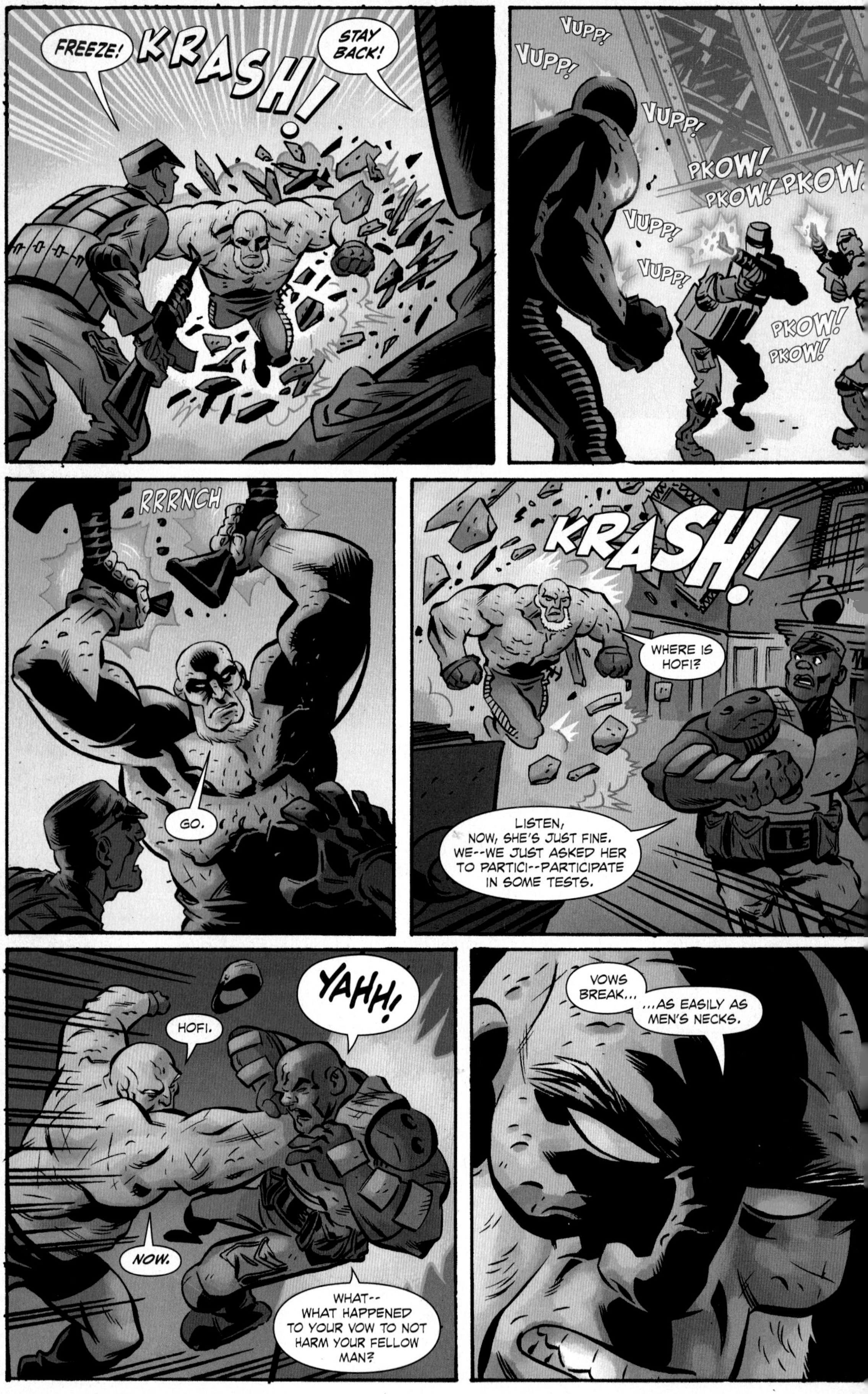
FREEZE!
KRASH!
STAY BACK!
VUPP!
VUPP!
VUPP!
PKOW!
PKOW! PKOW!
VUPP!
VUPP!
PKOW!
PKOW!
RRRNCH
GO.
KRASH!
WHERE IS HOFI?
LISTEN, NOW, SHE'S JUST FINE. WE--WE JUST ASKED HER TO PARTICI--PARTICIPATE IN SOME TESTS.
YAHH!
HOFI.
NOW.
WHAT-- WHAT HAPPENED TO YOUR VOW TO NOT HARM YOUR FELLOW MAN?
VOWS BREAK...
...AS EASILY AS MEN'S NECKS.

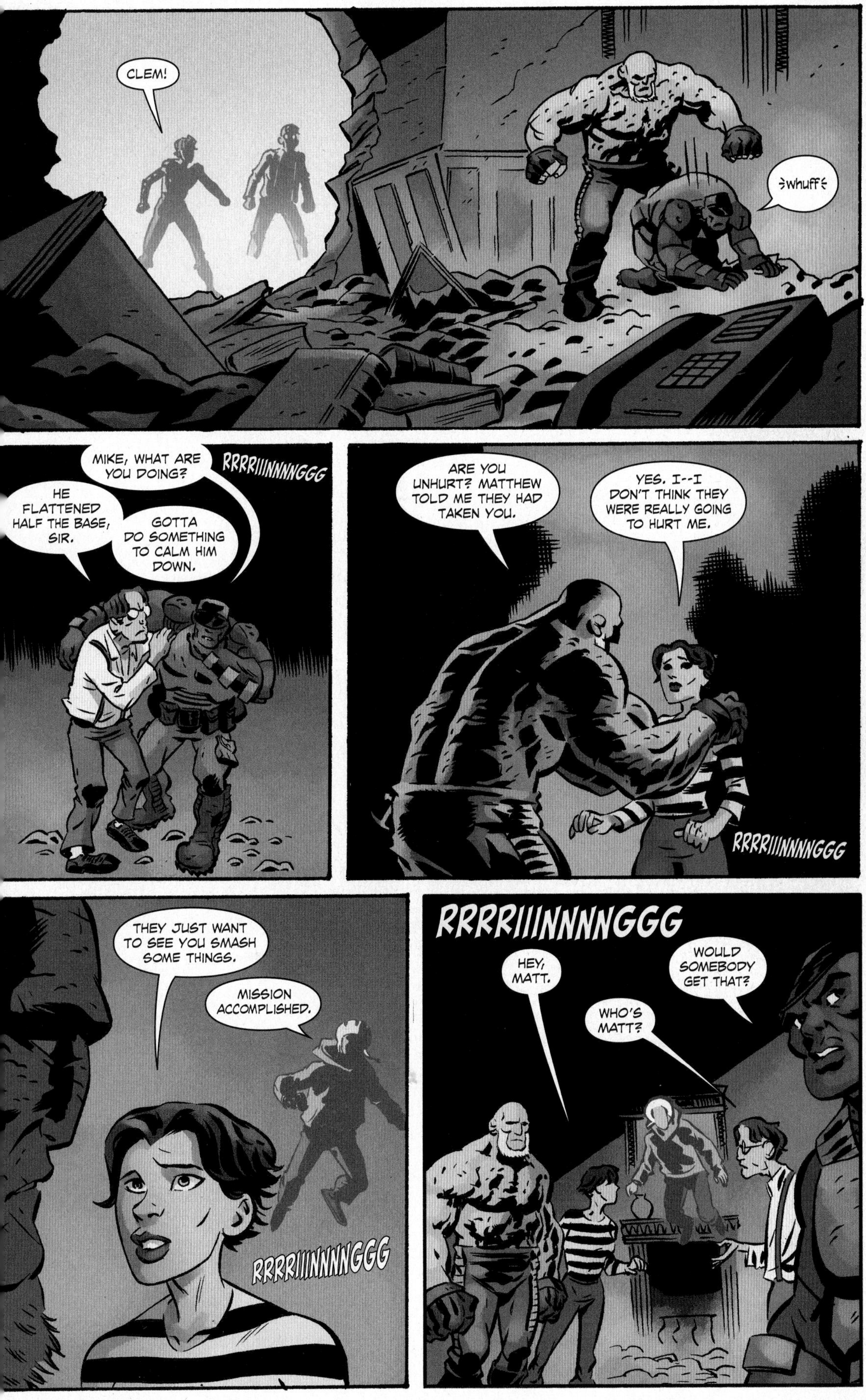

CLEM!
whuff
MIKE, WHAT ARE YOU DOING?
RRRRIIINNNNGGG
HE FLATTENED HALF THE BASE, SIR.
GOTTA DO SOMETHING TO CALM HIM DOWN.
ARE YOU UNHURT? MATTHEW TOLD ME THEY HAD TAKEN YOU.
YES. I--I DON'T THINK THEY WERE REALLY GOING TO HURT ME.
RRRRIIINNNNGGG
THEY JUST WANT TO SEE YOU SMASH SOME THINGS.
MISSION ACCOMPLISHED.
RRRRIIINNNNGGG
RRRRIIINNNNGGG
HEY, MATT.
WOULD SOMEBODY GET THAT?
WHO'S MATT?

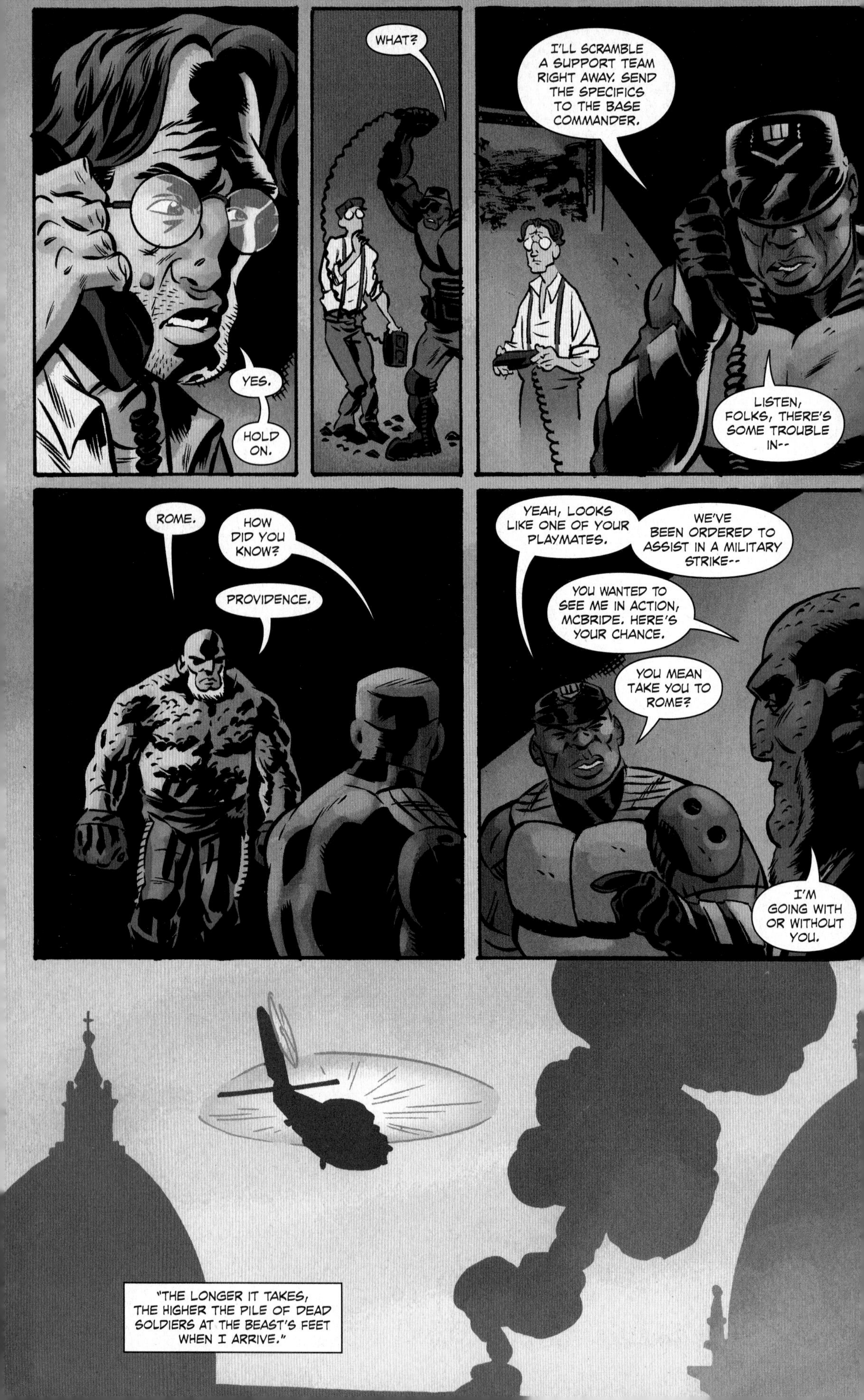
YES.
HOLD ON.
WHAT?
I'LL SCRAMBLE A SUPPORT TEAM RIGHT AWAY. SEND THE SPECIFICS TO THE BASE COMMANDER.
LISTEN, FOLKS, THERE'S SOME TROUBLE IN--
ROME.
HOW DID YOU KNOW?
PROVIDENCE.
YEAH, LOOKS LIKE ONE OF YOUR PLAYMATES.
WE'VE BEEN ORDERED TO ASSIST IN A MILITARY STRIKE--
YOU WANTED TO SEE ME IN ACTION, MCBRIDE. HERE'S YOUR CHANCE.
YOU MEAN TAKE YOU TO ROME?
I'M GOING WITH OR WITHOUT YOU.
"THE LONGER IT TAKES, THE HIGHER THE PILE OF DEAD SOLDIERS AT THE BEAST'S FEET WHEN I ARRIVE."

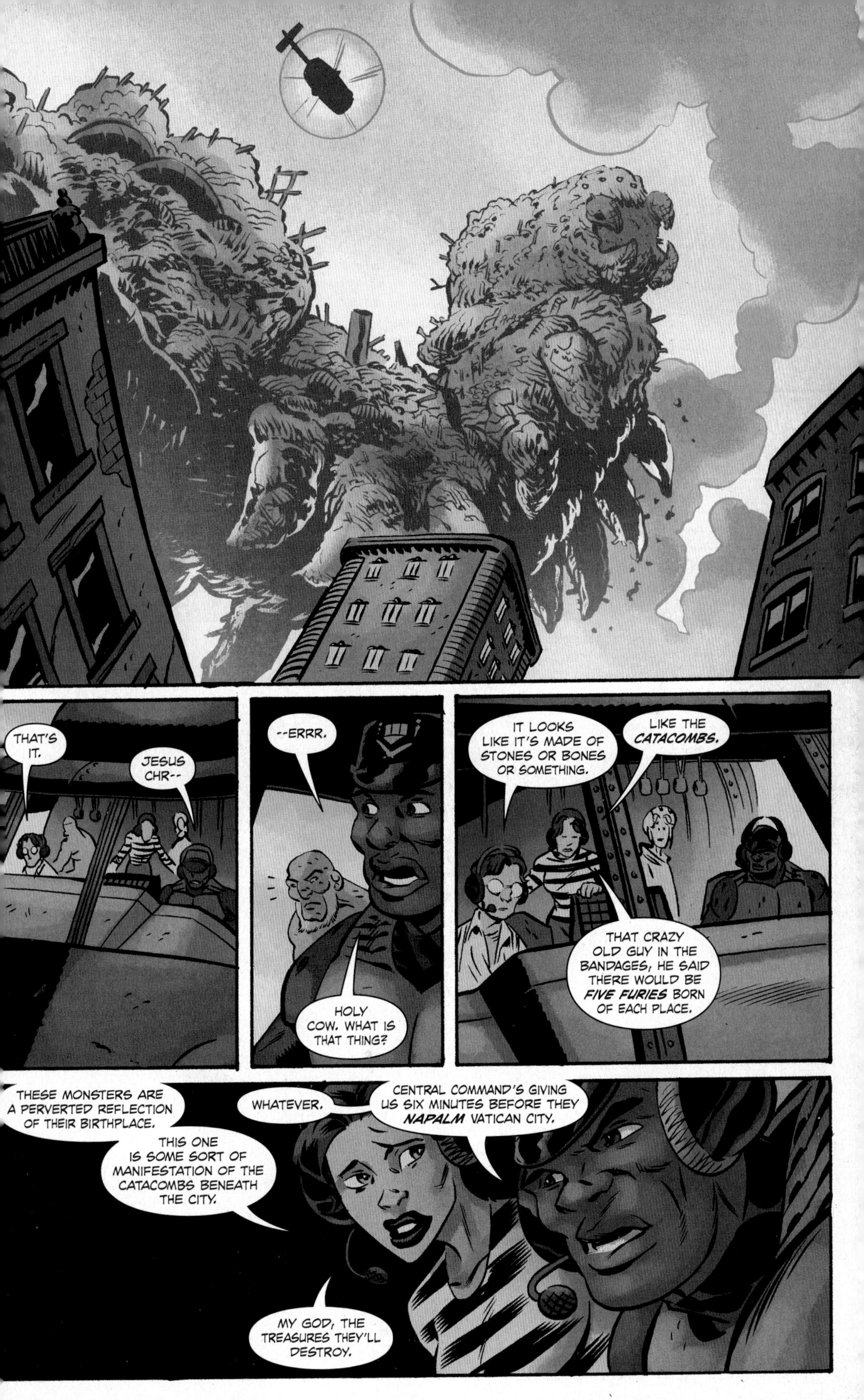
THAT'S IT.
JESUS CHR--
--ERRR.
HOLY COW. WHAT IS THAT THING?
IT LOOKS LIKE IT'S MADE OF STONES OR BONES OR SOMETHING.
LIKE THE *CATACOMBS.*
THAT CRAZY OLD GUY IN THE BANDAGES, HE SAID THERE WOULD BE *FIVE FURIES* BORN OF EACH PLACE.
THESE MONSTERS ARE A PERVERTED REFLECTION OF THEIR BIRTHPLACE.
THIS ONE IS SOME SORT OF MANIFESTATION OF THE CATACOMBS BENEATH THE CITY.
WHATEVER.
CENTRAL COMMAND'S GIVING US SIX MINUTES BEFORE THEY *NAPALM* VATICAN CITY.
MY GOD, THE TREASURES THEY'LL DESTROY.

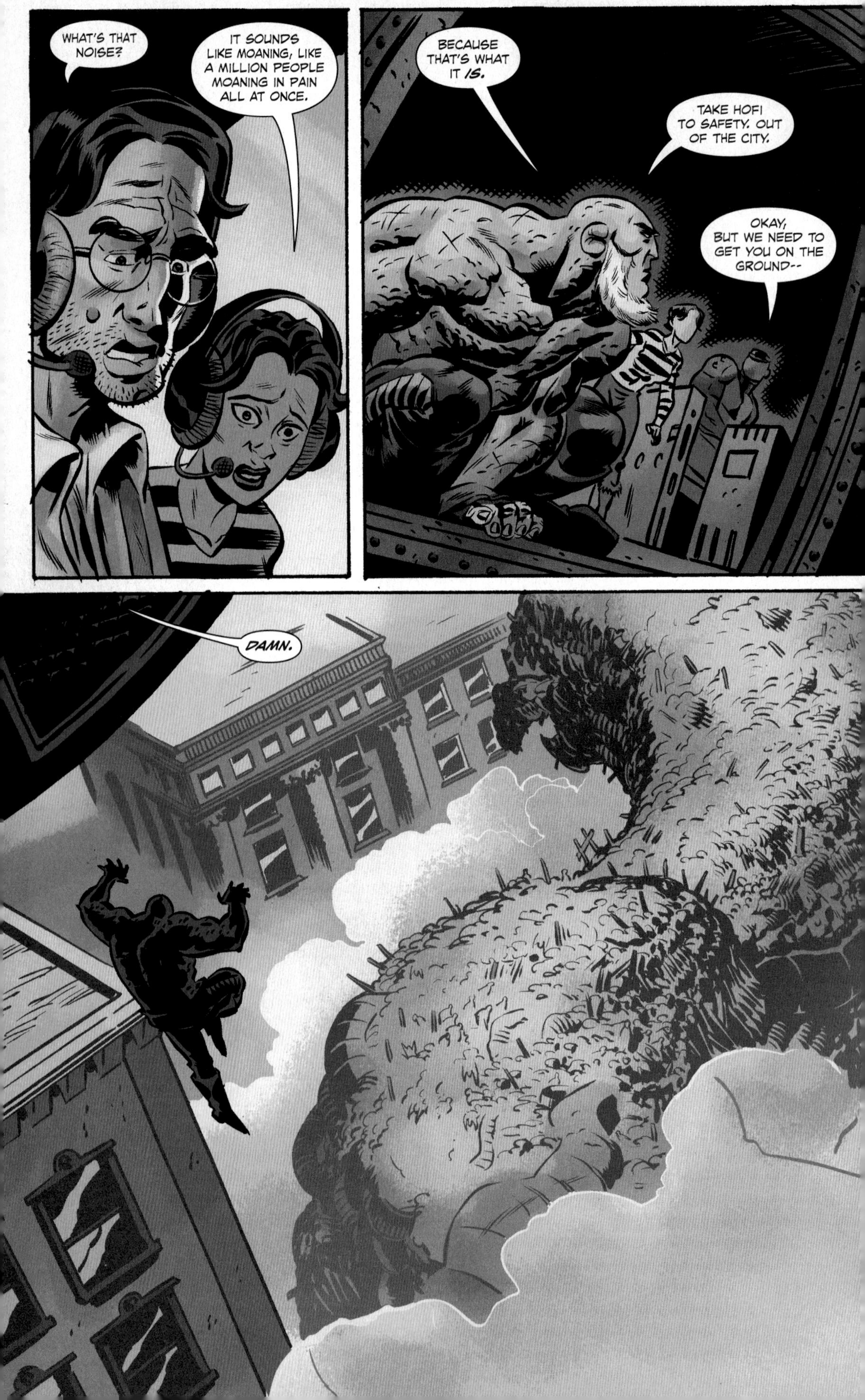
WHAT'S THAT NOISE?
IT SOUNDS LIKE MOANING, LIKE A MILLION PEOPLE MOANING IN PAIN ALL AT ONCE.
BECAUSE THAT'S WHAT IT *IS.*
TAKE HOFI TO SAFETY. OUT OF THE CITY.
OKAY, BUT WE NEED TO GET YOU ON THE GROUND--
DAMN.

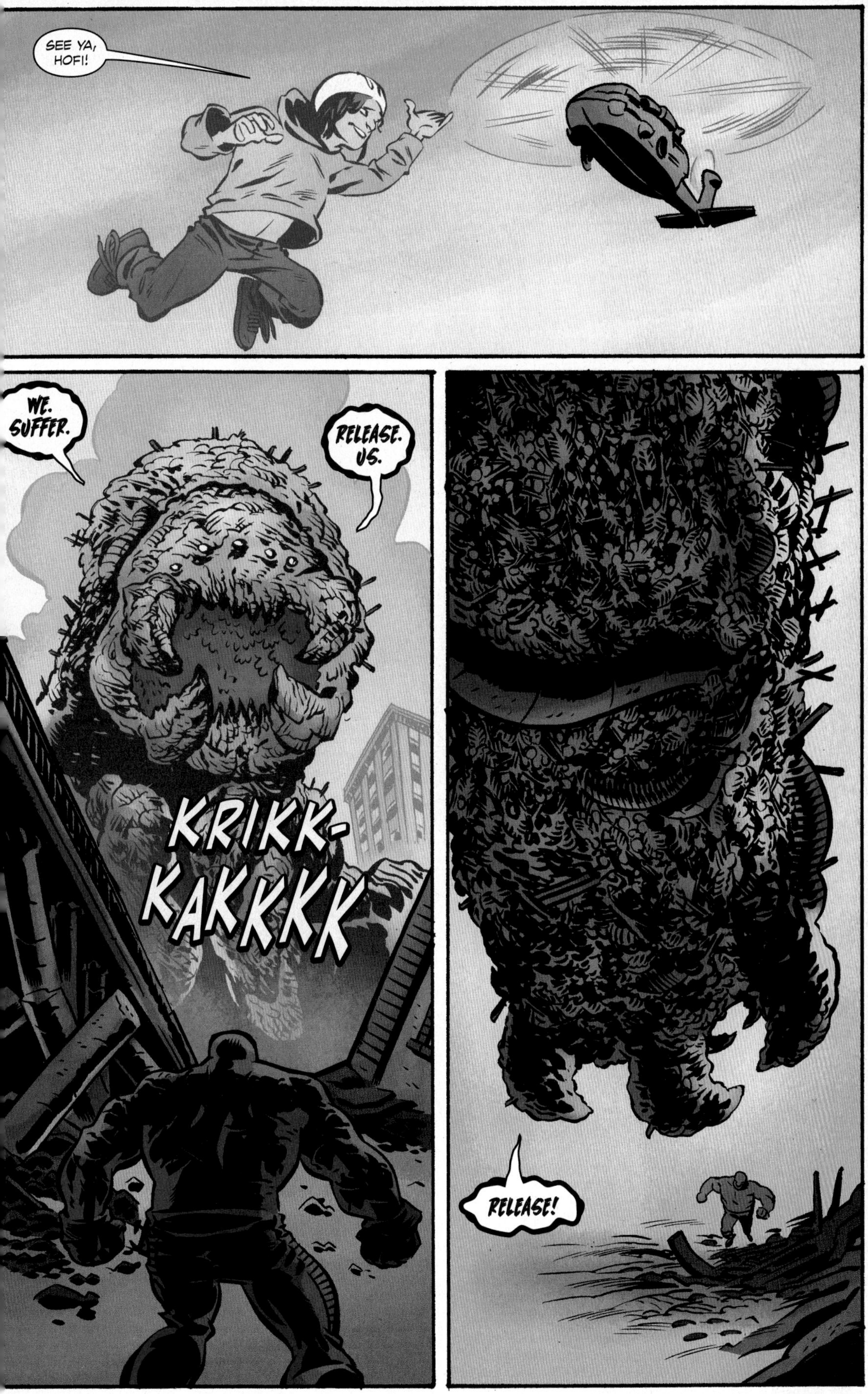
SEE YA, HOFI!
WE. SUFFER.
RELEASE. US.
KRIKK-KAKKKK
RELEASE!

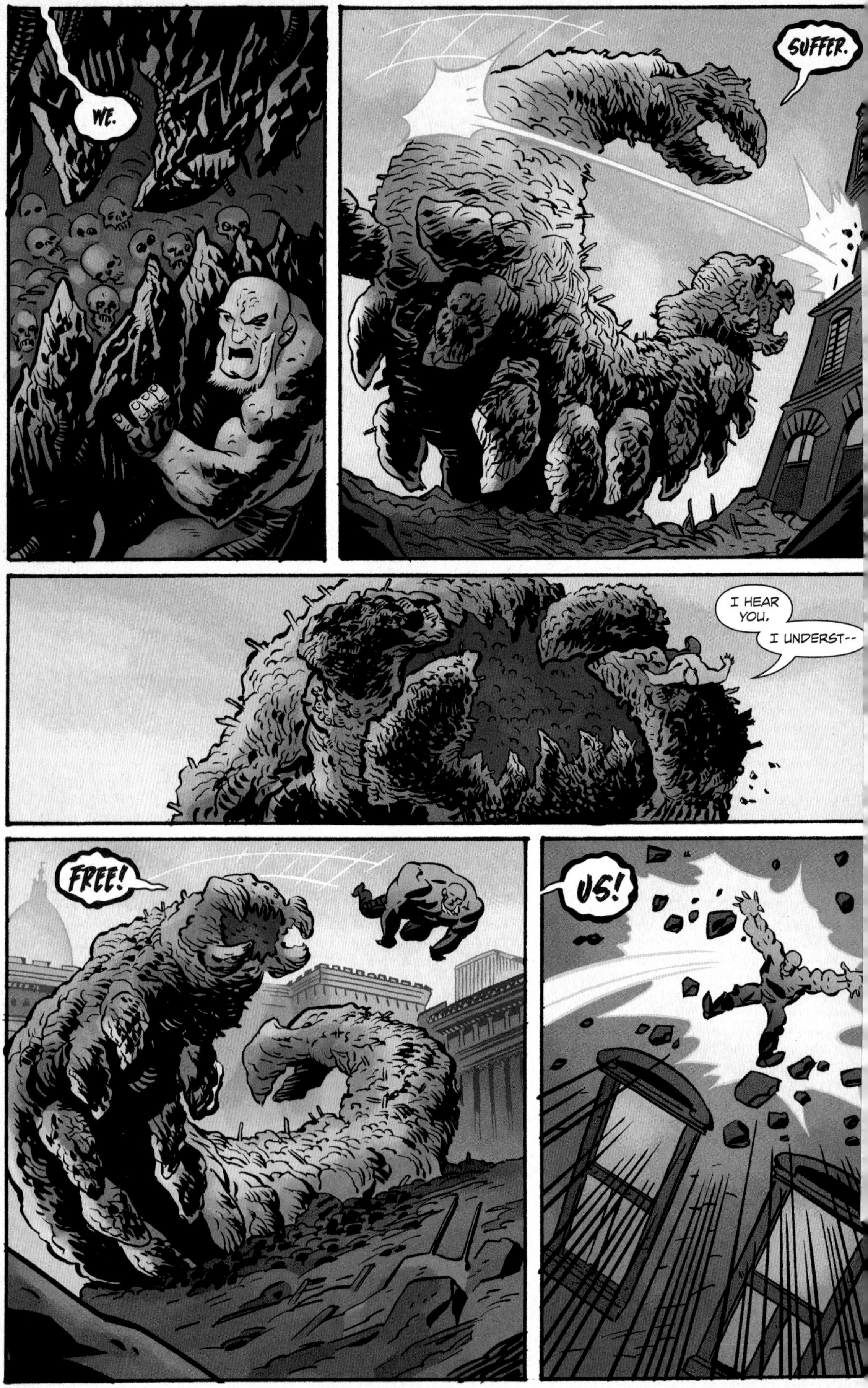
WE.
SUFFER.
I HEAR YOU.
I UNDERST--
FREE!
US!

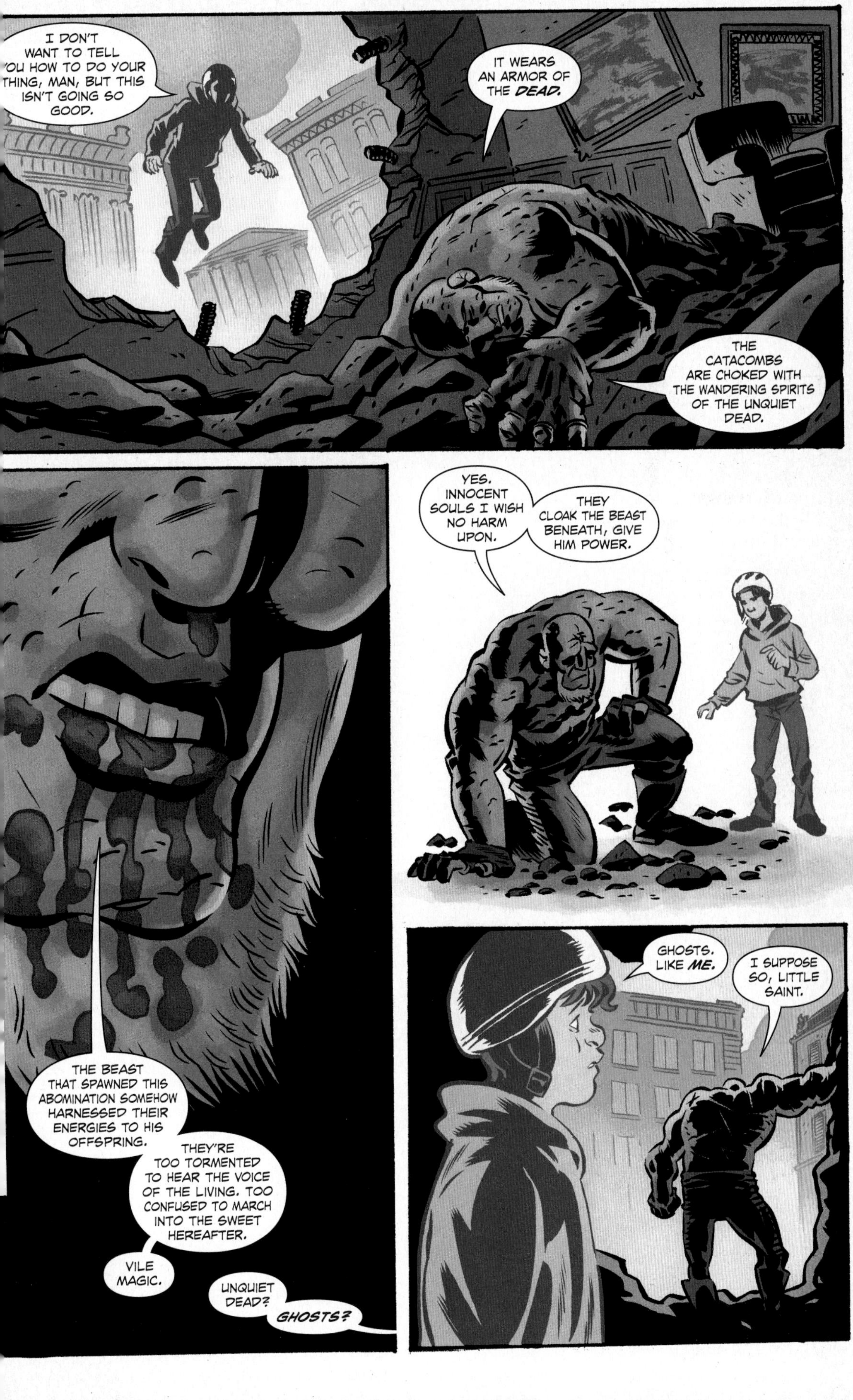
I DON'T WANT TO TELL YOU HOW TO DO YOUR THING, MAN, BUT THIS ISN'T GOING SO GOOD.
IT WEARS AN ARMOR OF THE *DEAD.*
THE CATACOMBS ARE CHOKED WITH THE WANDERING SPIRITS OF THE UNQUIET DEAD.
YES. INNOCENT SOULS I WISH NO HARM UPON.
THEY CLOAK THE BEAST BENEATH, GIVE HIM POWER.
THE BEAST THAT SPAWNED THIS ABOMINATION SOMEHOW HARNESSED THEIR ENERGIES TO HIS OFFSPRING.
THEY'RE TOO TORMENTED TO HEAR THE VOICE OF THE LIVING. TOO CONFUSED TO MARCH INTO THE SWEET HEREAFTER.
VILE MAGIC.
UNQUIET DEAD? *GHOSTS?*
GHOSTS. LIKE *ME.*
I SUPPOSE SO, LITTLE SAINT.

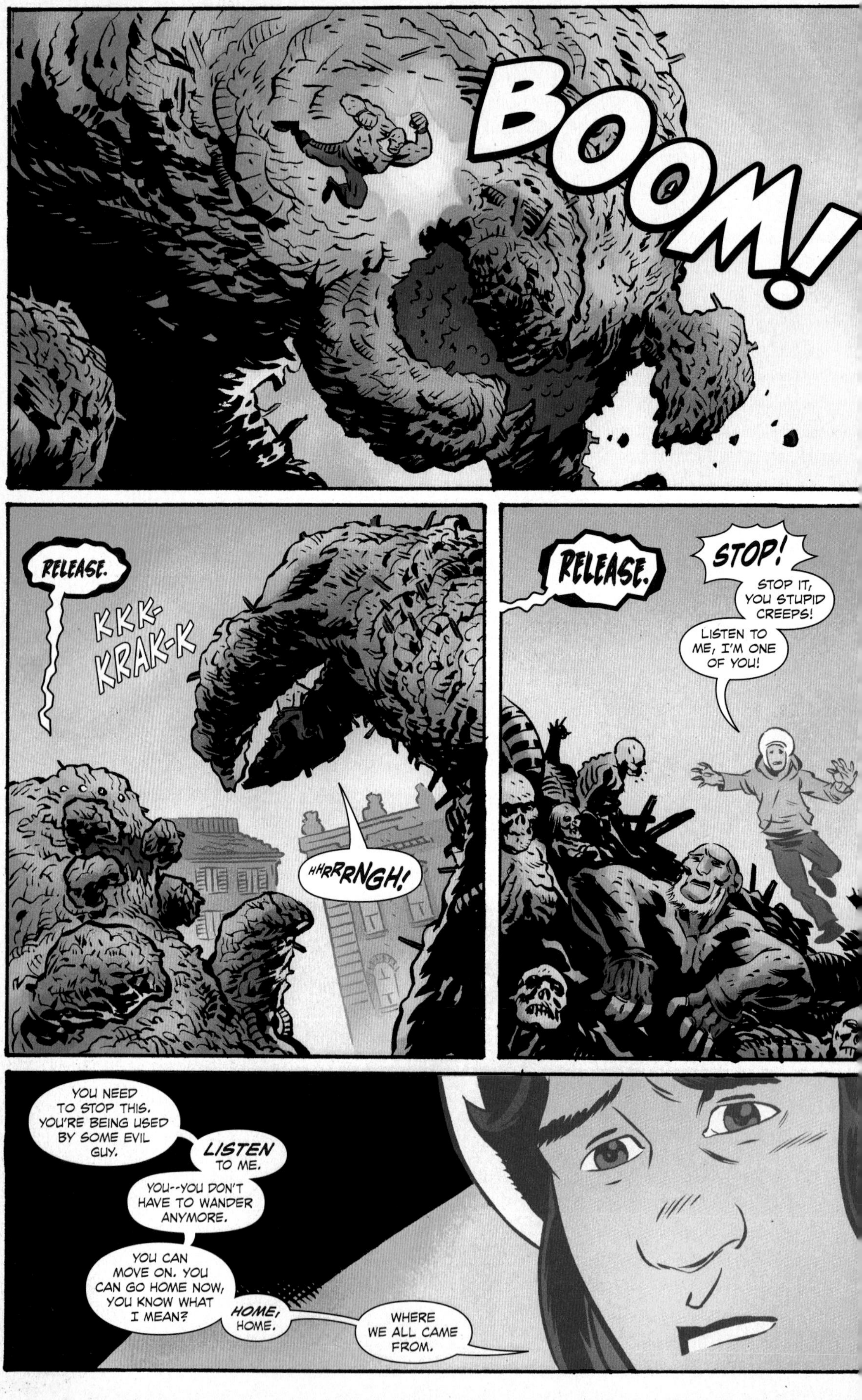
BOOM!
RELEASE.
KKK-KRAK-K
HHRRRNGH!
RELEASE.
STOP!
STOP IT, YOU STUPID CREEPS!
LISTEN TO ME, I'M ONE OF YOU!
YOU NEED TO STOP THIS. YOU'RE BEING USED BY SOME EVIL GUY.
LISTEN TO ME.
YOU--YOU DON'T HAVE TO WANDER ANYMORE.
YOU CAN MOVE ON. YOU CAN GO HOME NOW, YOU KNOW WHAT I MEAN?
HOME, HOME.
WHERE WE ALL CAME FROM.

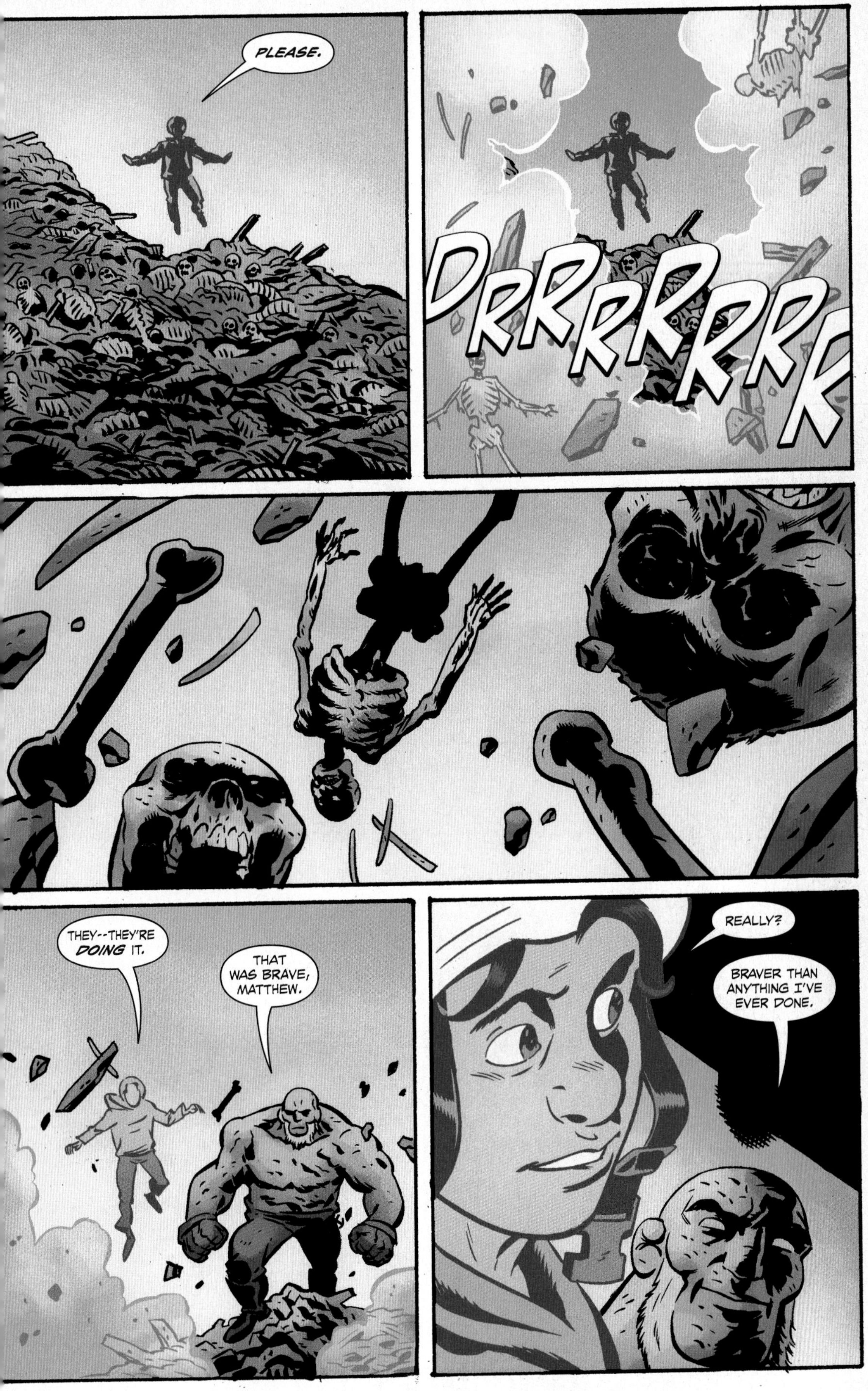
PLEASE.
DRRRRRRRRK
THEY--THEY'RE DOING IT.
THAT WAS BRAVE, MATTHEW.
REALLY?
BRAVER THAN ANYTHING I'VE EVER DONE.

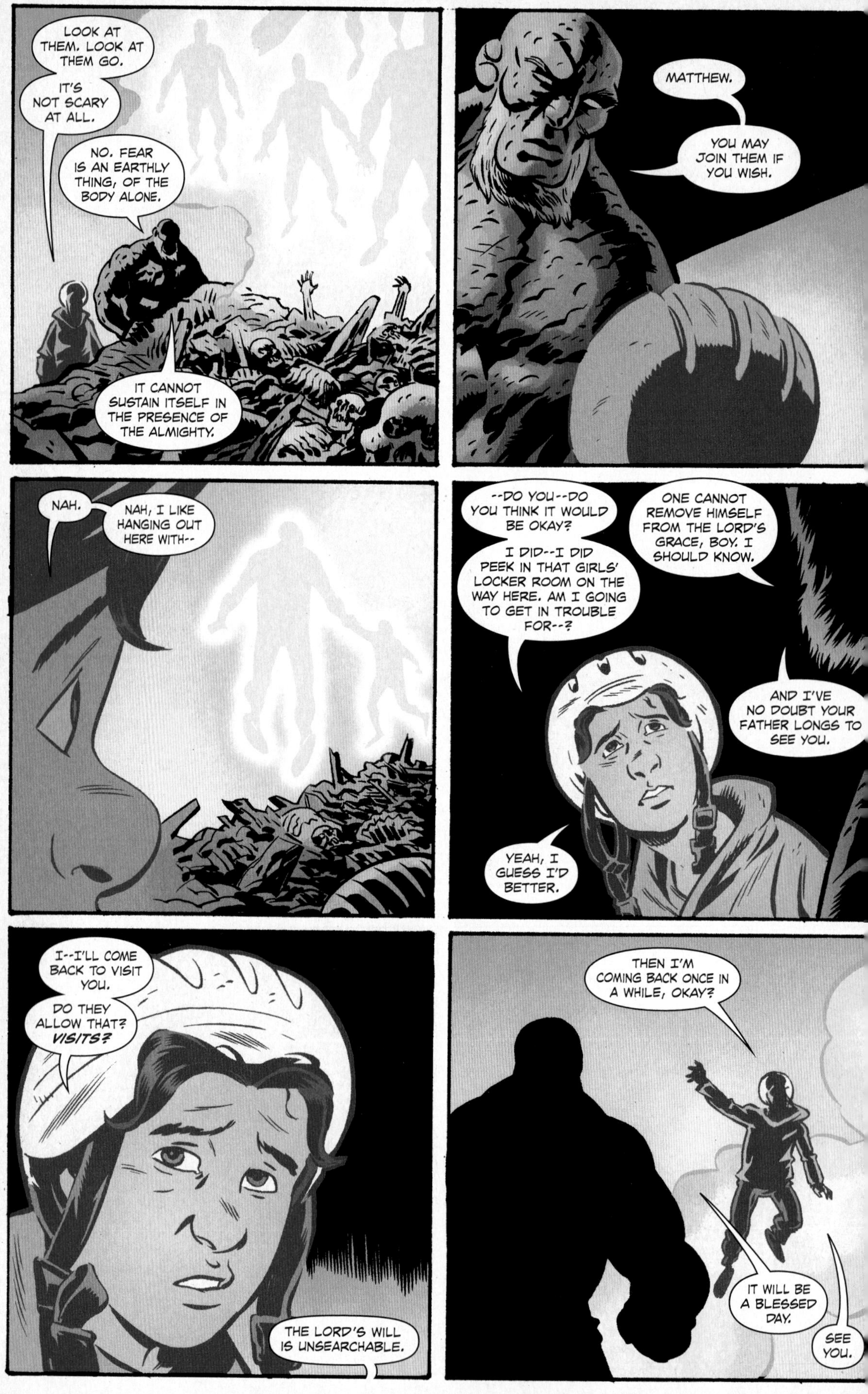
LOOK AT THEM. LOOK AT THEM GO.
IT'S NOT SCARY AT ALL.
NO. FEAR IS AN EARTHLY THING, OF THE BODY ALONE.
IT CANNOT SUSTAIN ITSELF IN THE PRESENCE OF THE ALMIGHTY.
MATTHEW.
YOU MAY JOIN THEM IF YOU WISH.
NAH.
NAH, I LIKE HANGING OUT HERE WITH--
--DO YOU--DO YOU THINK IT WOULD BE OKAY?
I DID--I DID PEEK IN THAT GIRLS' LOCKER ROOM ON THE WAY HERE. AM I GOING TO GET IN TROUBLE FOR--?
ONE CANNOT REMOVE HIMSELF FROM THE LORD'S GRACE, BOY. I SHOULD KNOW.
AND I'VE NO DOUBT YOUR FATHER LONGS TO SEE YOU.
YEAH, I GUESS I'D BETTER.
I--I'LL COME BACK TO VISIT YOU.
DO THEY ALLOW THAT? *VISITS?*
THE LORD'S WILL IS UNSEARCHABLE.
THEN I'M COMING BACK ONCE IN A WHILE, OKAY?
IT WILL BE A BLESSED DAY.
SEE YOU.

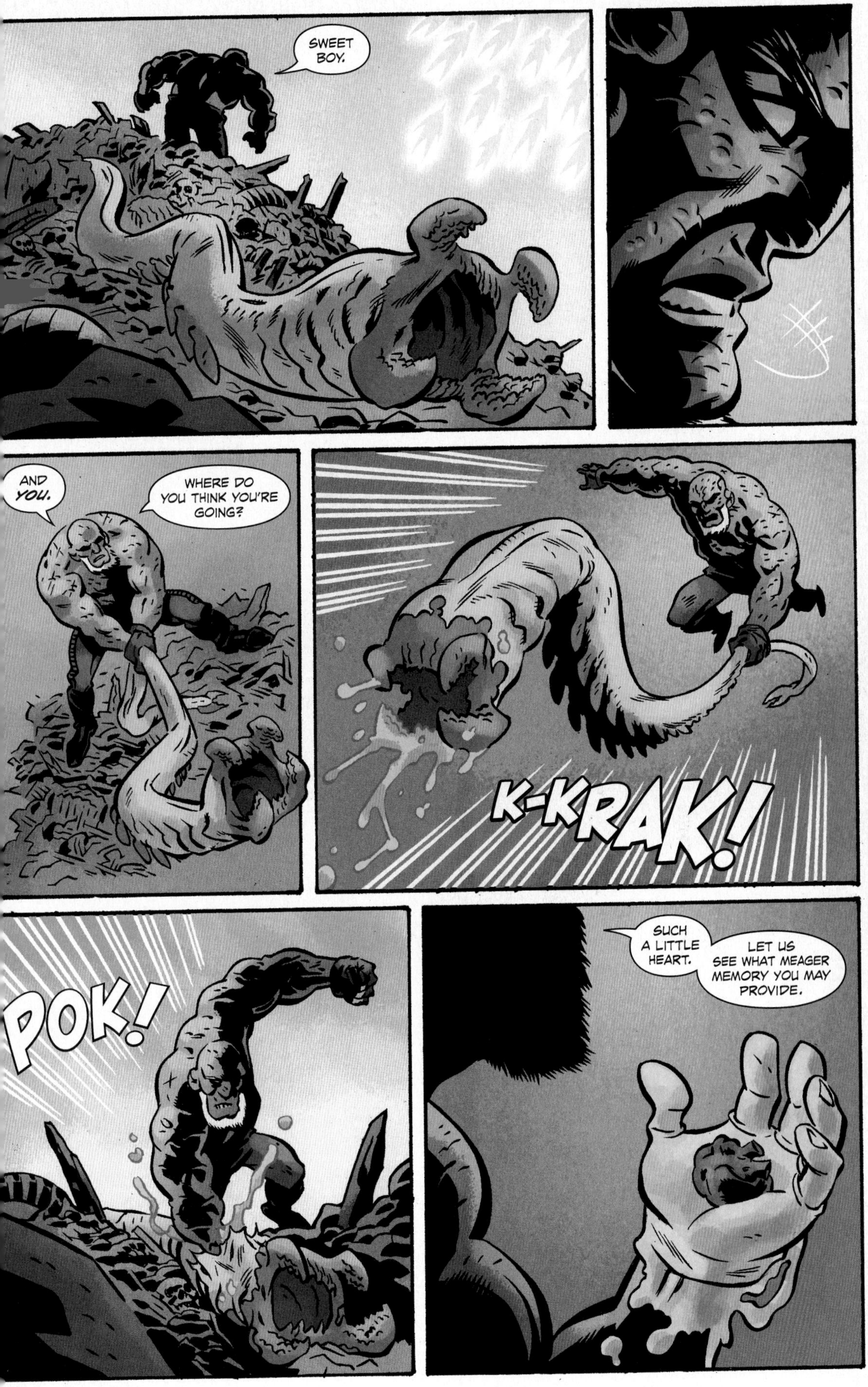
SWEET BOY.
AND YOU.
WHERE DO YOU THINK YOU'RE GOING?
K-KRAK!
POK!
SUCH A LITTLE HEART.
LET US SEE WHAT MEAGER MEMORY YOU MAY PROVIDE.

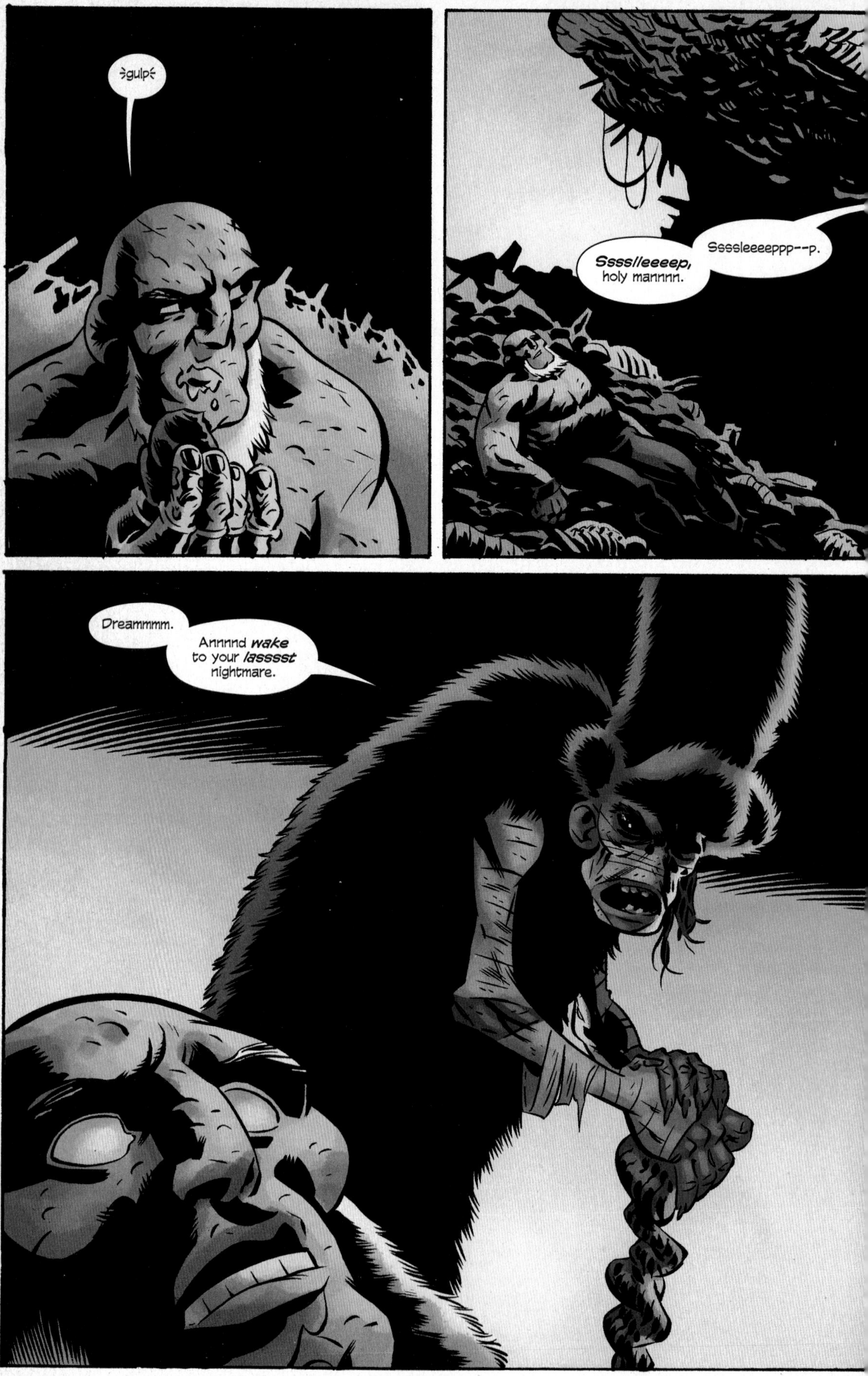
gulp
Ssssleeeeppp--p.
Sssslleeeep, holy mannnn.
Dreammmm.
Annnnd wake to your lasssst nightmare.

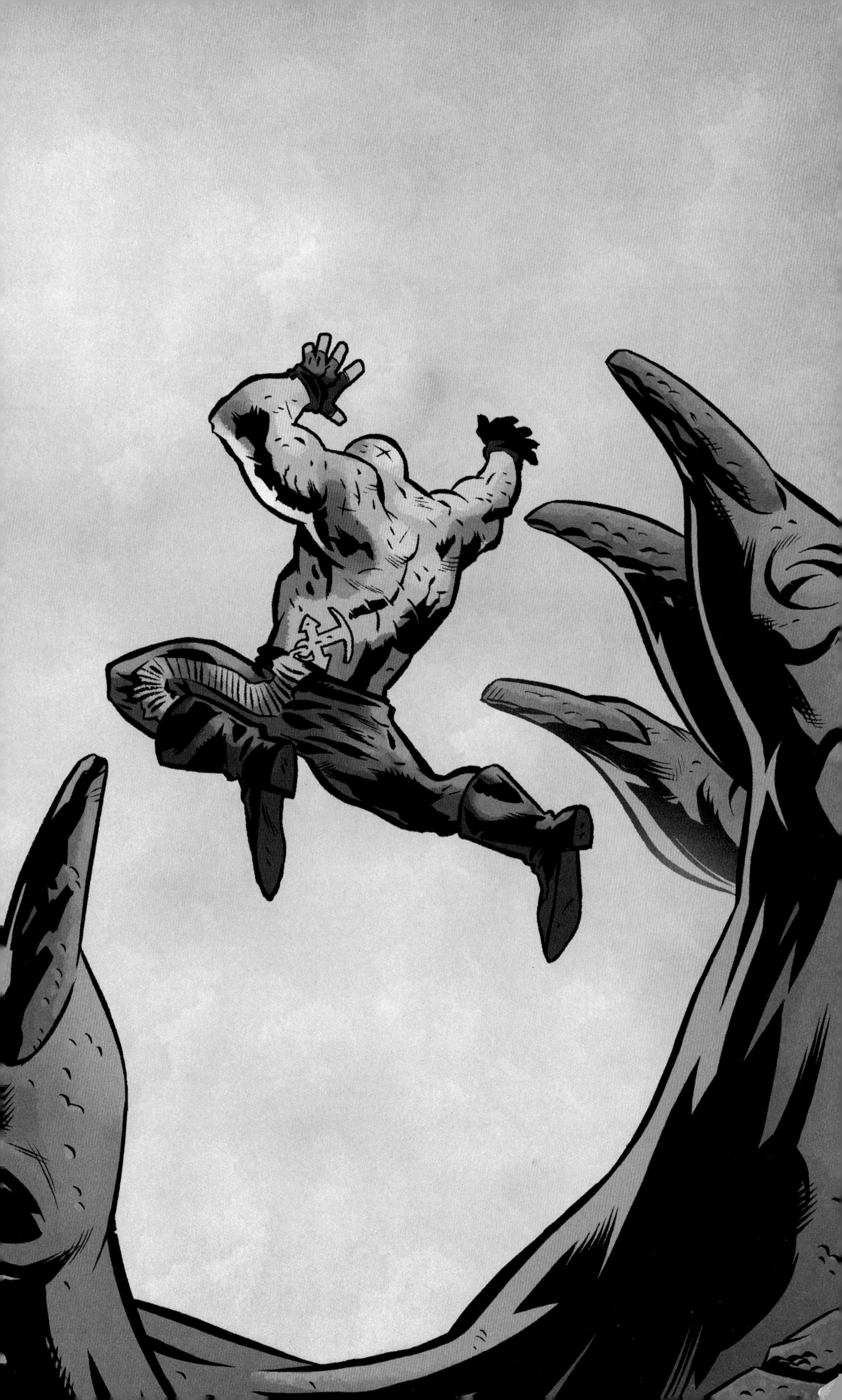

Chapter Four

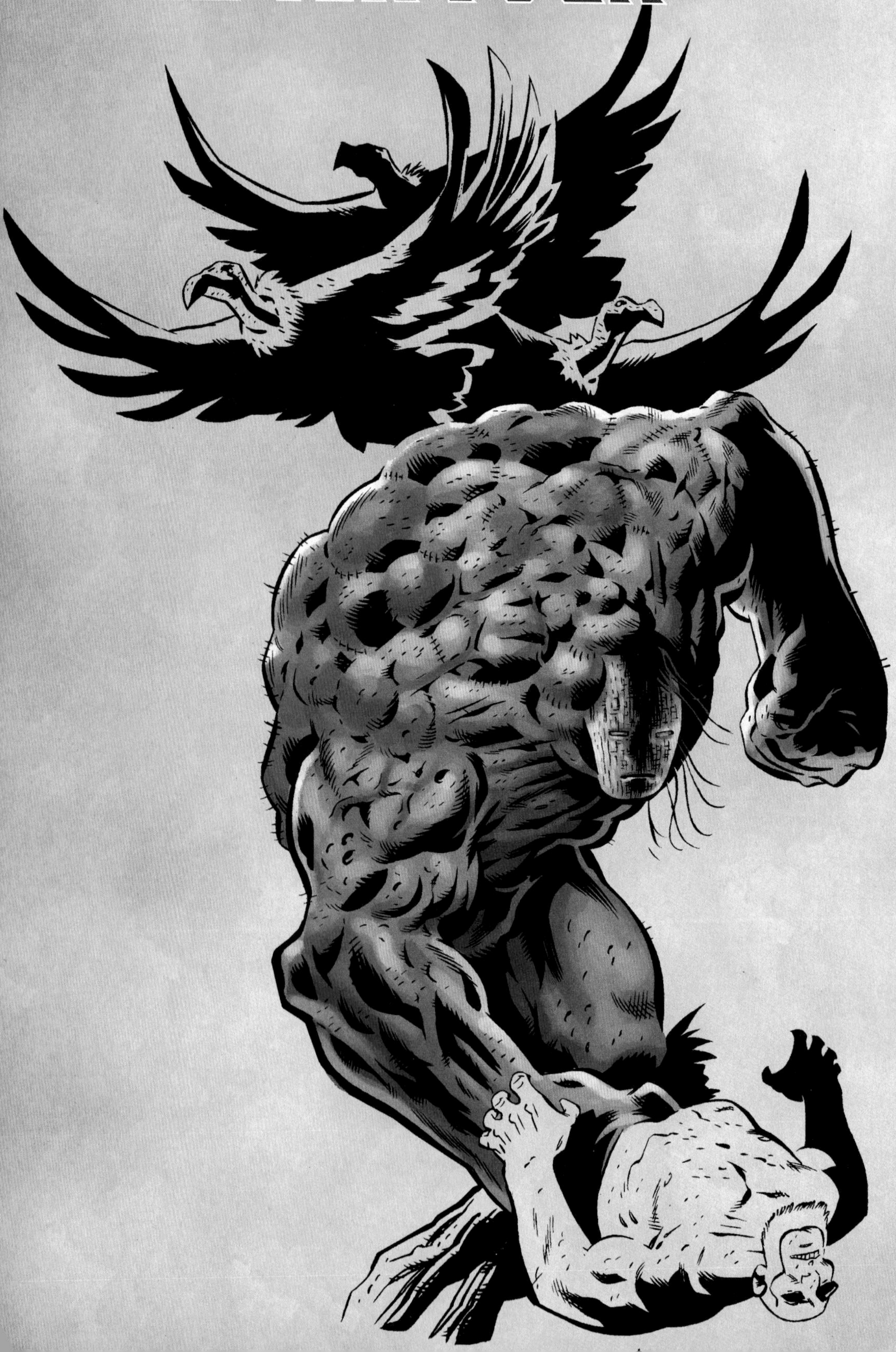

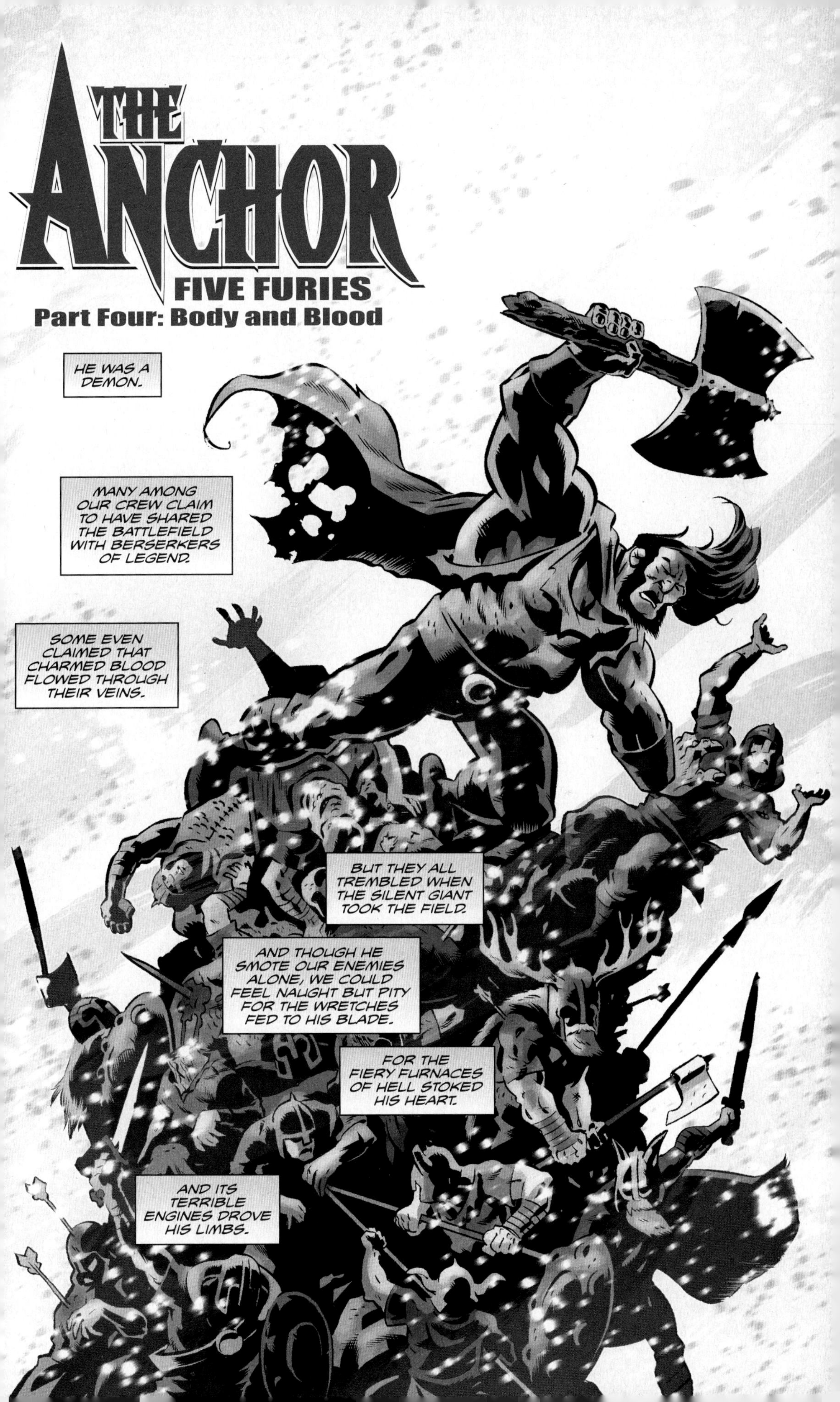
THE ANCHOR
FIVE FURIES
Part Four: Body and Blood
HE WAS A DEMON.
MANY AMONG OUR CREW CLAIM TO HAVE SHARED THE BATTLEFIELD WITH BERSERKERS OF LEGEND.
SOME EVEN CLAIMED THAT CHARMED BLOOD FLOWED THROUGH THEIR VEINS.
BUT THEY ALL TREMBLED WHEN THE SILENT GIANT TOOK THE FIELD.
AND THOUGH HE SMOTE OUR ENEMIES ALONE, WE COULD FEEL NAUGHT BUT PITY FOR THE WRETCHES FED TO HIS BLADE.
FOR THE FIERY FURNACES OF HELL STOKED HIS HEART.
AND ITS TERRIBLE ENGINES DROVE HIS LIMBS.

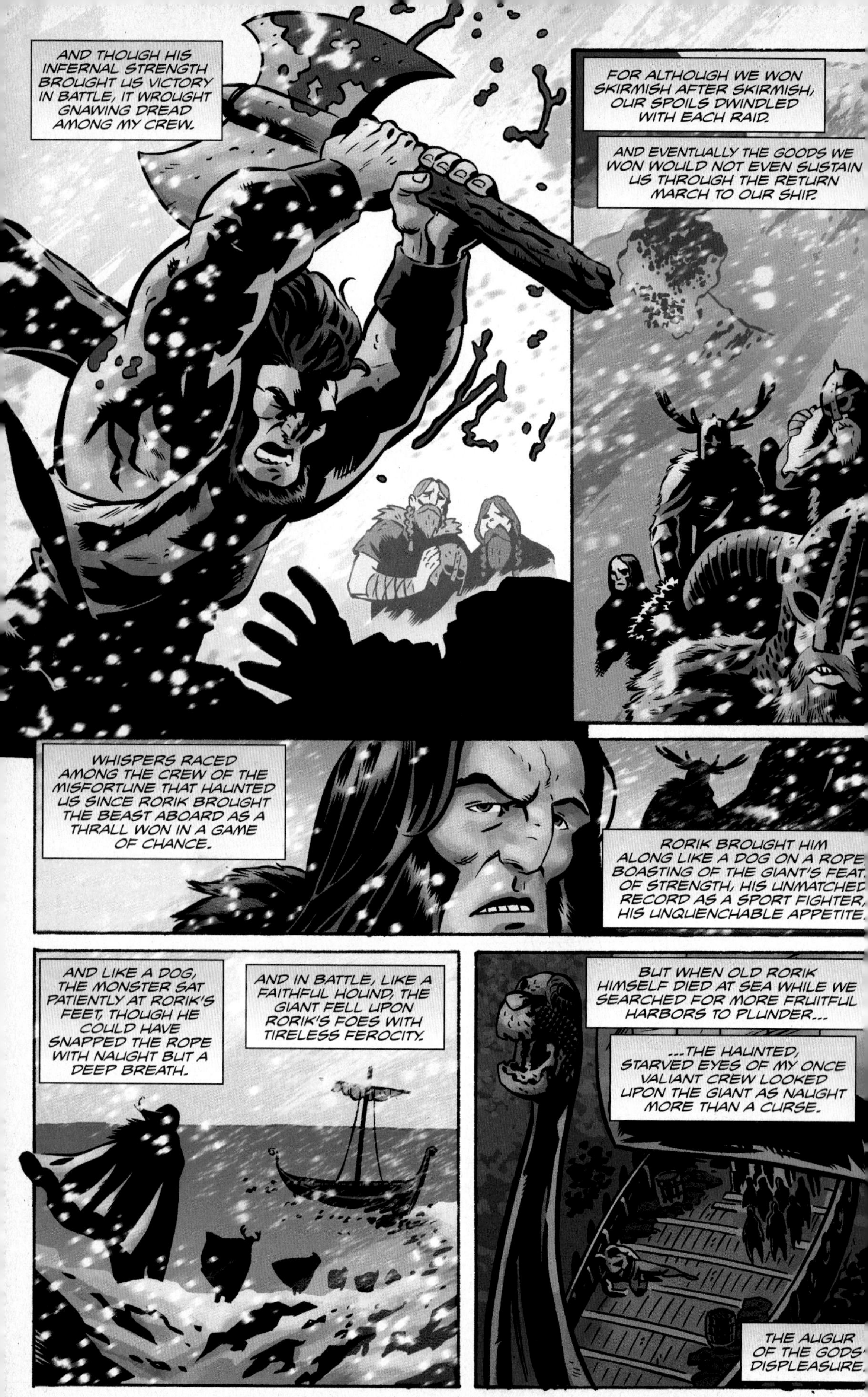
AND THOUGH HIS INFERNAL STRENGTH BROUGHT US VICTORY IN BATTLE, IT WROUGHT GNAWING DREAD AMONG MY CREW.
FOR ALTHOUGH WE WON SKIRMISH AFTER SKIRMISH, OUR SPOILS DWINDLED WITH EACH RAID.
AND EVENTUALLY THE GOODS WE WON WOULD NOT EVEN SUSTAIN US THROUGH THE RETURN MARCH TO OUR SHIP.
WHISPERS RACED AMONG THE CREW OF THE MISFORTUNE THAT HAUNTED US SINCE RORIK BROUGHT THE BEAST ABOARD AS A THRALL WON IN A GAME OF CHANCE.
RORIK BROUGHT HIM ALONG LIKE A DOG ON A ROPE BOASTING OF THE GIANT'S FEAT OF STRENGTH, HIS UNMATCHED RECORD AS A SPORT FIGHTER, HIS UNQUENCHABLE APPETITE.
AND LIKE A DOG, THE MONSTER SAT PATIENTLY AT RORIK'S FEET, THOUGH HE COULD HAVE SNAPPED THE ROPE WITH NAUGHT BUT A DEEP BREATH.
AND IN BATTLE, LIKE A FAITHFUL HOUND, THE GIANT FELL UPON RORIK'S FOES WITH TIRELESS FEROCITY.
BUT WHEN OLD RORIK HIMSELF DIED AT SEA WHILE WE SEARCHED FOR MORE FRUITFUL HARBORS TO PLUNDER...
...THE HAUNTED, STARVED EYES OF MY ONCE VALIANT CREW LOOKED UPON THE GIANT AS NAUGHT MORE THAN A CURSE.
THE AUGUR OF THE GODS' DISPLEASURE.

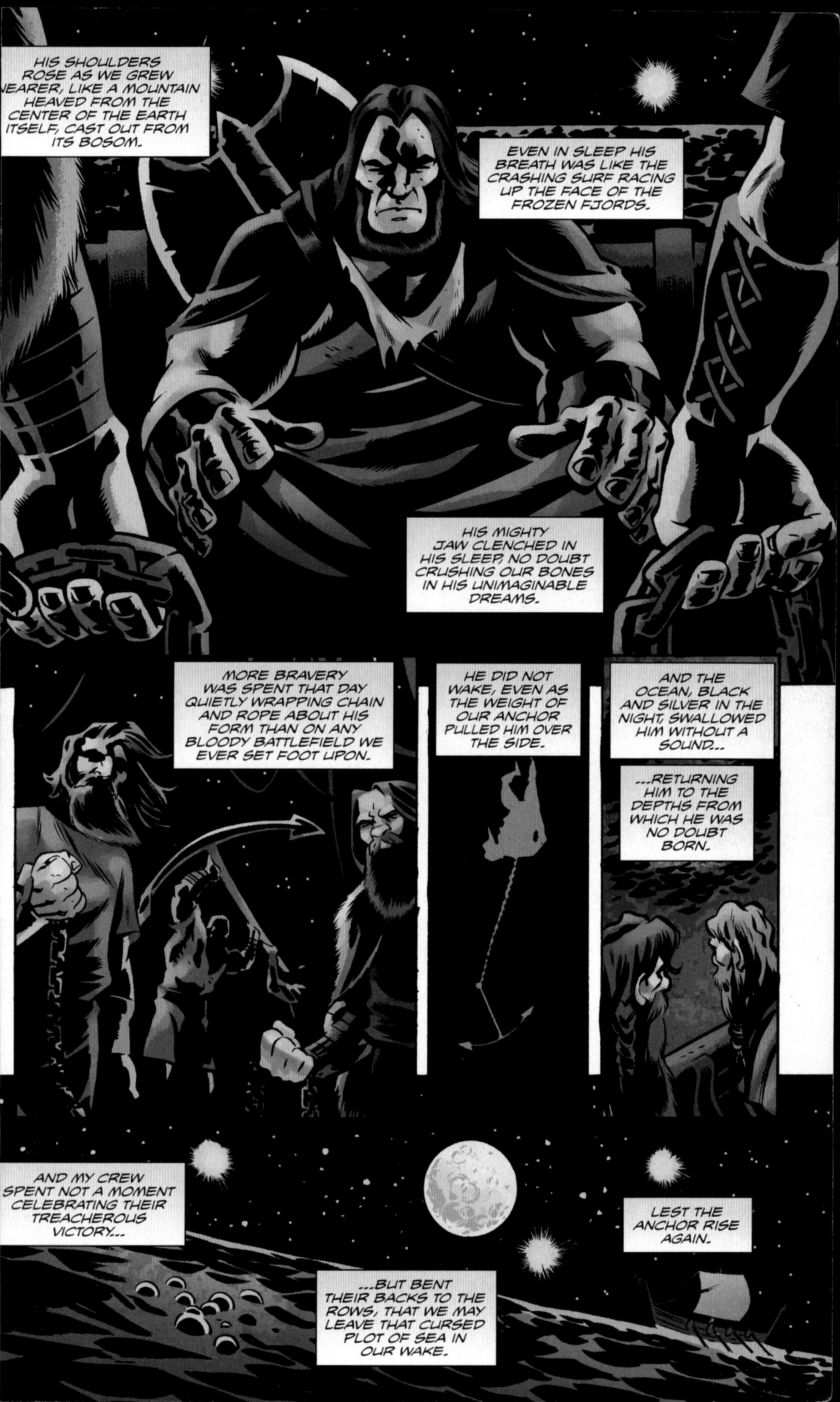
HIS SHOULDERS ROSE AS WE GREW NEARER, LIKE A MOUNTAIN HEAVED FROM THE CENTER OF THE EARTH ITSELF, CAST OUT FROM ITS BOSOM.
EVEN IN SLEEP HIS BREATH WAS LIKE THE CRASHING SURF RACING UP THE FACE OF THE FROZEN FJORDS.
HIS MIGHTY JAW CLENCHED IN HIS SLEEP, NO DOUBT CRUSHING OUR BONES IN HIS UNIMAGINABLE DREAMS.
MORE BRAVERY WAS SPENT THAT DAY QUIETLY WRAPPING CHAIN AND ROPE ABOUT HIS FORM THAN ON ANY BLOODY BATTLEFIELD WE EVER SET FOOT UPON.
HE DID NOT WAKE, EVEN AS THE WEIGHT OF OUR ANCHOR PULLED HIM OVER THE SIDE.
AND THE OCEAN, BLACK AND SILVER IN THE NIGHT, SWALLOWED HIM WITHOUT A SOUND...
...RETURNING HIM TO THE DEPTHS FROM WHICH HE WAS NO DOUBT BORN.
AND MY CREW SPENT NOT A MOMENT CELEBRATING THEIR TREACHEROUS VICTORY...
...BUT BENT THEIR BACKS TO THE ROWS, THAT WE MAY LEAVE THAT CURSED PLOT OF SEA IN OUR WAKE.
LEST THE ANCHOR RISE AGAIN.

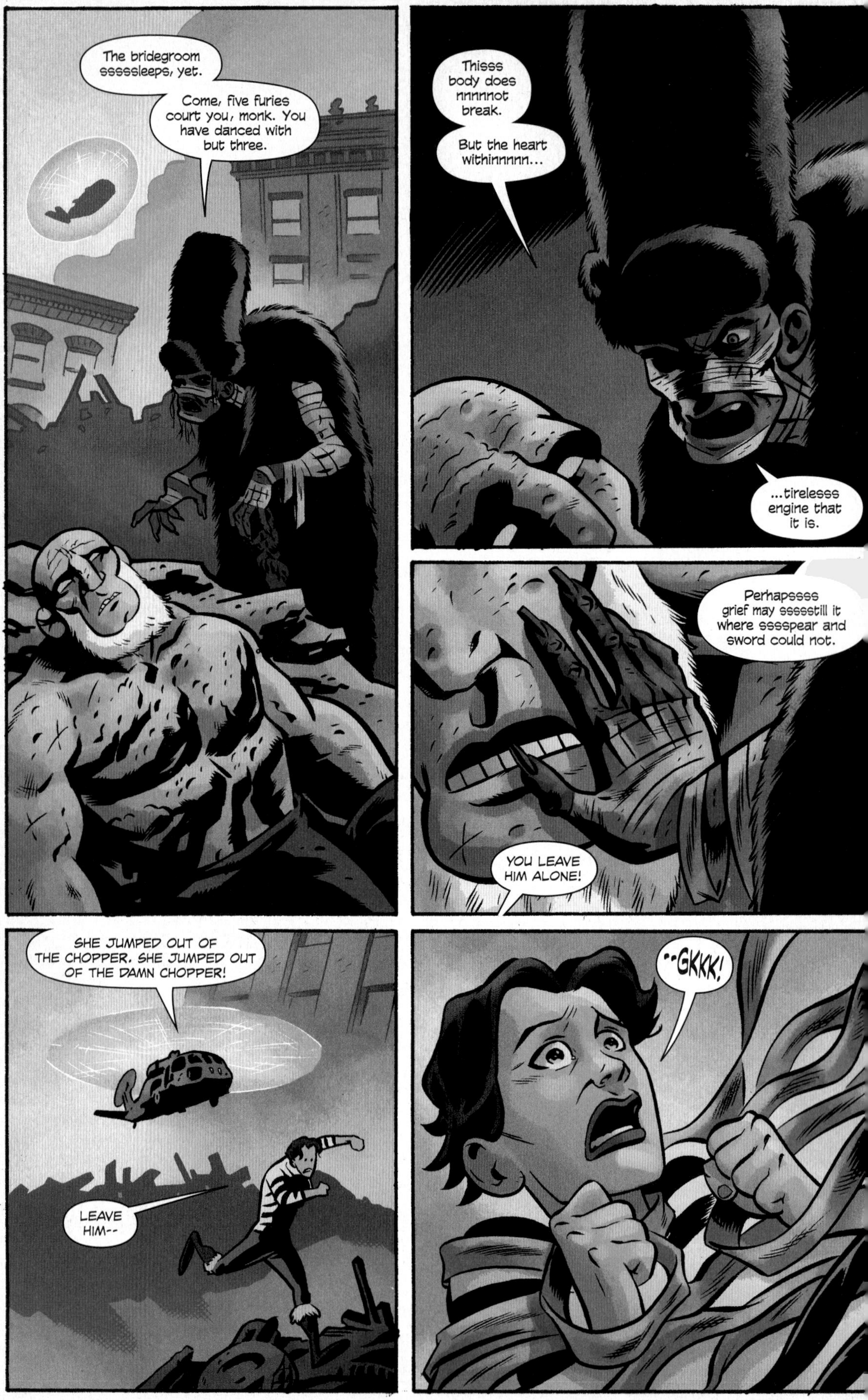
The bridegroom ssssssleeps, yet.
Come, five furies court you, monk. You have danced with but three.
Thisss body does nnnnnot break.
But the heart withinnnnn...
...tirelesss engine that it is.
Perhapssss grief may sssssstill it where sssspear and sword could not.
YOU LEAVE HIM ALONE!
SHE JUMPED OUT OF THE CHOPPER. SHE JUMPED OUT OF THE DAMN CHOPPER!
LEAVE HIM--
--GKKK!

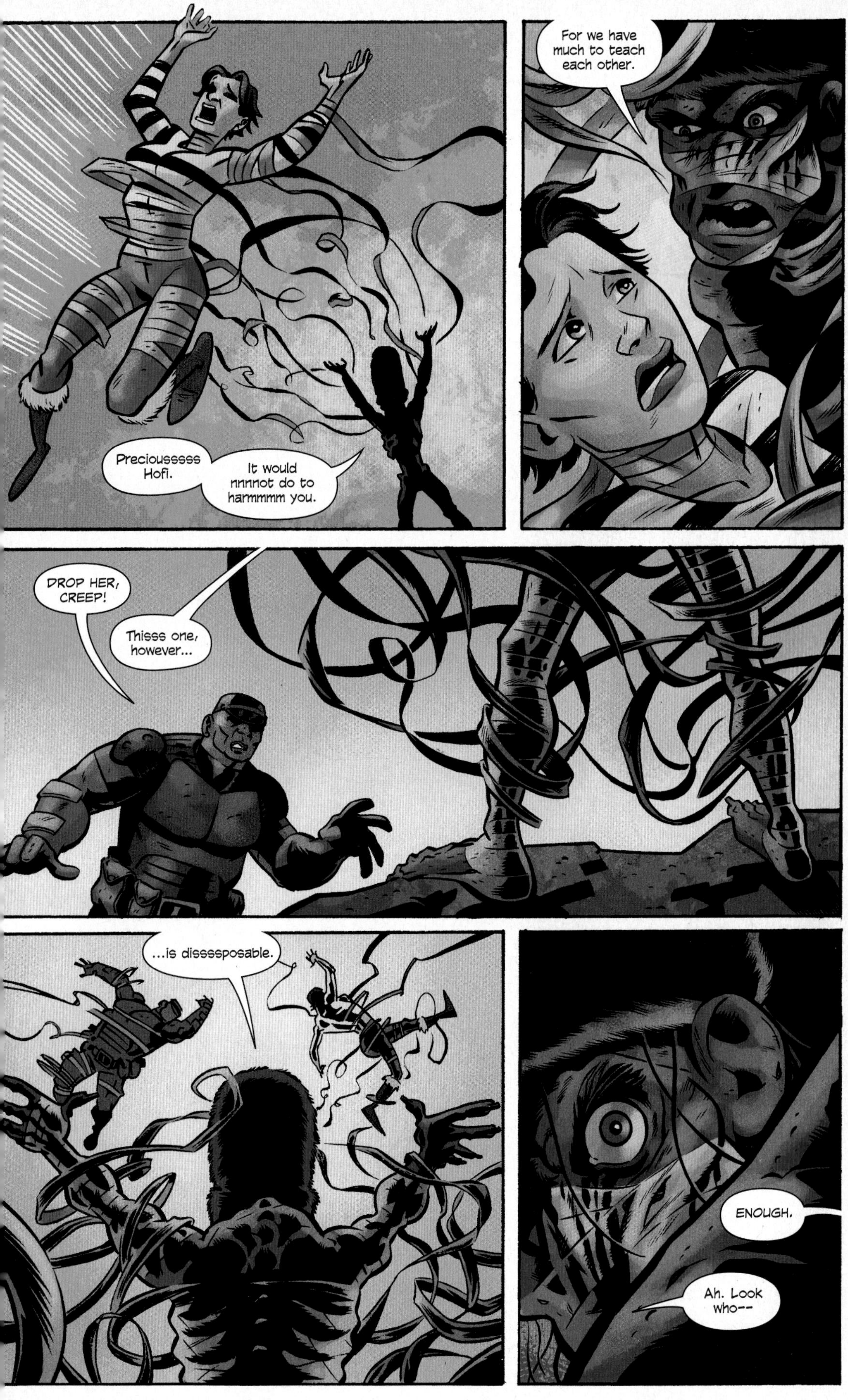
Precioussssss Hofi.
It would nnnnot do to harmmmm you.
For we have much to teach each other.
DROP HER, CREEP!
Thisss one, however...
...is dissssposable.
ENOUGH.
Ah. Look who--

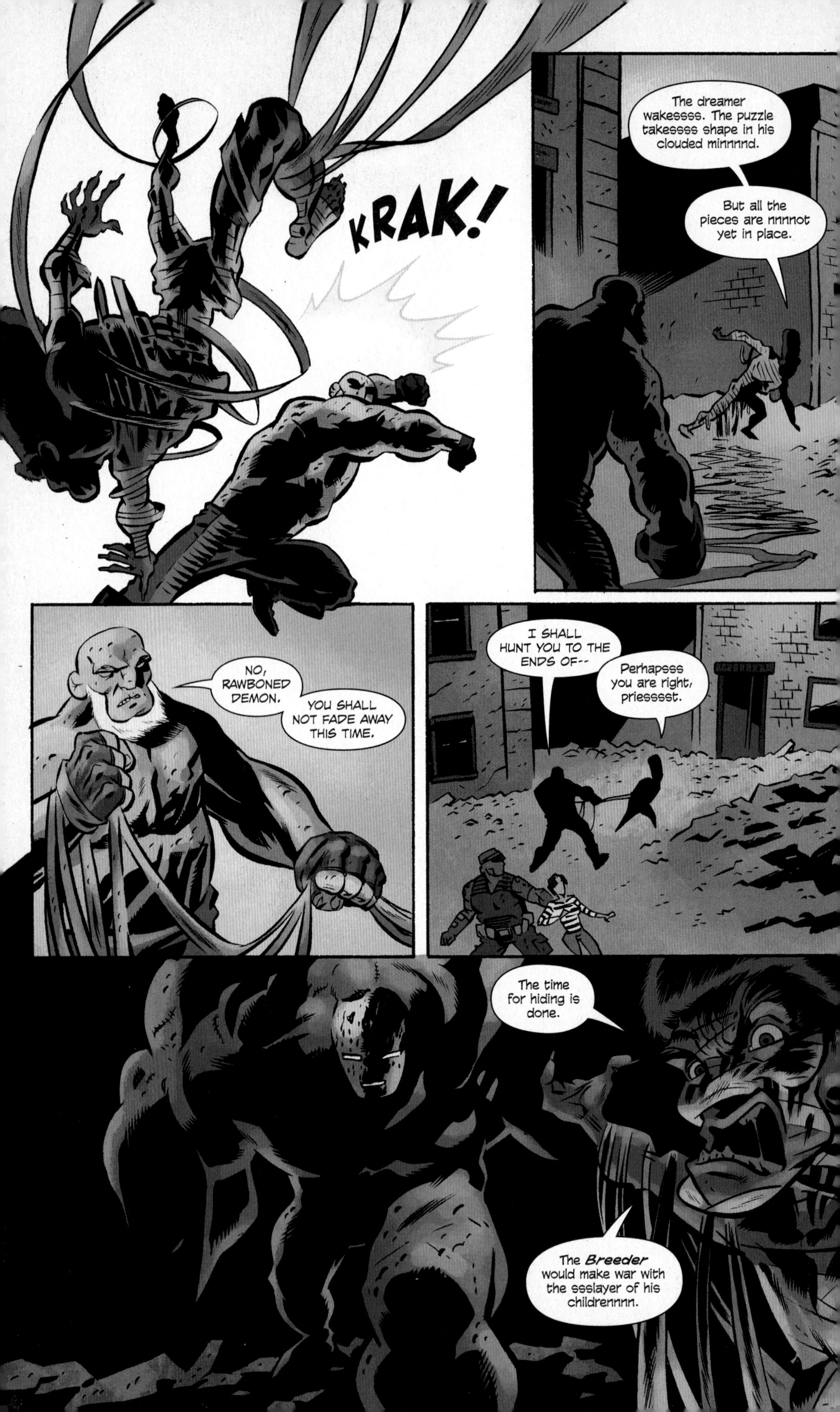
KRAK!
The dreamer wakessss. The puzzle takessss shape in his clouded minnnnd.
But all the pieces are nnnnot yet in place.
NO, RAWBONED DEMON.
YOU SHALL NOT FADE AWAY THIS TIME.
I SHALL HUNT YOU TO THE ENDS OF--
Perhapsss you are right, priessssst.
The time for hiding is done.
The *Breeder* would make war with the ssslayer of his childrennnn.

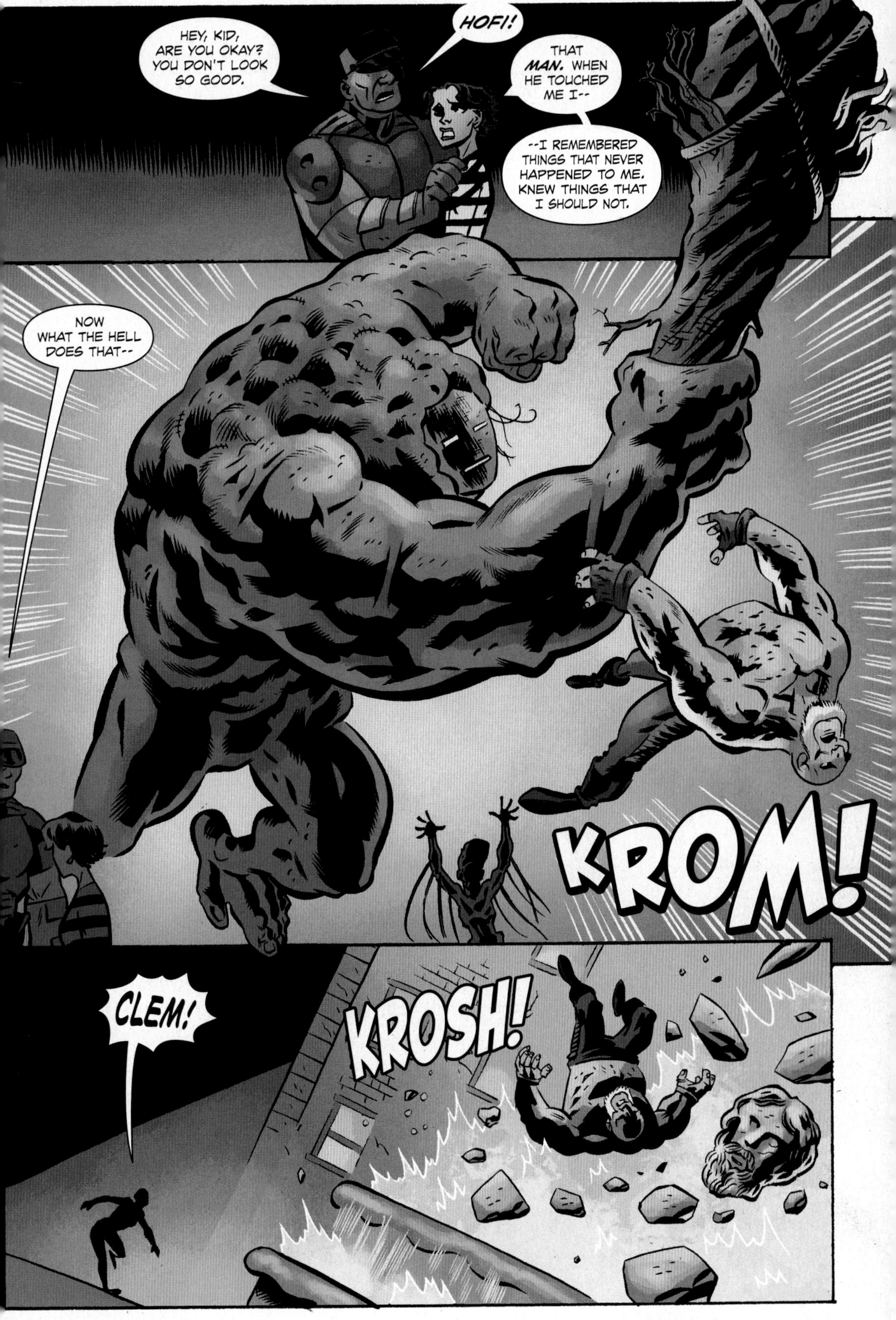
HEY, KID, ARE YOU OKAY? YOU DON'T LOOK SO GOOD.
HOFI!
THAT *MAN.* WHEN HE TOUCHED ME I--
--I REMEMBERED THINGS THAT NEVER HAPPENED TO ME. KNEW THINGS THAT I SHOULD NOT.
NOW WHAT THE HELL DOES THAT--
KROM!
CLEM!
KROSH!

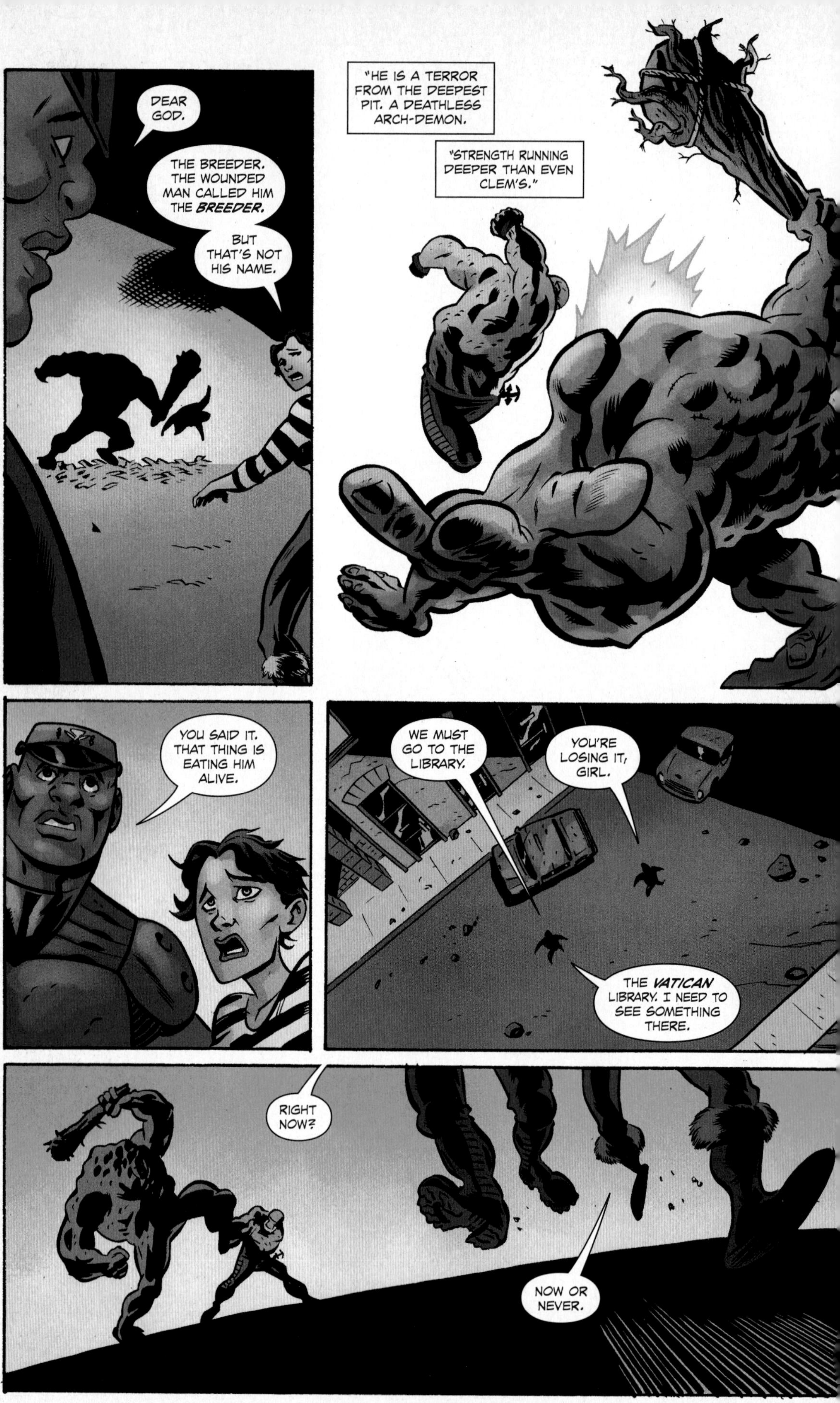
DEAR GOD.
THE BREEDER. THE WOUNDED MAN CALLED HIM THE *BREEDER.*
BUT THAT'S NOT HIS NAME.
"HE IS A TERROR FROM THE DEEPEST PIT. A DEATHLESS ARCH-DEMON.
"STRENGTH RUNNING DEEPER THAN EVEN CLEM'S."
YOU SAID IT. THAT THING IS EATING HIM ALIVE.
WE MUST GO TO THE LIBRARY.
YOU'RE LOSING IT, GIRL.
THE *VATICAN* LIBRARY. I NEED TO SEE SOMETHING THERE.
RIGHT NOW?
NOW OR NEVER.

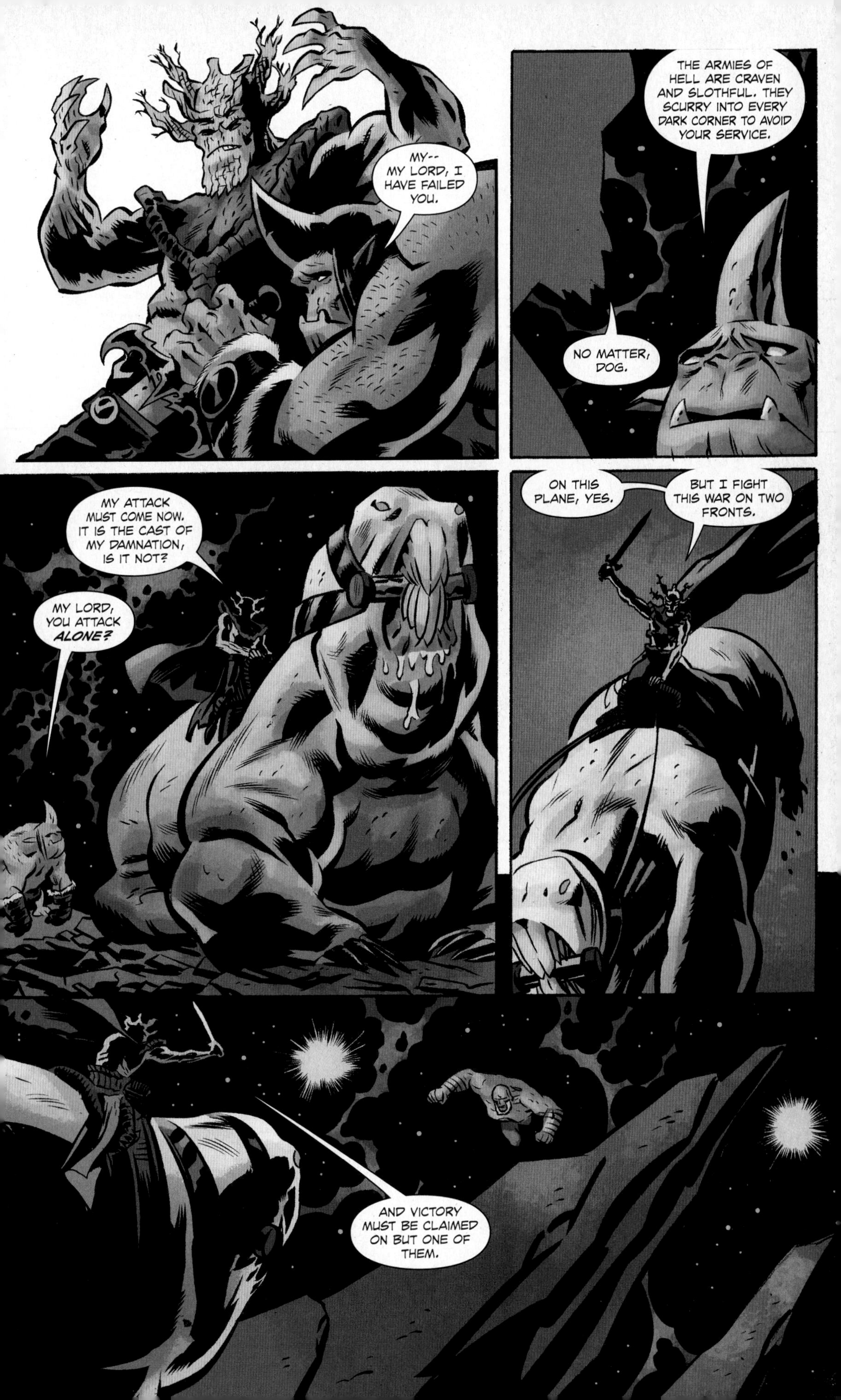
MY--
MY LORD, I HAVE FAILED YOU.
THE ARMIES OF HELL ARE CRAVEN AND SLOTHFUL. THEY SCURRY INTO EVERY DARK CORNER TO AVOID YOUR SERVICE.
NO MATTER, DOG.
MY ATTACK MUST COME NOW. IT IS THE CAST OF MY DAMNATION, IS IT NOT?
MY LORD, YOU ATTACK *ALONE?*
ON THIS PLANE, YES.
BUT I FIGHT THIS WAR ON TWO FRONTS.
AND VICTORY MUST BE CLAIMED ON BUT ONE OF THEM.

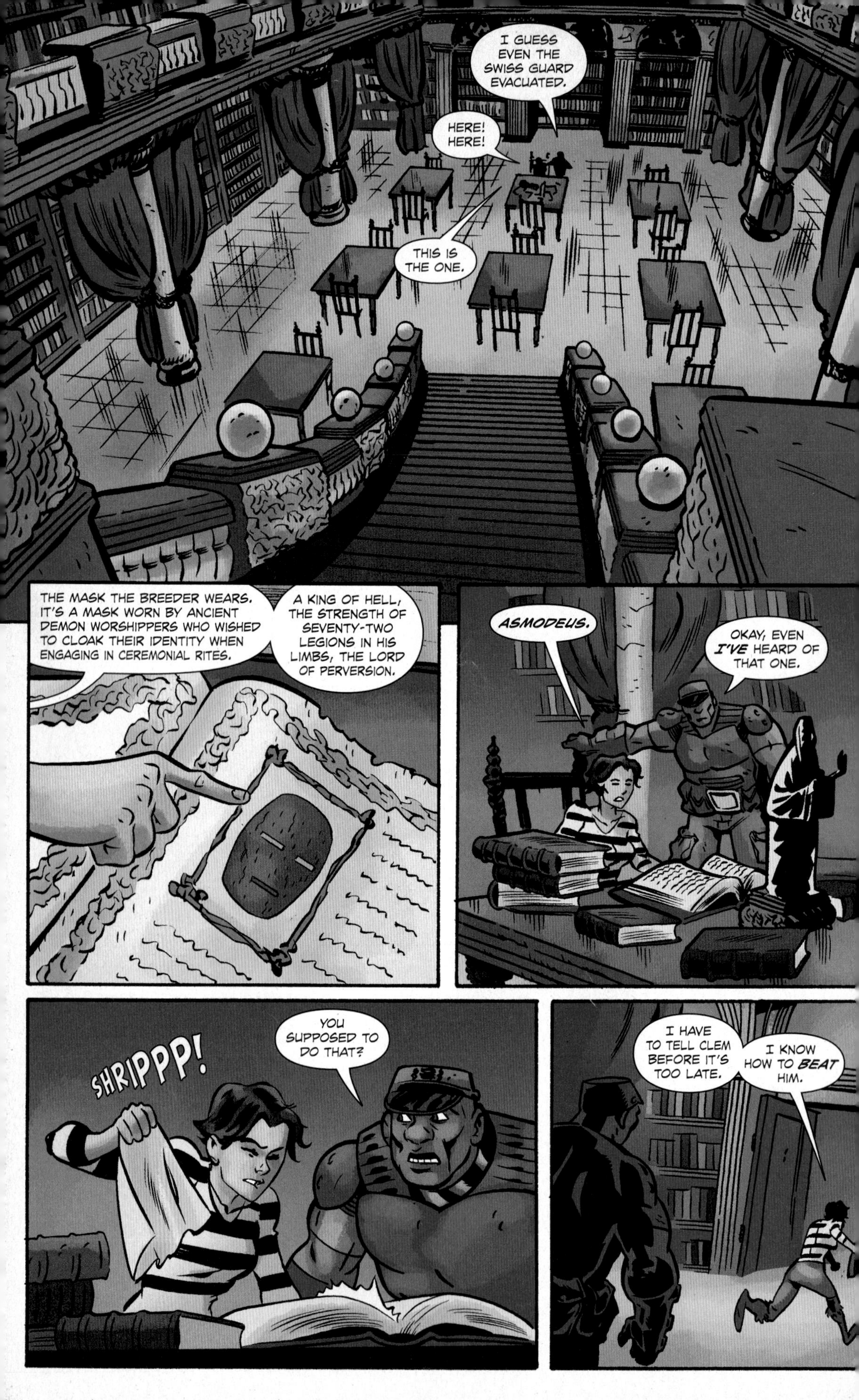
I GUESS EVEN THE SWISS GUARD EVACUATED.
HERE! HERE!
THIS IS THE ONE.
THE MASK THE BREEDER WEARS. IT'S A MASK WORN BY ANCIENT DEMON WORSHIPPERS WHO WISHED TO CLOAK THEIR IDENTITY WHEN ENGAGING IN CEREMONIAL RITES.
A KING OF HELL, THE STRENGTH OF SEVENTY-TWO LEGIONS IN HIS LIMBS, THE LORD OF PERVERSION.
ASMODEUS.
OKAY, EVEN I'VE HEARD OF THAT ONE.
SHRIPPP!
YOU SUPPOSED TO DO THAT?
I HAVE TO TELL CLEM BEFORE IT'S TOO LATE.
I KNOW HOW TO BEAT HIM.

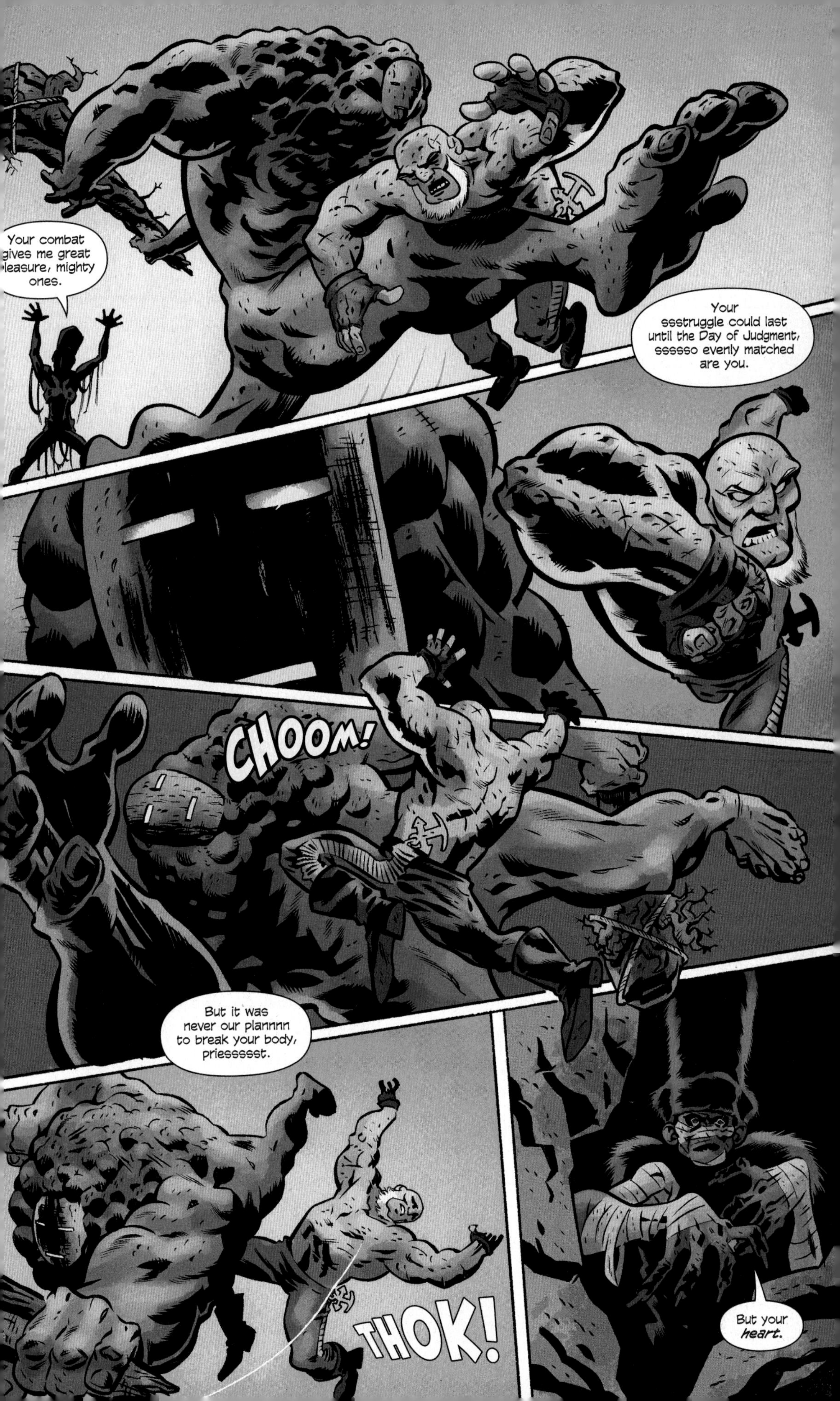
Your combat gives me great pleasure, mighty ones.
Your ssstruggle could last until the Day of Judgment, ssssso evenly matched are you.
CHOOM!
But it was never our plannnn to break your body, priesssssst.
THOK!
But your *heart.*

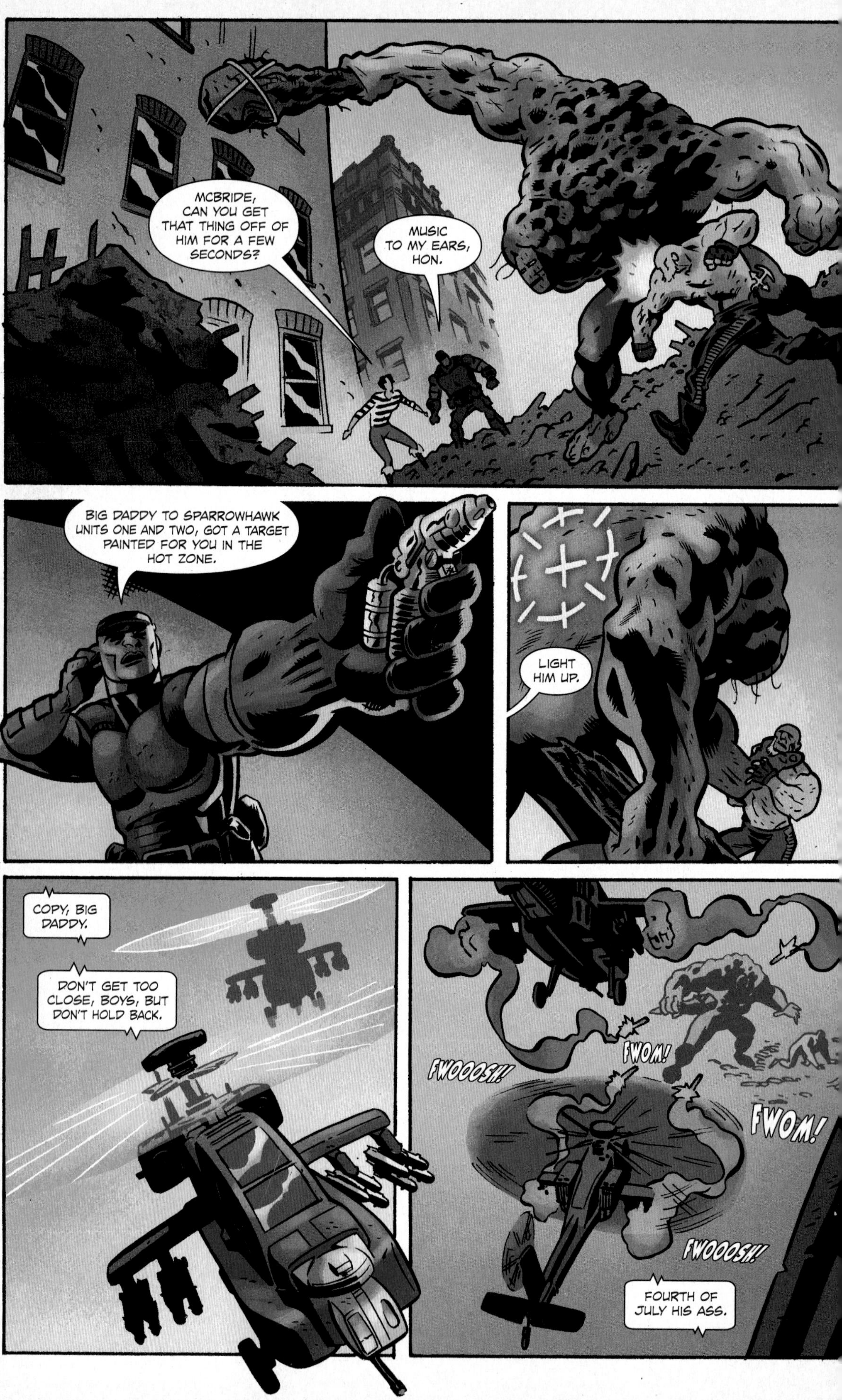
MCBRIDE, CAN YOU GET THAT THING OFF OF HIM FOR A FEW SECONDS?
MUSIC TO MY EARS, HON.
BIG DADDY TO SPARROWHAWK UNITS ONE AND TWO, GOT A TARGET PAINTED FOR YOU IN THE HOT ZONE.
LIGHT HIM UP.
COPY, BIG DADDY.
DON'T GET TOO CLOSE, BOYS, BUT DON'T HOLD BACK.
FWOOOSH!
FWOM!
FWOM!
FWOOOSH!
FOURTH OF JULY HIS ASS.

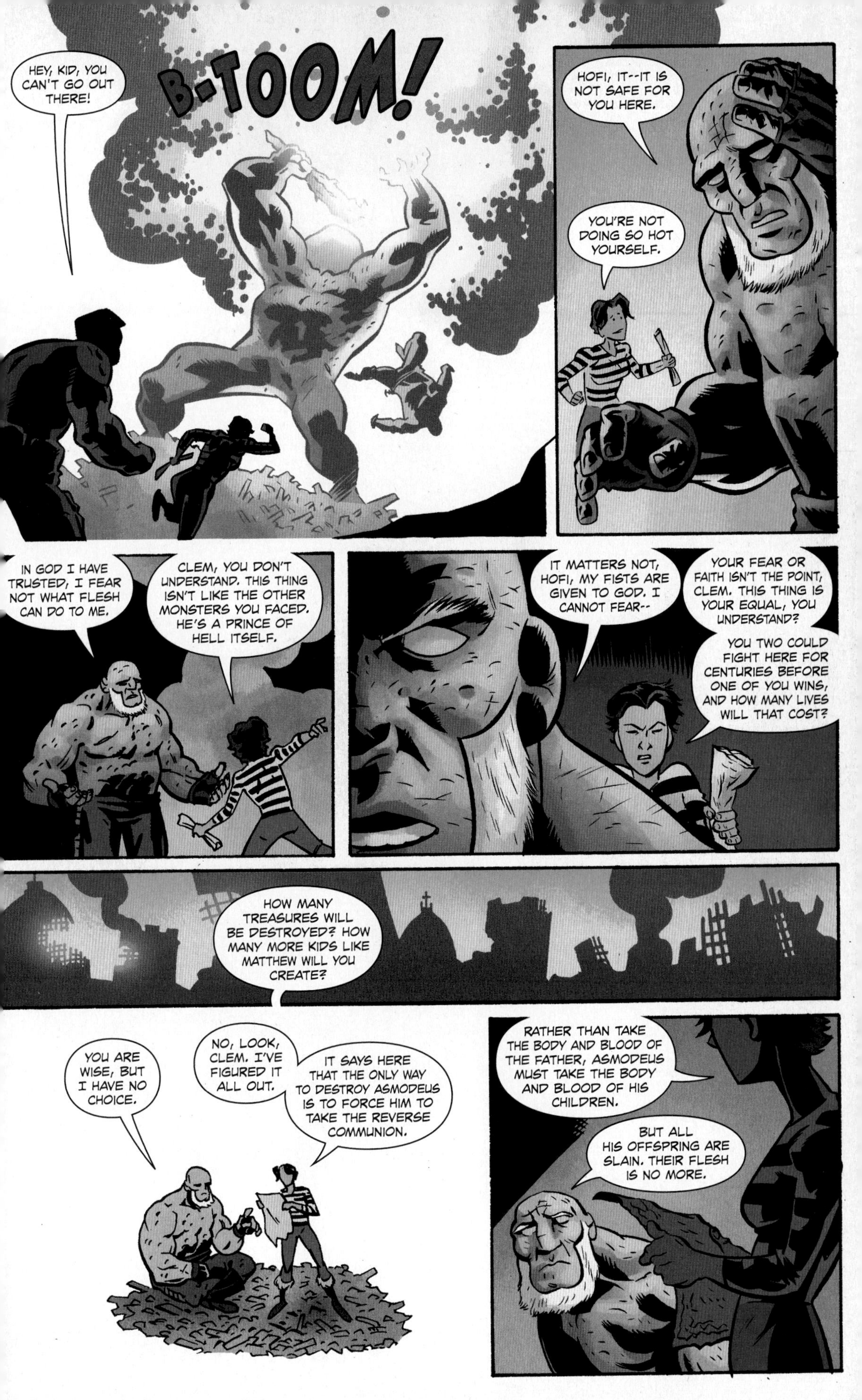
HEY, KID, YOU CAN'T GO OUT THERE!
B-TOOM!
HOFI, IT--IT IS NOT SAFE FOR YOU HERE.
YOU'RE NOT DOING SO HOT YOURSELF.
IN GOD I HAVE TRUSTED, I FEAR NOT WHAT FLESH CAN DO TO ME.
CLEM, YOU DON'T UNDERSTAND. THIS THING ISN'T LIKE THE OTHER MONSTERS YOU FACED. HE'S A PRINCE OF HELL ITSELF.
IT MATTERS NOT, HOFI, MY FISTS ARE GIVEN TO GOD. I CANNOT FEAR--
YOUR FEAR OR FAITH ISN'T THE POINT, CLEM. THIS THING IS YOUR EQUAL, YOU UNDERSTAND?
YOU TWO COULD FIGHT HERE FOR CENTURIES BEFORE ONE OF YOU WINS, AND HOW MANY LIVES WILL THAT COST?
HOW MANY TREASURES WILL BE DESTROYED? HOW MANY MORE KIDS LIKE MATTHEW WILL YOU CREATE?
YOU ARE WISE, BUT I HAVE NO CHOICE.
NO, LOOK, CLEM. I'VE FIGURED IT ALL OUT.
IT SAYS HERE THAT THE ONLY WAY TO DESTROY ASMODEUS IS TO FORCE HIM TO TAKE THE REVERSE COMMUNION.
RATHER THAN TAKE THE BODY AND BLOOD OF THE FATHER, ASMODEUS MUST TAKE THE BODY AND BLOOD OF HIS CHILDREN.
BUT ALL HIS OFFSPRING ARE SLAIN. THEIR FLESH IS NO MORE.

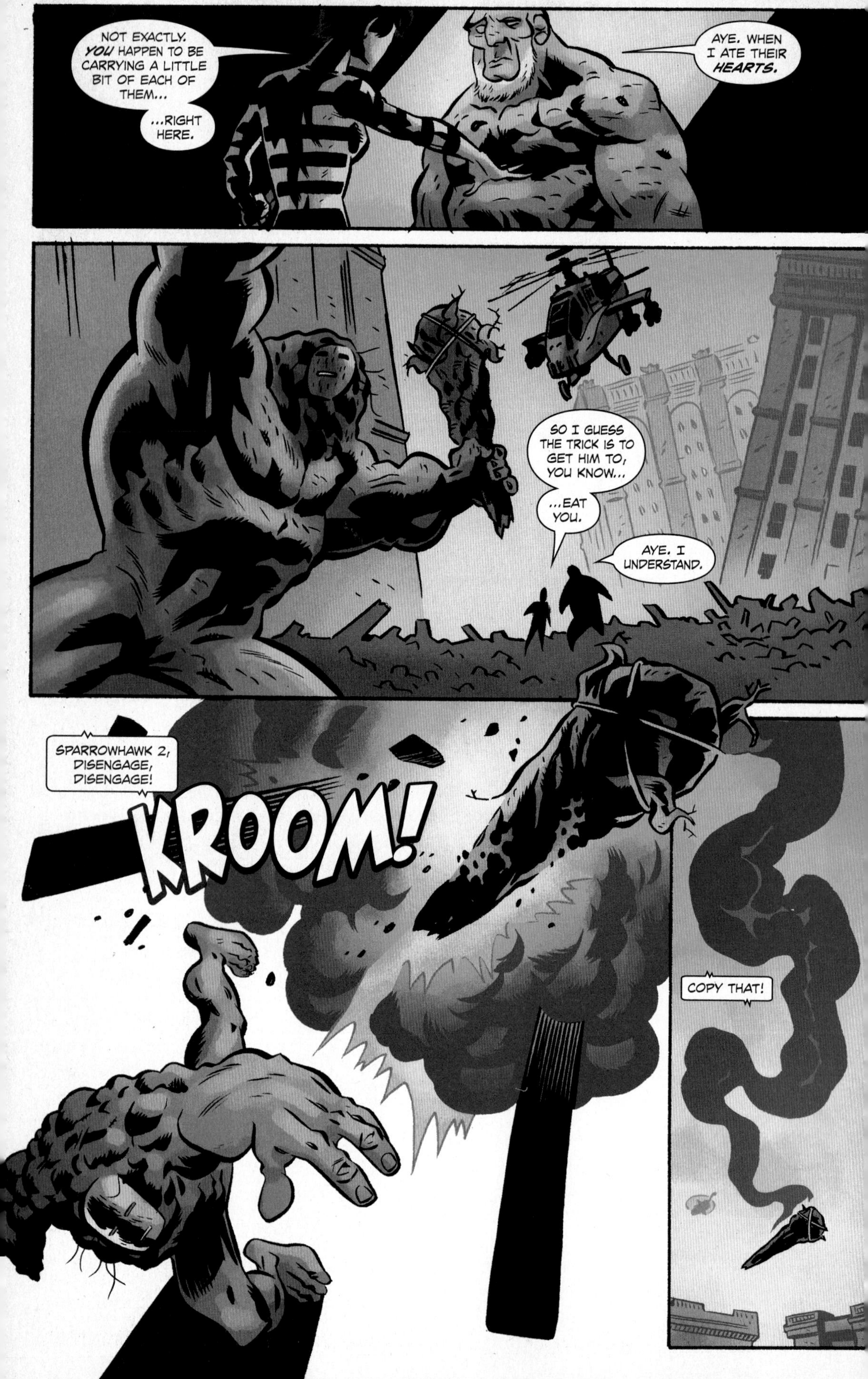

NOT EXACTLY. *YOU* HAPPEN TO BE CARRYING A LITTLE BIT OF EACH OF THEM...
...RIGHT HERE.
AYE. WHEN I ATE THEIR *HEARTS.*
SO I GUESS THE TRICK IS TO GET HIM TO, YOU KNOW...
...EAT YOU.
AYE. I UNDERSTAND.
SPARROWHAWK 2, DISENGAGE, DISENGAGE!
KROOM!
COPY THAT!

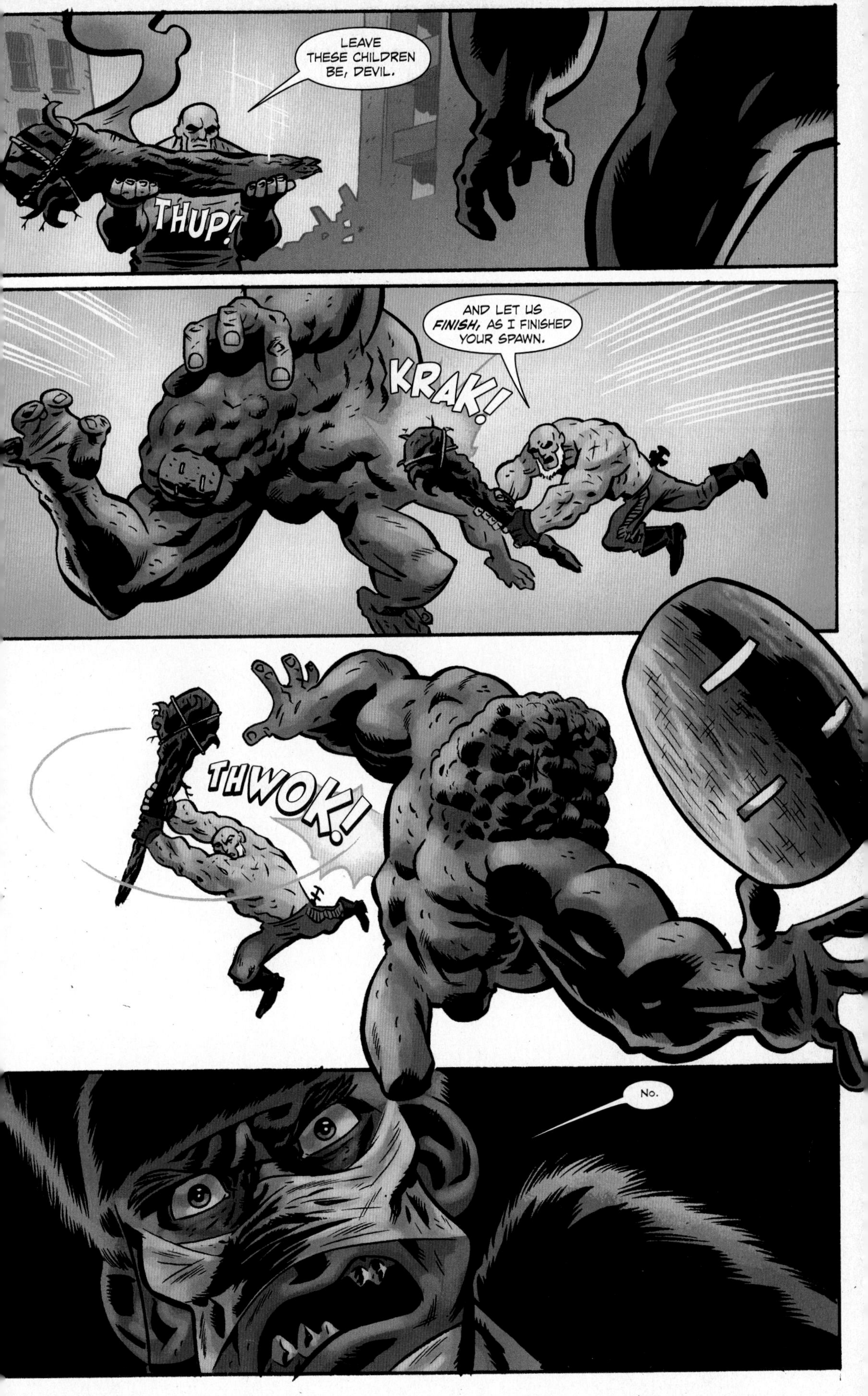
LEAVE THESE CHILDREN BE, DEVIL.
THUP!
AND LET US *FINISH,* AS I FINISHED YOUR SPAWN.
KRAK!
THWOK!
No.

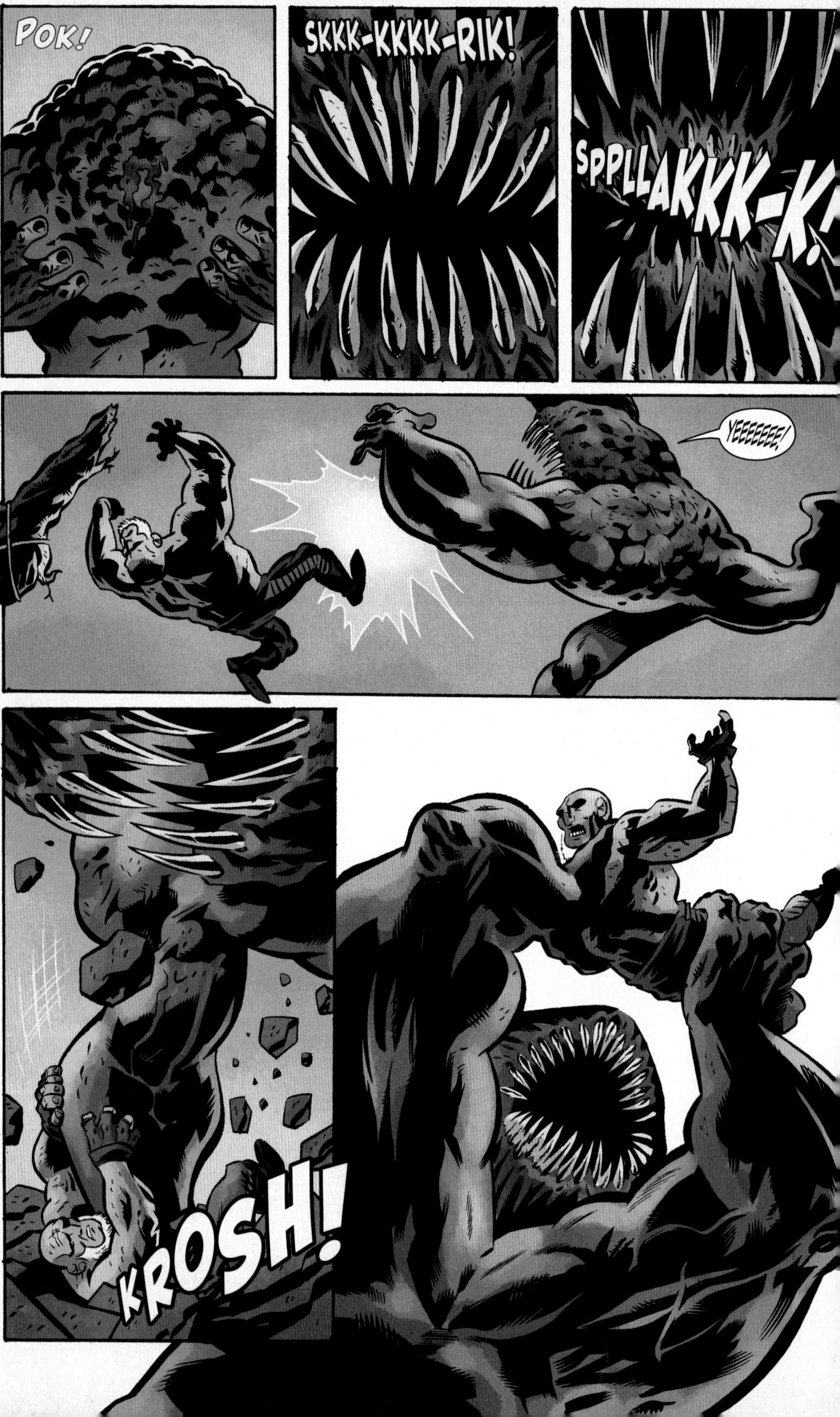
POK!
SKKK-KKKK-RIK!
SPPLLAKKK-K!
YEEEEEEE!
KROSH!

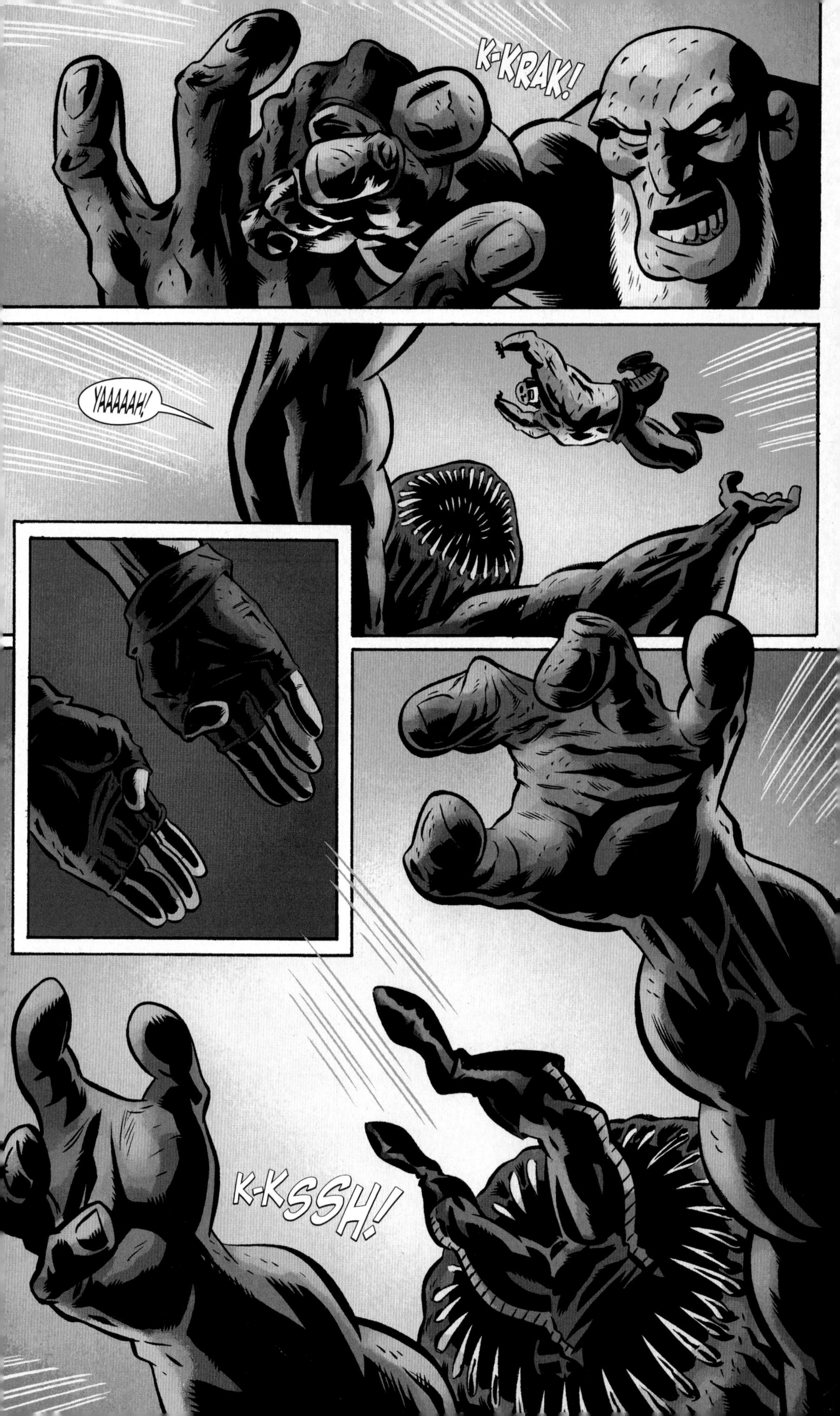
K-KRAK!
YAAAAAH!
K-KSSH!

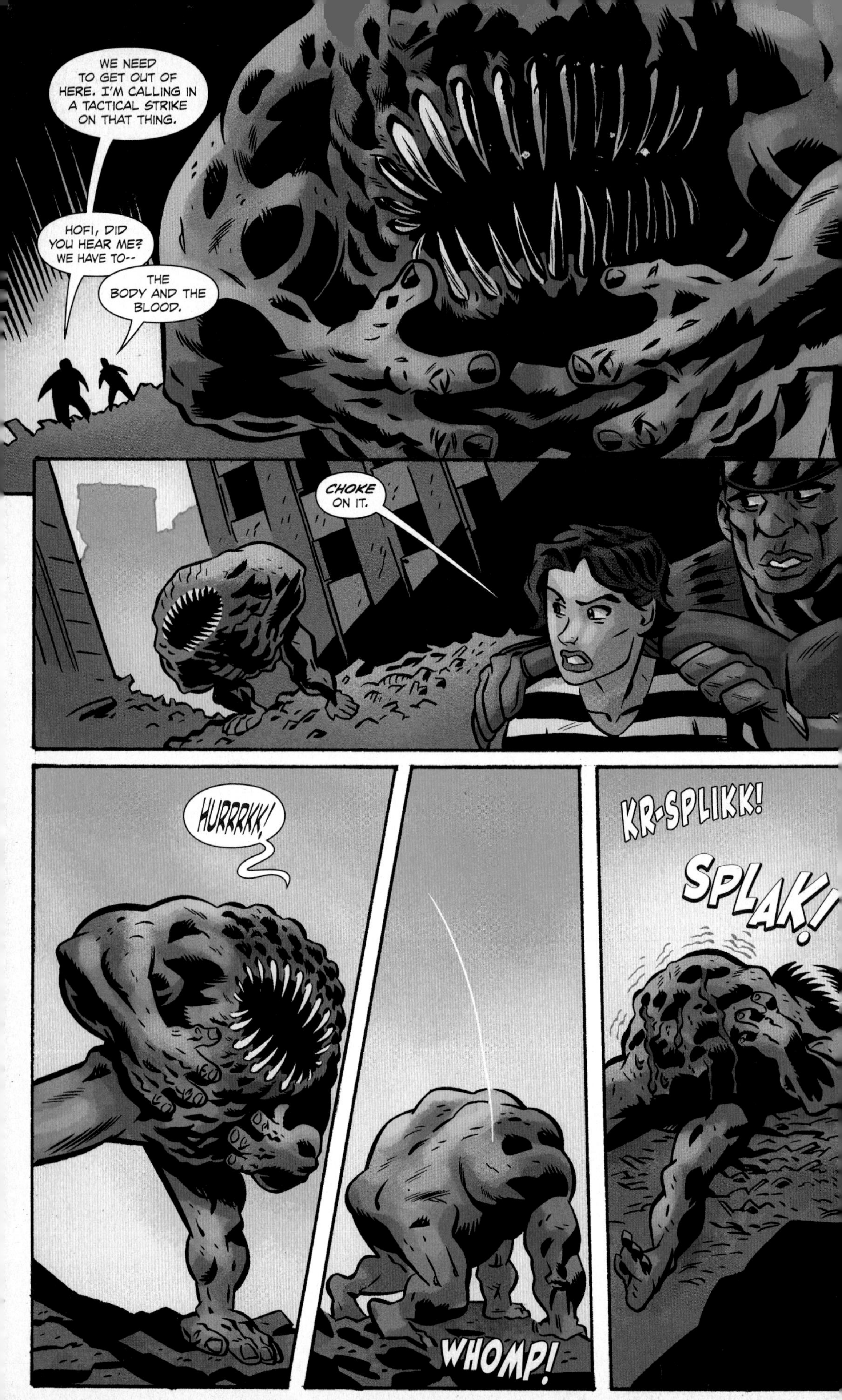
WE NEED TO GET OUT OF HERE. I'M CALLING IN A TACTICAL STRIKE ON THAT THING.
HOFI, DID YOU HEAR ME? WE HAVE TO--
THE BODY AND THE BLOOD.
CHOKE ON IT.
HURRRKK!
WHOMP!
KR-SPLIKK!
SPLAK!

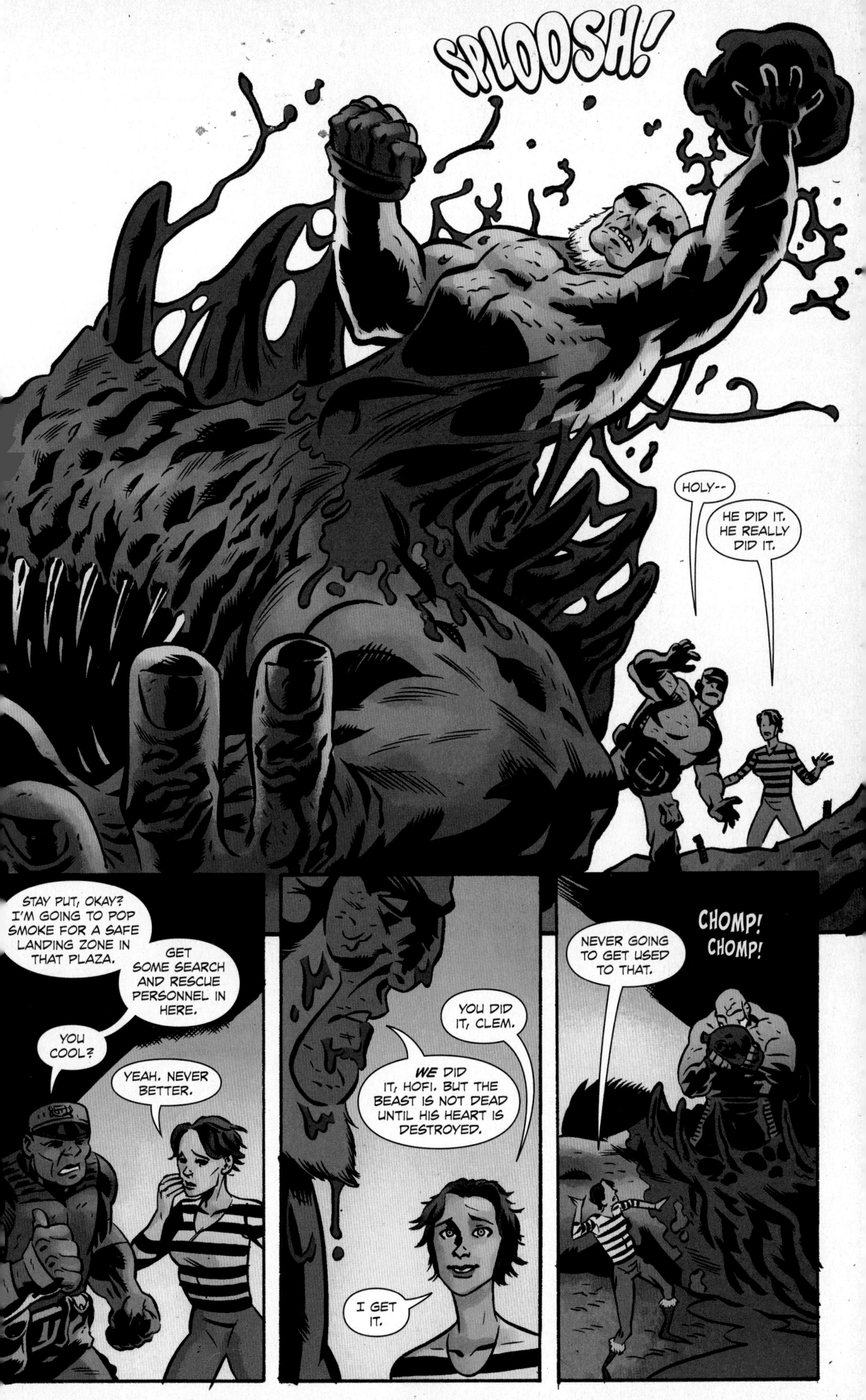
SPLOOSH!
HOLY--
HE DID IT. HE REALLY DID IT.
STAY PUT, OKAY? I'M GOING TO POP SMOKE FOR A SAFE LANDING ZONE IN THAT PLAZA.
GET SOME SEARCH AND RESCUE PERSONNEL IN HERE.
YOU COOL?
YEAH. NEVER BETTER.
YOU DID IT, CLEM.
WE DID IT, HOFI. BUT THE BEAST IS NOT DEAD UNTIL HIS HEART IS DESTROYED.
I GET IT.
CHOMP! CHOMP!
NEVER GOING TO GET USED TO THAT.

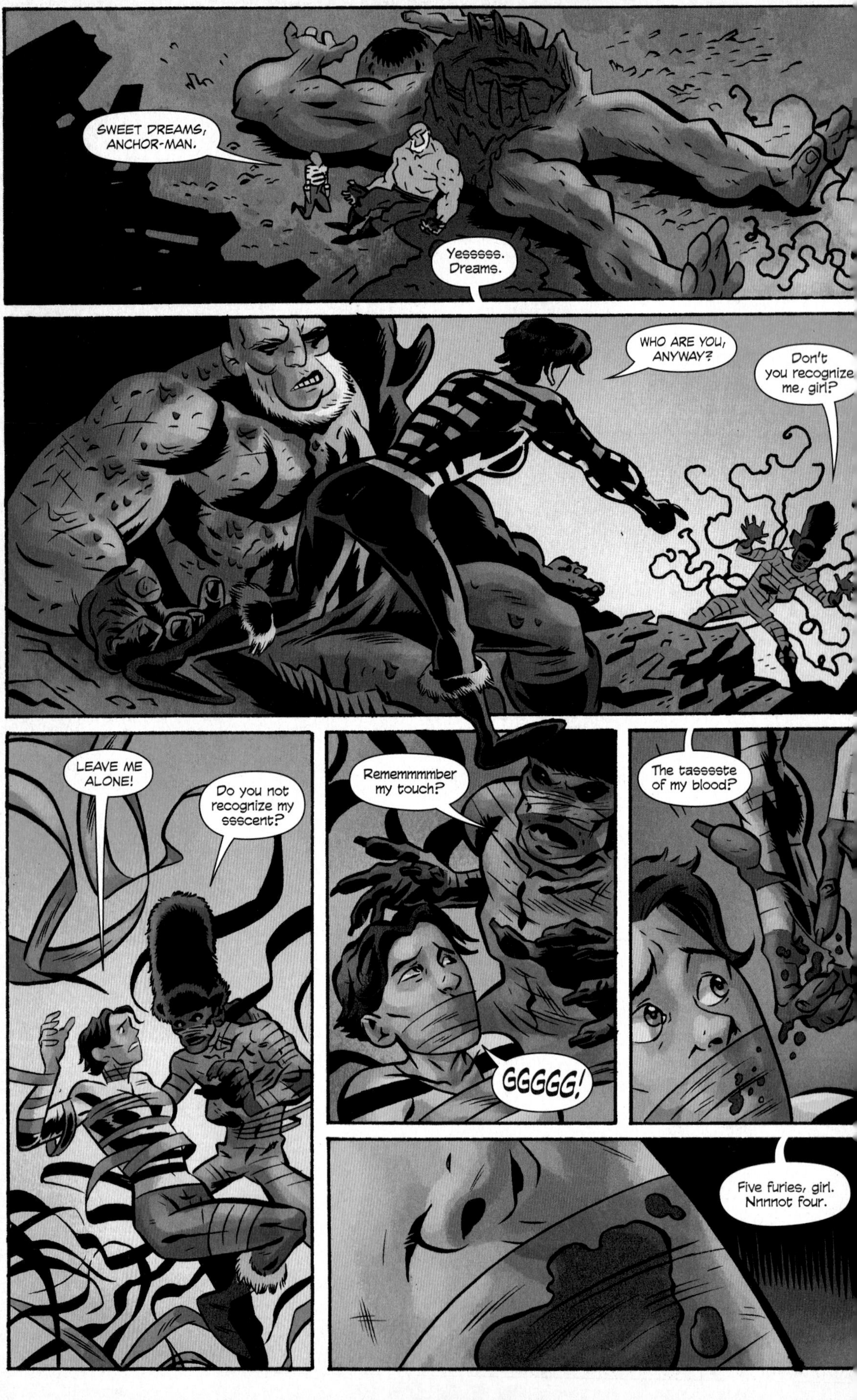

SWEET DREAMS, ANCHOR-MAN.
Yessssss. Dreams.
WHO ARE YOU, ANYWAY?
Don't you recognize me, girl?
LEAVE ME ALONE!
Do you not recognize my ssscent?
Rememmmmber my touch?
GGGGG!
The tasssste of my blood?
Five furies, girl. Nnnnot four.

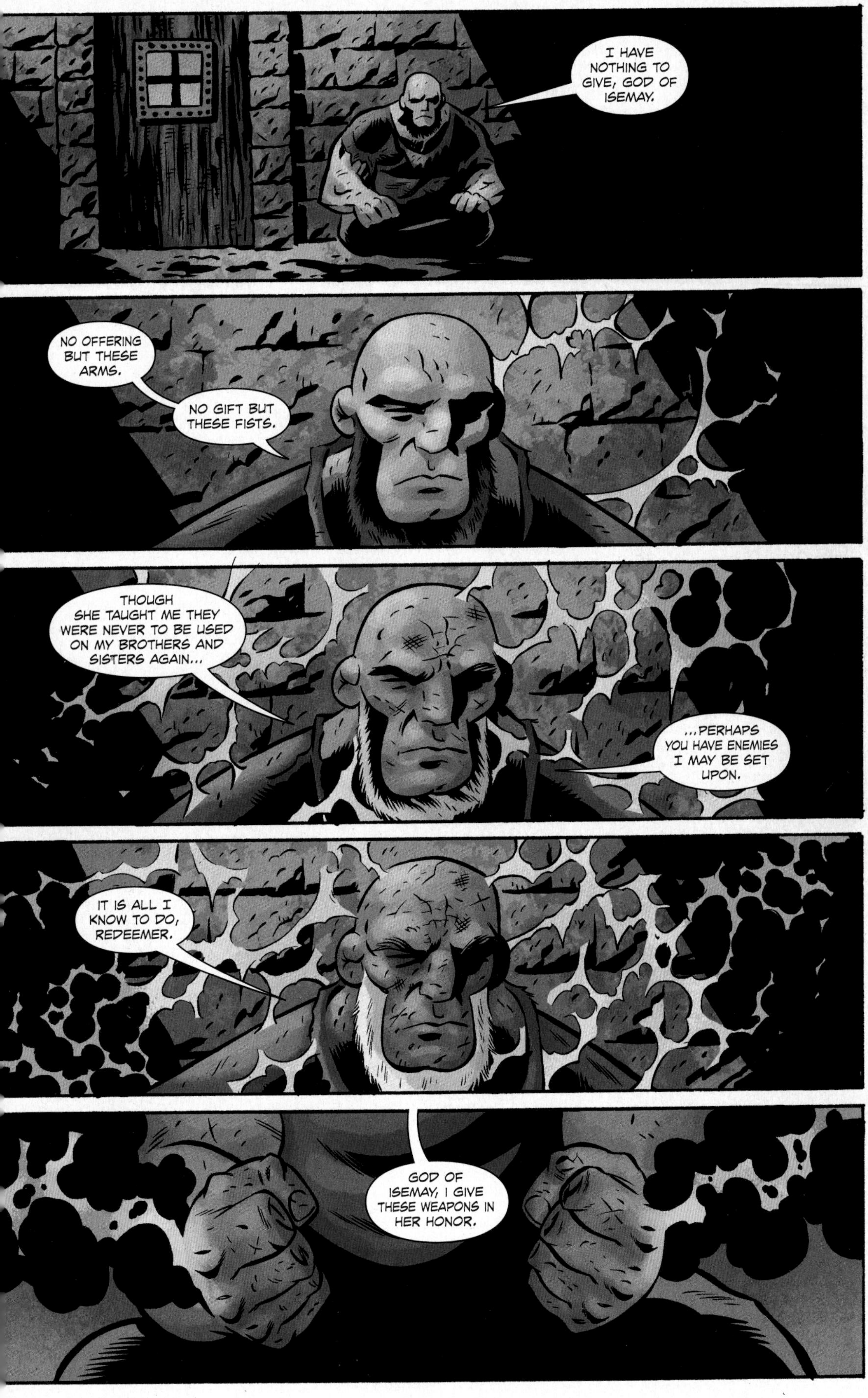
I HAVE NOTHING TO GIVE, GOD OF ISEMAY.
NO OFFERING BUT THESE ARMS.
NO GIFT BUT THESE FISTS.
THOUGH SHE TAUGHT ME THEY WERE NEVER TO BE USED ON MY BROTHERS AND SISTERS AGAIN...
...PERHAPS YOU HAVE ENEMIES I MAY BE SET UPON.
IT IS ALL I KNOW TO DO, REDEEMER.
GOD OF ISEMAY, I GIVE THESE WEAPONS IN HER HONOR.

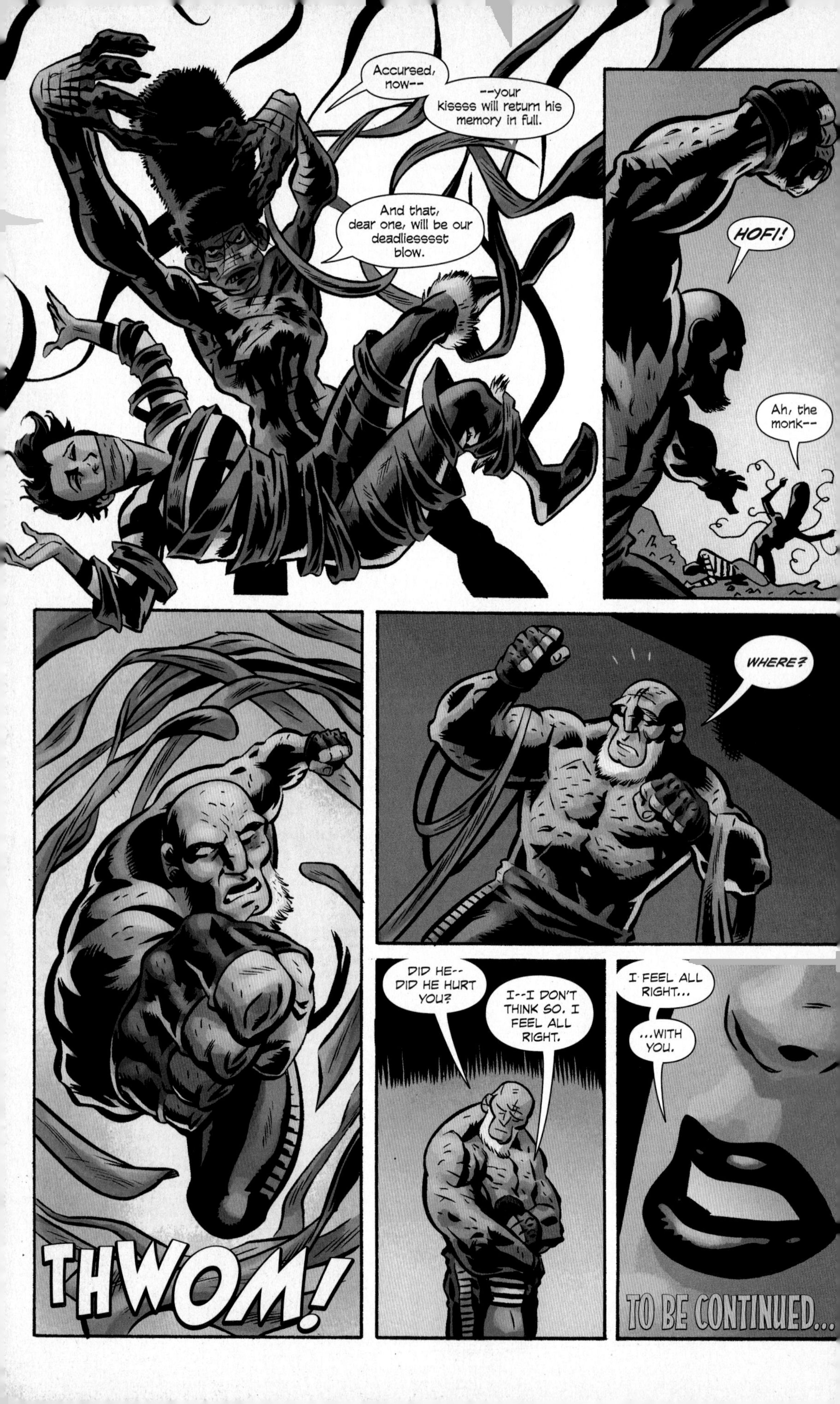

Accursed, now--
--your kissss will return his memory in full.
And that, dear one, will be our deadliessssst blow.
HOFI!
Ah, the monk--
THWOM!
WHERE?
DID HE-- DID HE HURT YOU?
I--I DON'T THINK SO. I FEEL ALL RIGHT.
I FEEL ALL RIGHT...
...WITH YOU.
TO BE CONTINUED...

COVER GALLERY

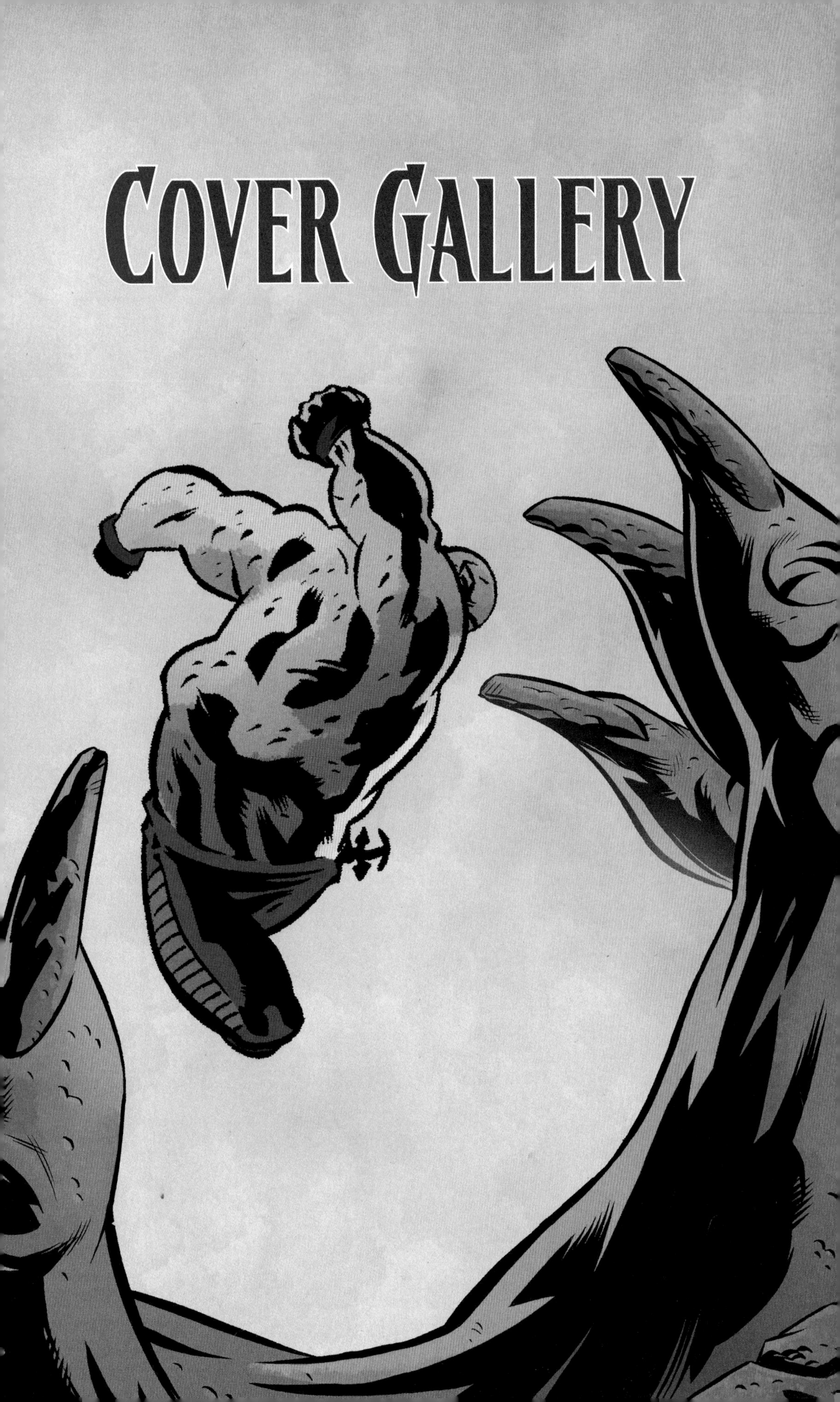

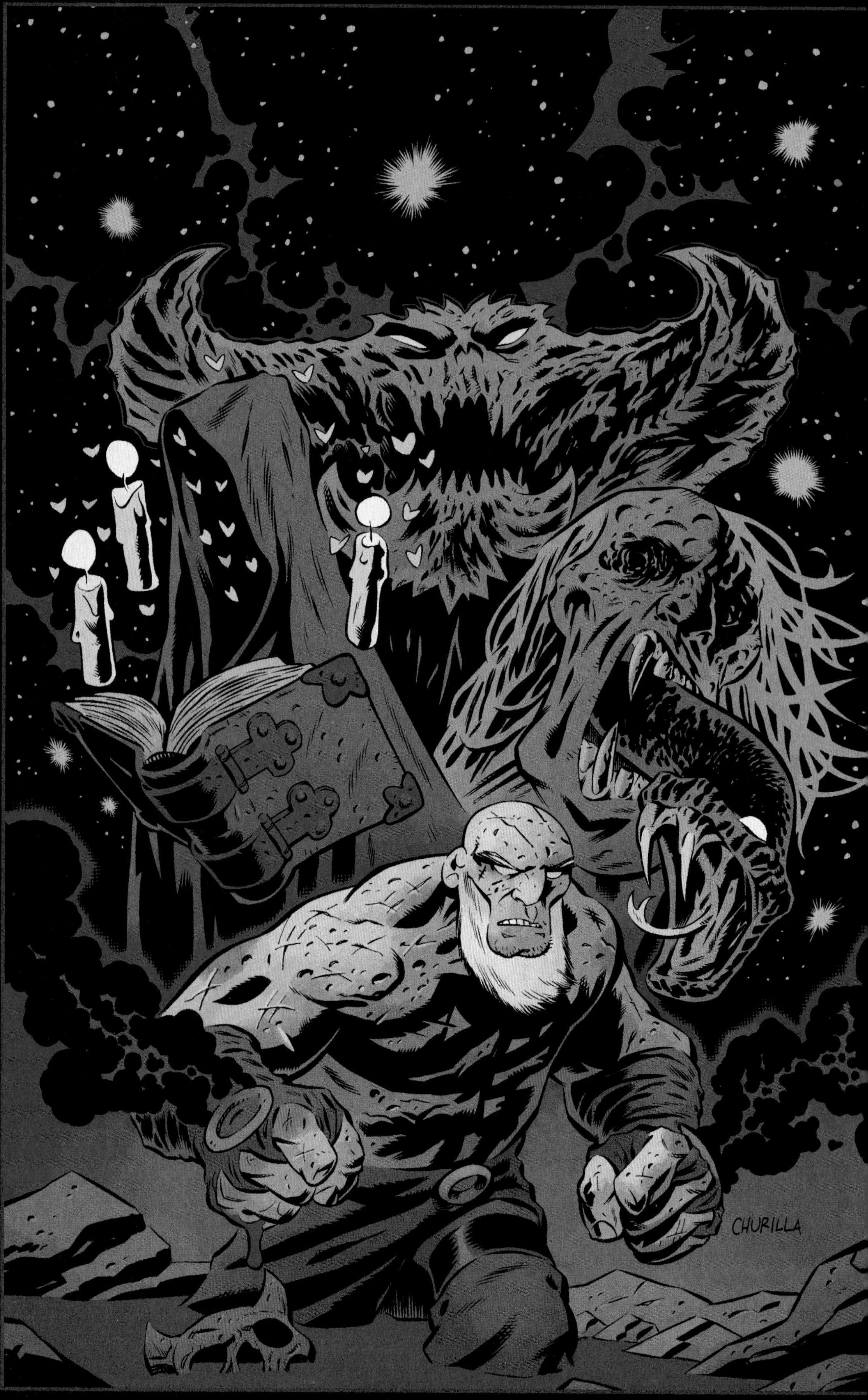
CHURILLA

COVER 1A
BRIAN CHURILLA / COLORS BY DAVE STEWART

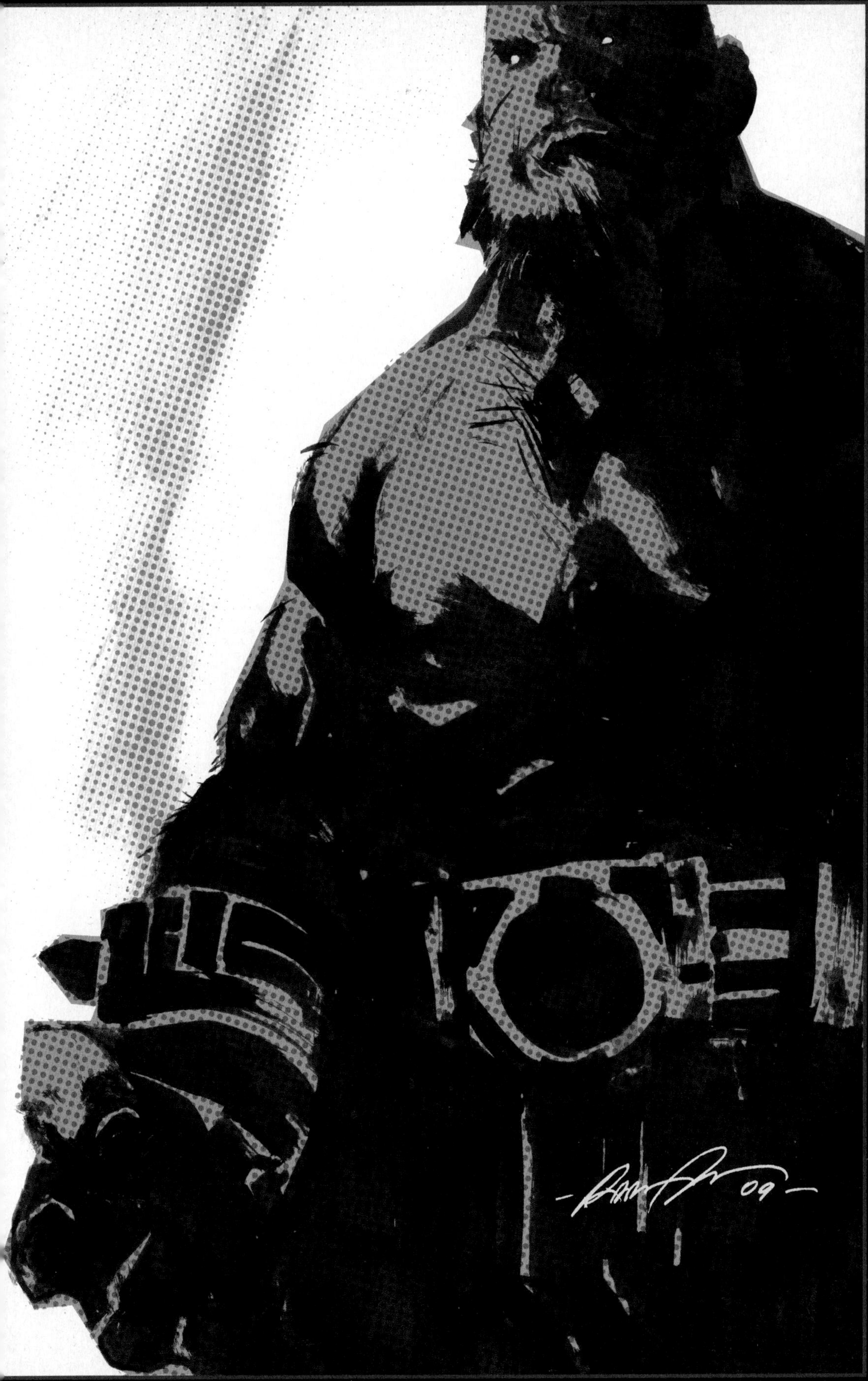

COVER 1B
RAFAEL ALBUQUERQUE

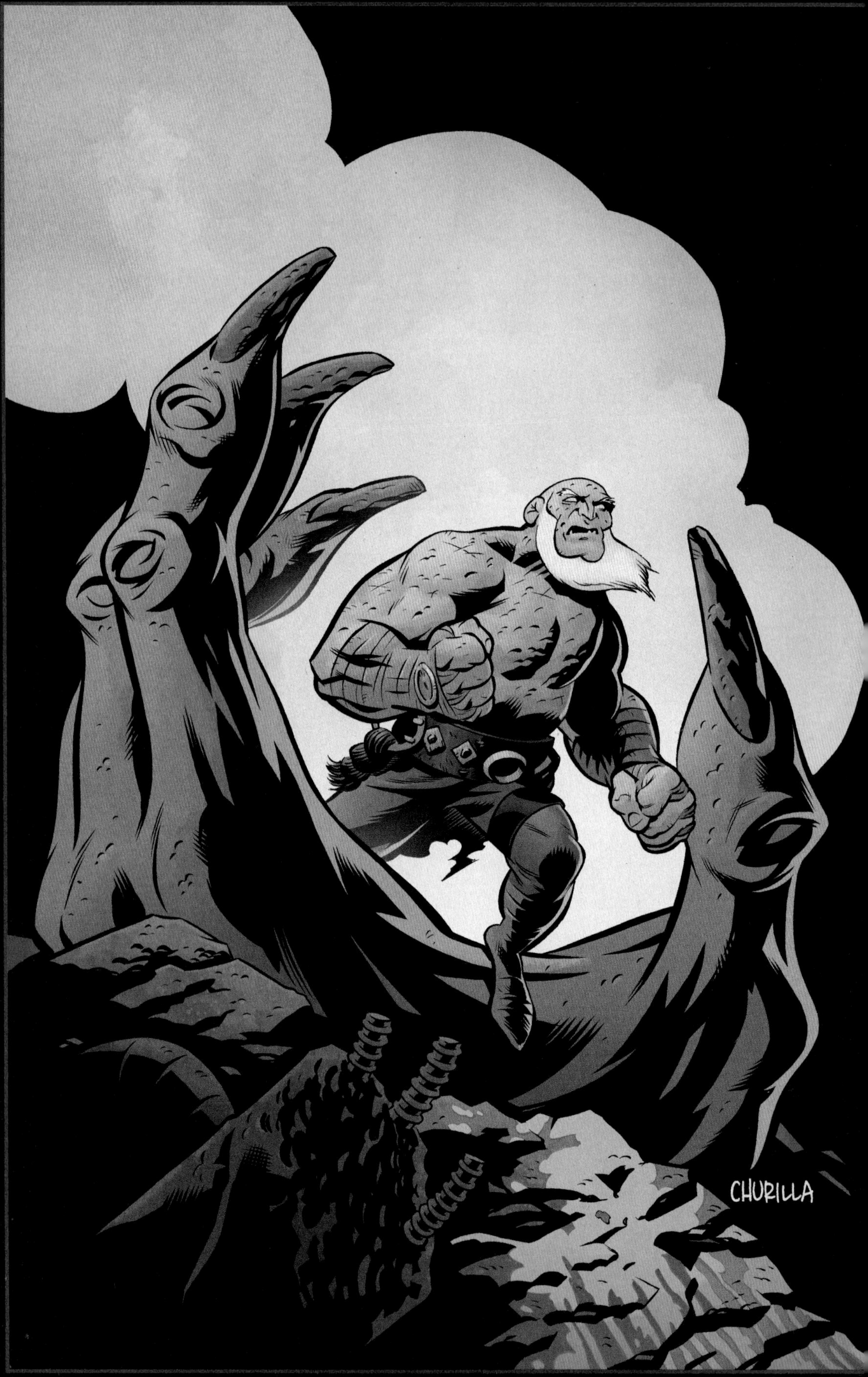
CHURILLA

COVER 1C
BRIAN CHURILLA / COLORS BY DAVE STEWART

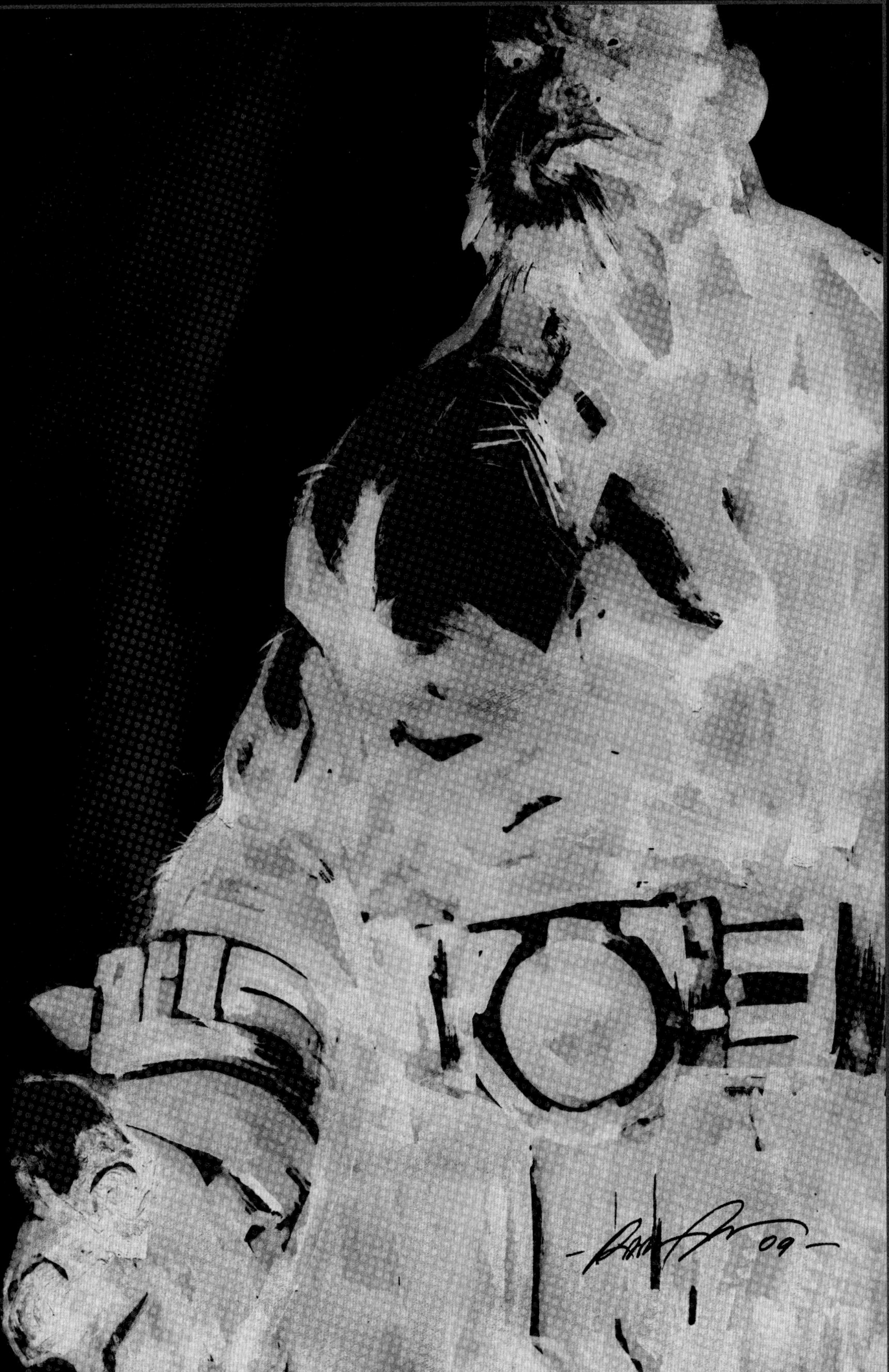

2ND PRINT - ISSUE 1
RAFAEL ALBUQUERQUE

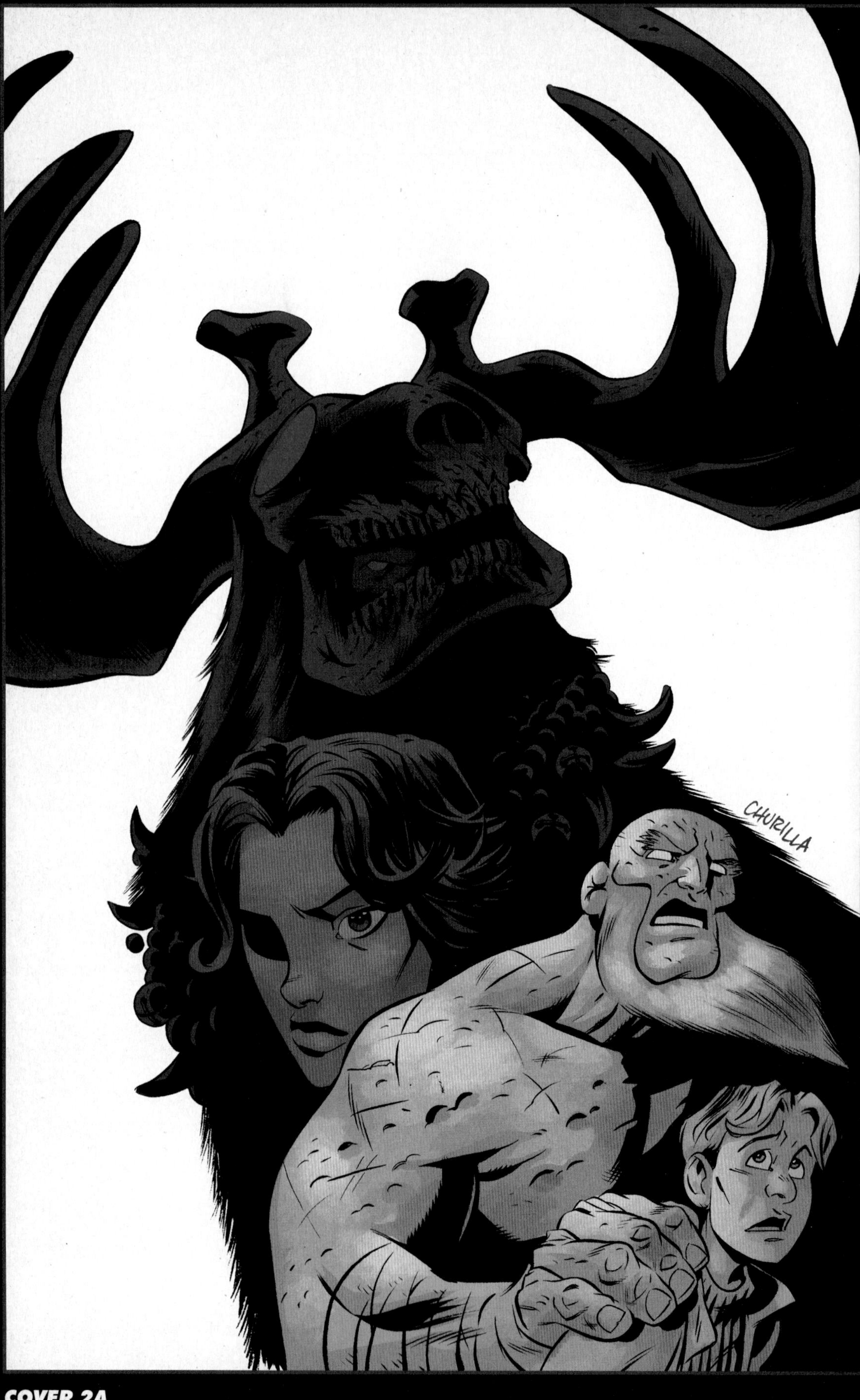
CHURILLA

COVER 2A
BRIAN CHURILLA / COLORS BY MATTHEW WILSON

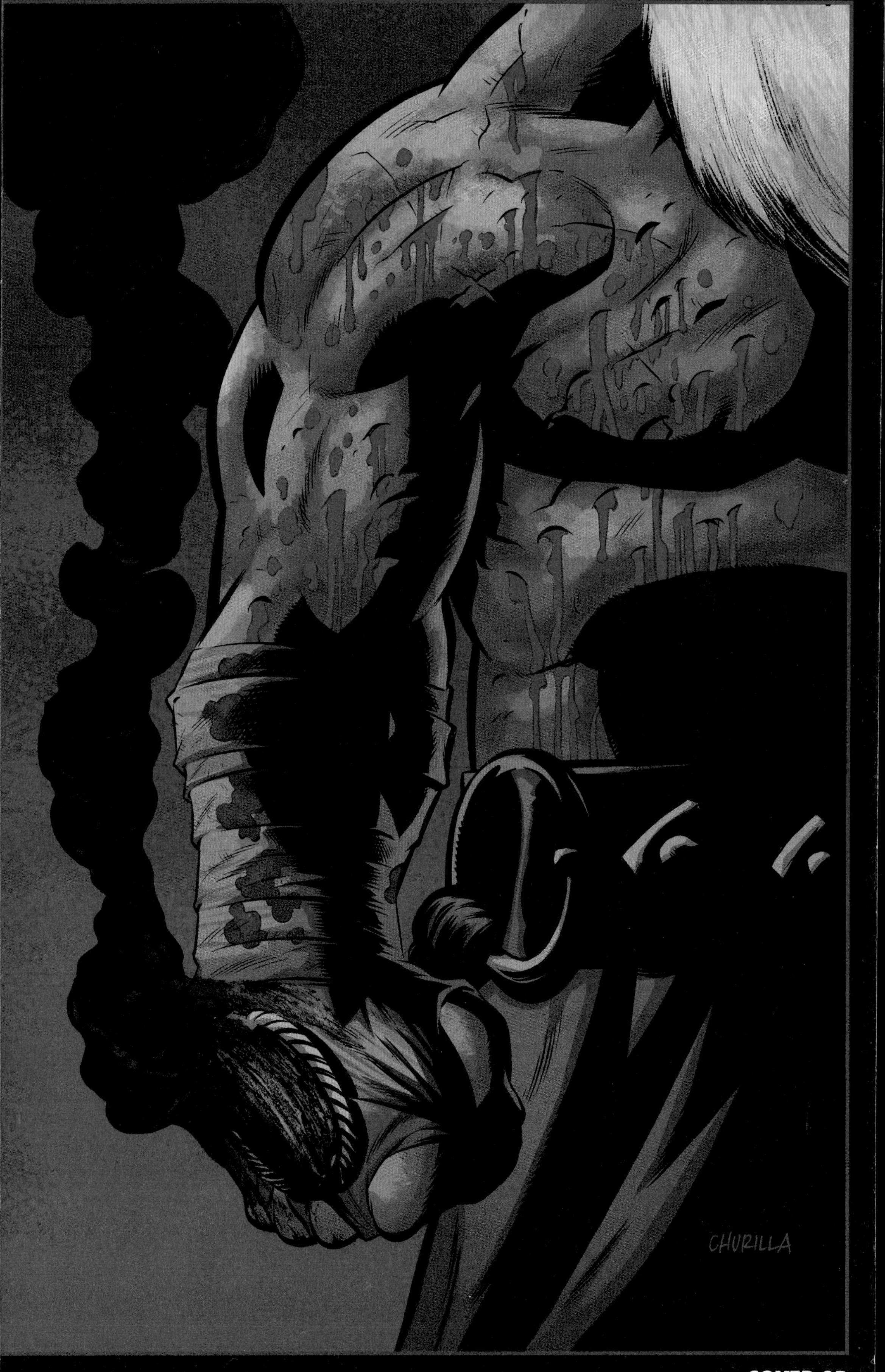
CHURILLA

COVER 2B
BRIAN CHURILLA / COLORS BY MATTHEW WILSON

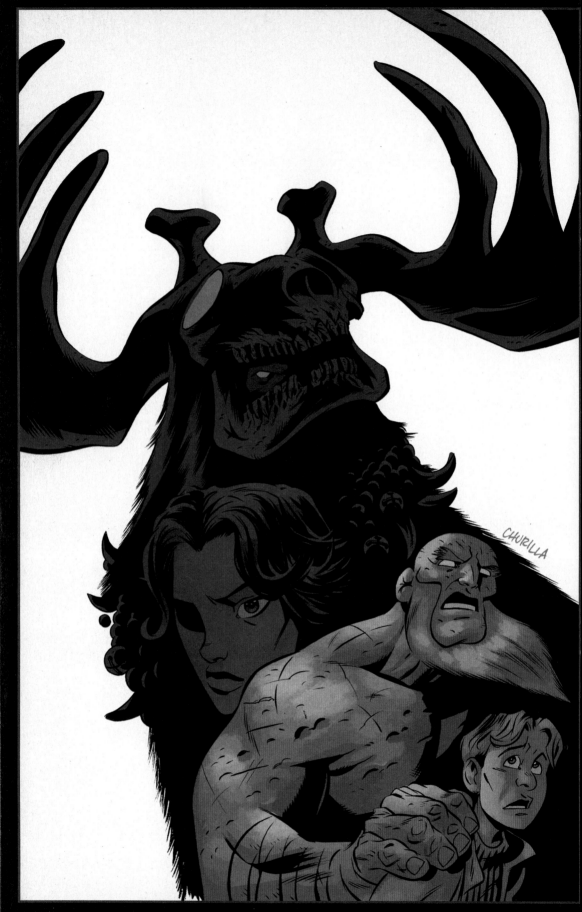

2ND PRINT - ISSUE 2
BRIAN CHURILLA / COLORS BY MATTHEW WILSON

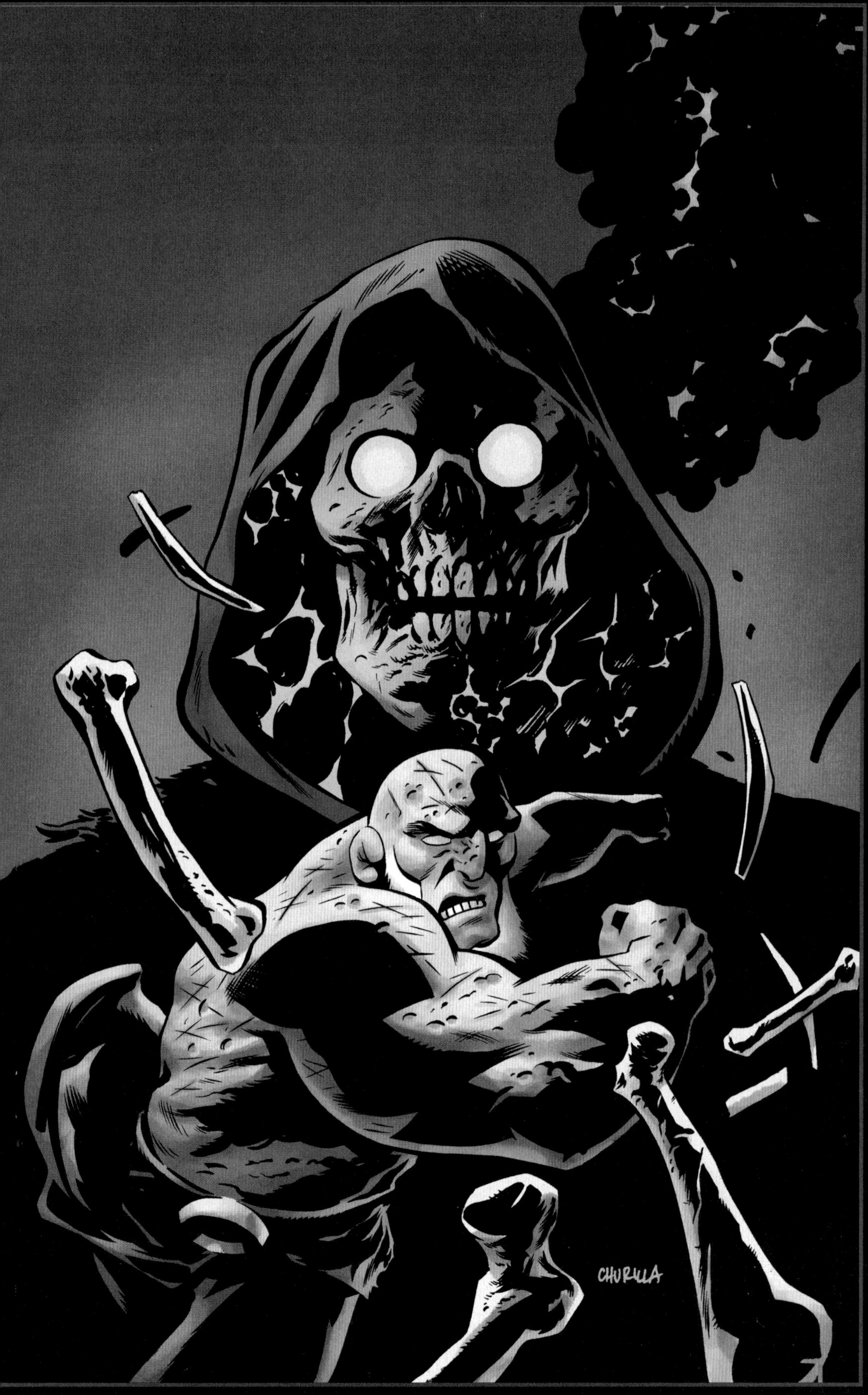
CHURILLA

COVER 3A
BRIAN CHURILLA / COLORS BY MATTHEW WILSON

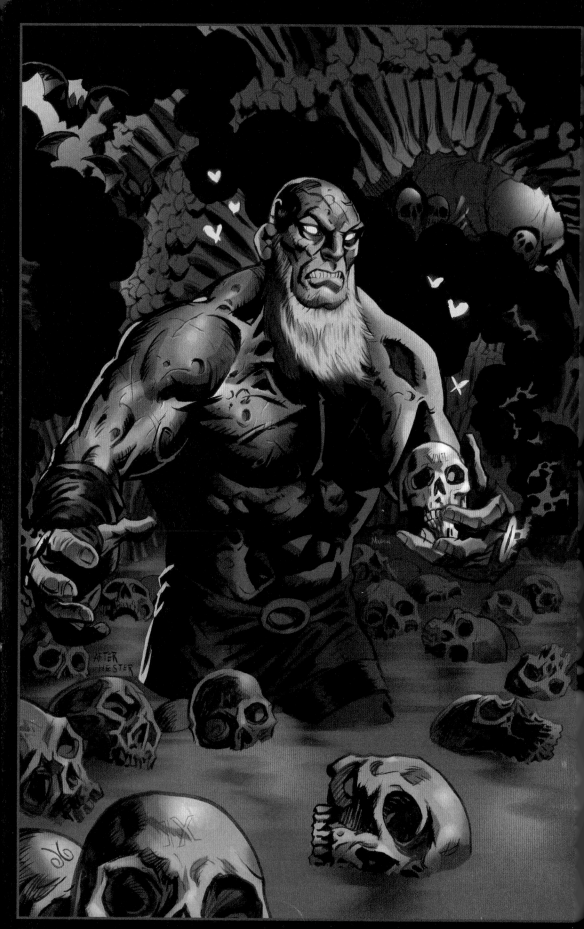

COVER 3B
DAN BRERETON / COLORS BY MARTIN THOMAS

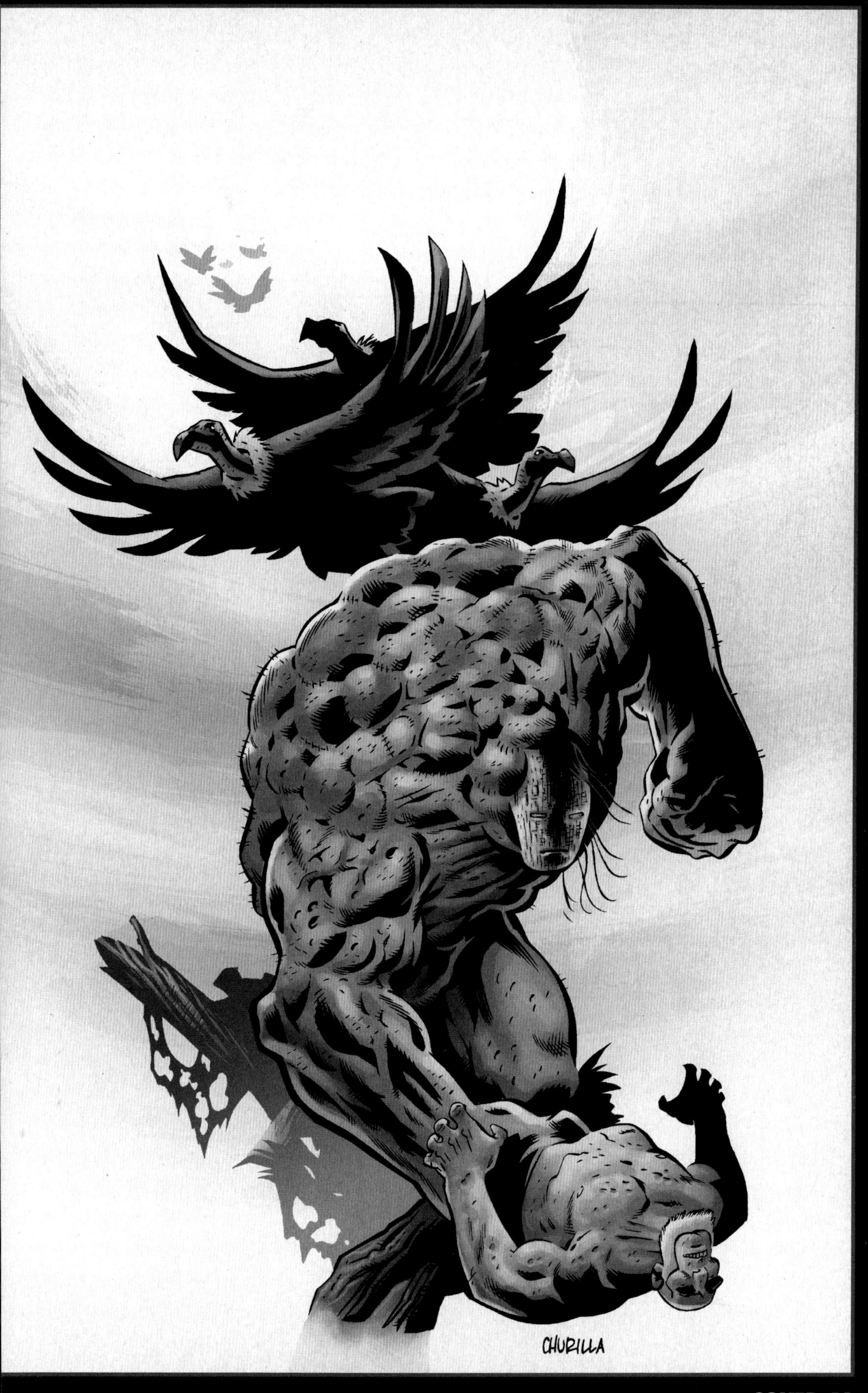
CHURILLA

COVER 4A
BRIAN CHURILLA / COLORS BY MATTHEW WILSON

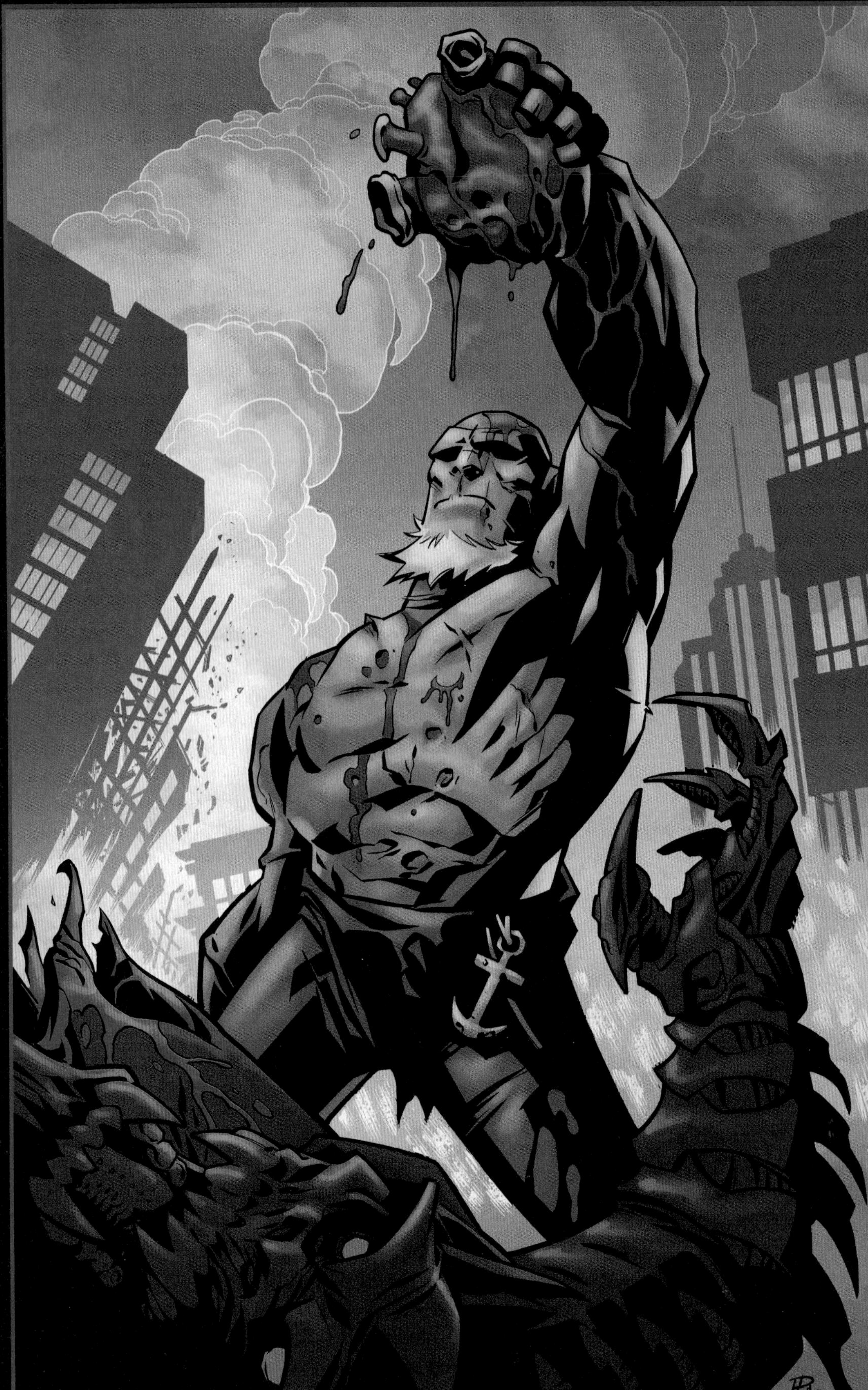

COVER 4B
PHIL HESTER / INKS BY ANDE PARKS / COLORS BY MATTHEW WILSON

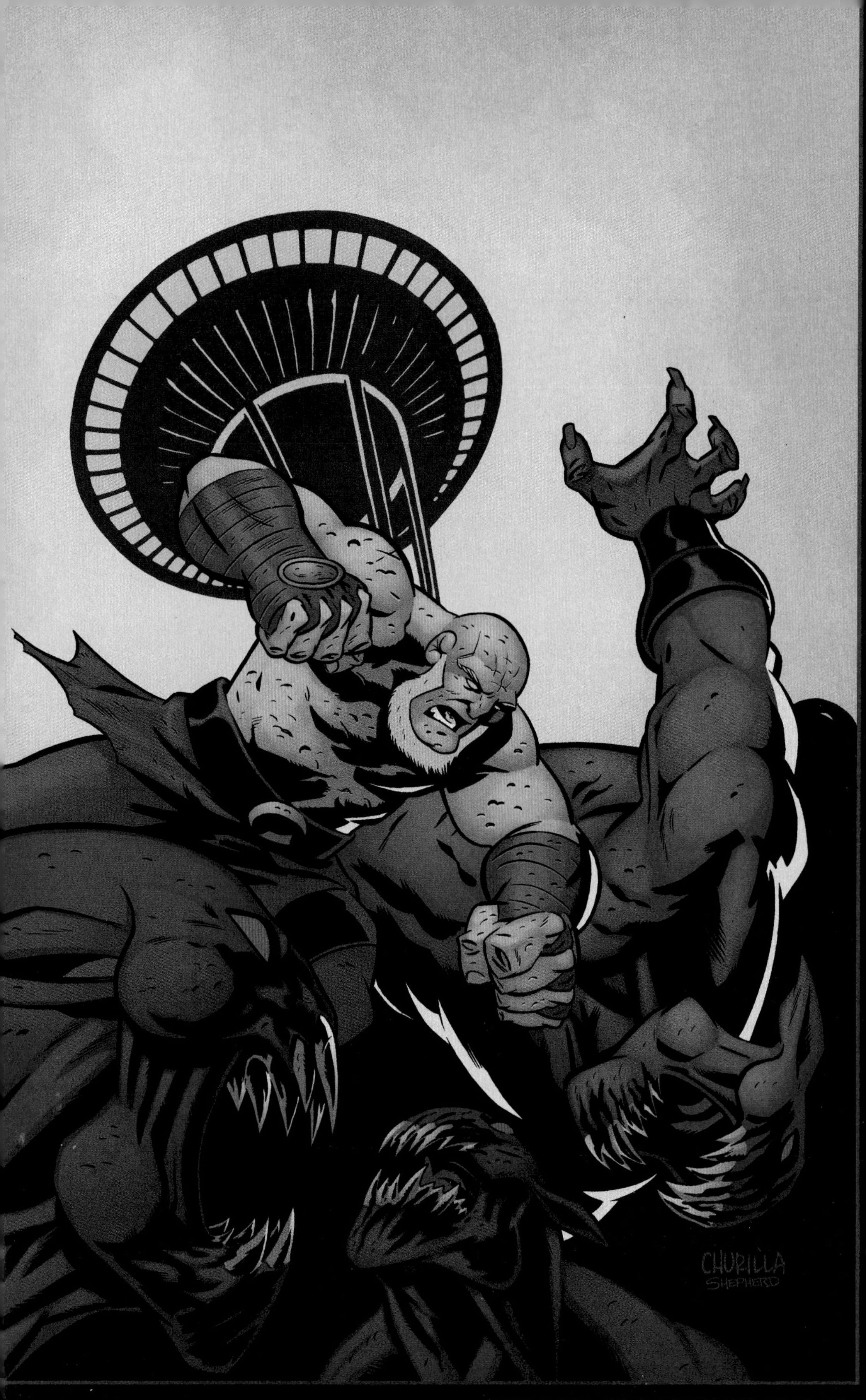
CHURILLA
SHEPHERD

EMERALD CITY COMICON 2010 AD:
BRIAN CHURILLA / COLORS BY JEREMY SHEPHERD

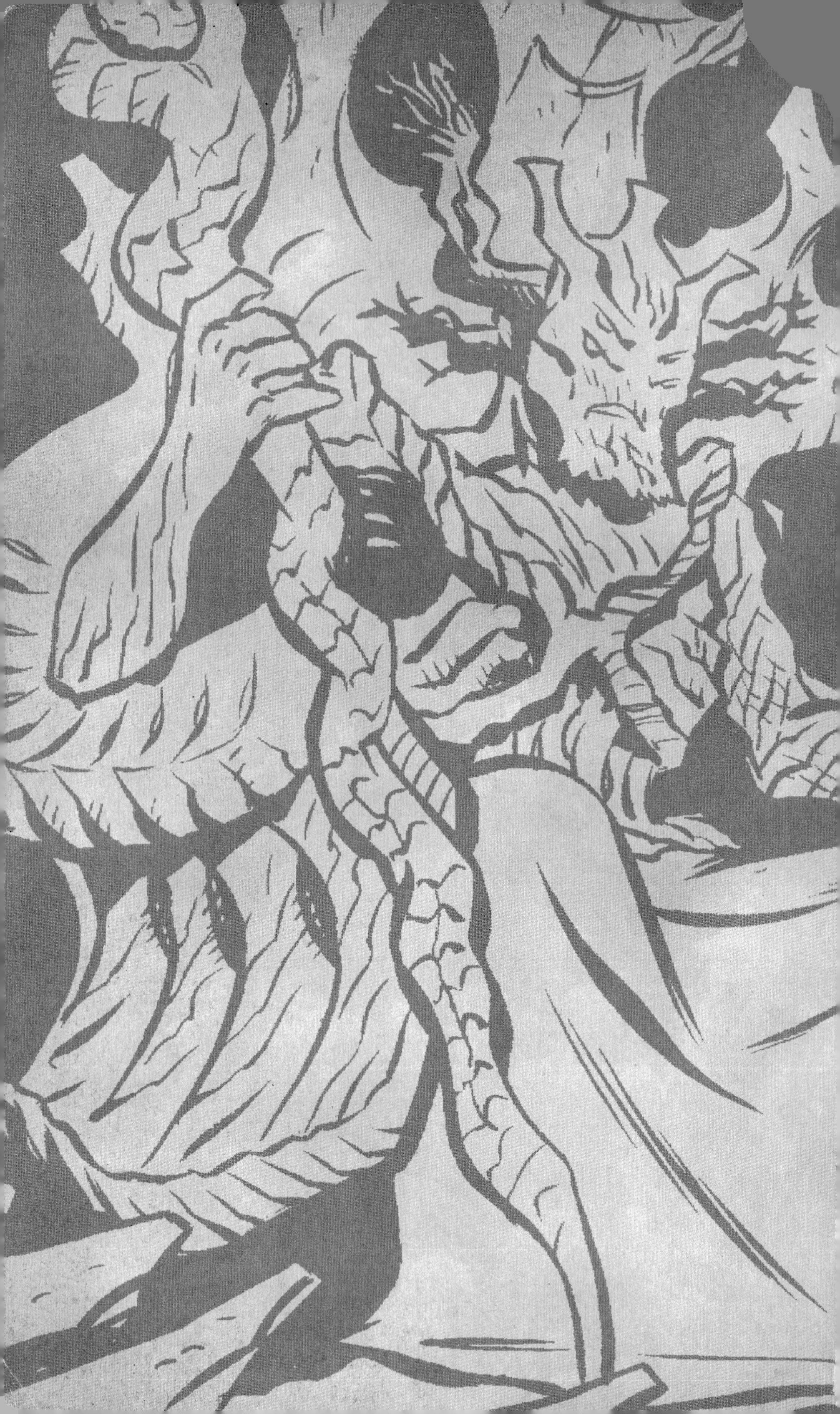